Beckett the
shape changer

Beckett the shape changer

a symposium edited by

Katharine Worth

Department of English, Royal Holloway College,
University of London

Routledge & Kegan Paul
London and Boston

First published in 1975
by Routledge & Kegan Paul Ltd
Broadway House, 68–74 Carter Lane,
London EC4V 5EL and
9 Park Street,
Boston, Mass. 02108, USA
Set in Monotype Scotch Roman
and printed in Great Britain by
The Camelot Press Ltd, Southampton
© Routledge & Kegan Paul 1975
No part of this book may be reproduced in
any form without permission from the
publisher, except for the quotation of brief
passages in criticism
ISBN 0 7100 8123 5

Contents

Contributors

JOHN CHALKER holds the chair of English at Westfield College, London. His main interests are in eighteenth- and twentieth-century literature, and he has contributed to a symposium on T. S. Eliot. He has published *The English Georgic: A Study in the Development of a Form.*

HARRY COCKERHAM is Lecturer in French at Royal Holloway College, London. He has written on nineteenth-century French literature and has published a critical edition of Gautier's *Poésies* (*1830*).

MARTIN DODSWORTH is Lecturer in English at Royal Holloway College, London. He has contributed articles to *Encounter, Essays in Criticism, The Review* and various symposia and newspapers. He has edited a book of essays, *The Survival of Poetry: A Contemporary Survey.*

BRIAN FINNEY teaches English for the Extra-mural Department, London University. He has written articles and a booklet, *Since How It Is,* on Beckett.

BARBARA HARDY holds the chair of English Literature at Birkbeck College, London, and was previously Professor of English at Royal Holloway College. She has written on nineteenth-century literature and modern poetry. Her critical works include studies of George Eliot, Charles Dickens and Thackeray, and *The Appropriate Form: An Essay on the Novel.*

CHARLES PEAKE is Reader in English at Queen Mary College, London. His main interests are in eighteenth-century literature and the modern novel. He has published *Poetry of the Landscape and of the Night* (an edited anthology), *Johnson: 'Rasselas' and Essays,* and contributed to various journals on subjects that include Defoe, Richardson and James Joyce. He is at present completing a critical study of Joyce.

VICTOR SAGE is Lecturer in English in the School of English and American Studies, East Anglia. He has made a special study of Beckett's fiction.

KATHARINE WORTH is Reader in English at Royal Holloway College, London. She is the author of *Revolutions in Modern English Drama*, and several of her essays on modern playwrights have appeared in symposia. She was an assistant editor of the *New Cambridge Bibliography of English Literature*, volume 4, to which she contributed the Beckett bibliography.

Acknowledgments

The editor wishes to acknowledge the kindness of Samuel Beckett in permitting quotation from his work and from correspondence with Brian Finney.

Acknowledgments are due to the following publishers for permission to print extracts from Beckett's works: Calder & Boyars Ltd and Editions de Minuit: *No's Knife, Lessness*; Calder & Boyars Ltd and Grove Press Inc.: *Molloy, Malone Dies, Proust, Murphy, How It Is, The Unnamable*; Faber & Faber Ltd and Grove Press Inc.: *Waiting for Godot, Endgame, Krapp's Last Tape and Embers, All That Fall, Happy Days, Play and Two Short Pieces for Radio* (*Words and Music* and *Cascando*), *Film, Eh Joe, Not I*; George G. Harrap & Co. Ltd and Editions de Minuit, Paris: *En attendant Godot*; Olympia Press Ltd: *Watt* ('Traveller's Companion' edition).

Acknowledgments are also due to Calder & Boyars and the Wesleyan University Press (copyright © 1958, 1959 by John Cage) for use of quotations from John Cage's *Silence*.

Chapter 1

Introduction

Katharine Worth

The god of shapes in the Greek myth was an old man of the sea with a marvellous gift for answering and also for eluding questions. He gave true answers, but only to a questioner who could keep a grip on him while he went through a series of shocking and witty shape changes; lion, bull, fire, water; the repertoire was formidable and seemingly endless.

It is as an artist of the Protean kind that Beckett has appealed to the contributors to this volume. The transformation process is our subject; how Beckett renews and reshapes himself from one form, language, genre, medium to another; how the characters take us into the pains, terrors and jokes of the reshaping, the Unnamable panting 'If I could be like Worm', the Voice in *Cascando* stretching itself to 'get' Woburn, say him, know him and change him; above all, how the illusion draws its strength from being exposed, handled, turned round for us to see how it is done, until finally there is no way of distinguishing how it is done from how it is. The freshness, variety, inventiveness of the process is our recurring refrain.

The symposium grew out of a series of lectures on Beckett I was invited to organise for the University of London Extra-mural Department, in response to various expressions of interest in his work. Its dazzling range and variety were, it seemed, what attracted people and also rather frightened them: they came to him as someone familiar, a household world (who could not know Godot?), who was at the same time distant and difficult. There was a sense of unknown regions, peculiar dimensions: there were the strange, hard-to-class forms, the *contes-lyriques*, the 'residua'; the bilingualism; the erudition; the weight of the Beckett criticism. Getting to know Beckett could seem a rather formidable business. How best to approach him, how to read him, how to get closer to the concrete experience, those were the questions we pursued: perhaps they may be thought sufficiently real and pressing to justify our following them up in print.

Most of the essays have come out of the lectures; but three were written specially for this symposium. Additional material was needed, partly because one of the original contributors had been

3

obliged to withdraw, owing to copyright difficulties, and because there was not space in the lecture programme for as much as we should have liked on the fiction, especially the later fiction and short forms like the *nouvelles*, texts and 'residua'. Much of that material is still new (in the sense of being newly published) and relatively unfamiliar; our first audience's reactions suggested that fuller accounts of it would be helpful. There was also a need for some analysis of single works such as we already had for drama and film.

With this tilt, then, towards the fiction, the collection is shaped to bring out the full variegation of Beckett's art as story-teller and playwright (the poetry and criticism, if they come in at all, do so only incidentally). The startling variegation of the Beckettian landscape could be glimpsed in the barest list of his writings, in the many changes of form it would show, and especially in that strange leap from English to French titles in the 1950s, followed by the still stranger continuous oscillation between the two languages. How one would like to know if what the narrator in *More Pricks Than Kicks* says of Belacqua is also true of Beckett: 'The creature dreams in French.' After nearly thirty years of his unique literary bilingualism it must surely be hard for him to say what his 'natural' language is.

That has often been a hard question for Irishmen to answer, being born with two languages as their equivocal inheritance. Perhaps Beckett's linguistic restlessness has to be seen, along with so many other features of his art, as an aspect of his Irishness. Early critics of his work tended to discuss it against a French background, naturally enough, since the trilogy and the two plays that made him universally known were all written in French. But in the last decade it has become easier to see how deep his Irish roots go, how much he has in common with predecessors like Yeats and Synge, how he shares with them the complex fate of being Anglo-Irish.

It seems an apt coincidence that he was born in Dublin in 1906, the year Synge completed *The Playboy of the Western World*, a play that raised troubling questions about the nature of Irishness and drew attention to the linguistic dilemma confronting Irish writers. The essence of Synge's characters was a Gaelic essence; it was in their Gaelic tongue that they lived with such fire and richness, a people, as he said, who had not shut their lips on poetry. Yet the language so brimful of life from one viewpoint, from another was practically dead; 'Irish as a living language is dying out year by year,' Synge wrote:[1]

the day the last old man or woman who can speak Irish
only dies in Connacht or Munster – a day that is coming near
– will mark a station in the Irish decline which will be final
a few years later. . . . the supreme good sense of childhood
will not cumber itself with two languages where one is enough.

To project into the future those characters whose language had
no future, he had to create his linguistic hybrid, or bastard, as
some have thought it: English words to an Irish tune, English
flesh on Gaelic bones. 'It's there your treachery is spurring me, till
I'm hard set to think you're the one I'm after lacing in my heart-
strings half-an-hour gone by.' Speaking like this, Christy Mahon,
Pegeen Mike, the Douls, have acquired a hauntingly convincing
stage existence. They have impressed audiences as natural and
spontaneous by grace of a language that is anything but natural,
a language no one spoke, which Synge himself couldn't speak,
according to Willie Fay, and even his Irish actors had difficulty
getting their tongues round, a language that can be parodied with
the greatest of ease and often seems on the point of dropping into
self-parody, on the lines of the skit, 'The Mists That Do be Rising
On the Bog'.

Beckett's characters are not drawn from the Gaelic-speaking
peasants of Aran, but he is very much in tune with Synge and often
echoes him. Even if he had not spoken of his special feeling for
The Well of the Saints[2] we should know it from the atmosphere
and setting of his own imagined world with its many Synge-like
beings; those tramps and homeless wanderers who meet under
trees in country lanes, are familiar with the inside of ditches, take
lonely journeys through sparsely-peopled countryside, telling tall
tales, if only to themselves. The dangerous closeness to unconscious self-parody in Synge's idiom was something Beckett
could use, although it may have taken him some time to see just
how: a knowing self-parody becomes a major means of expressing
self-consciousness in his fiction and his drama. His Molloys and
Malones have the gift of the gab and can tell a gallus story with
the same lilt and gusto as a Christy Mahon, making it seem as large
as life and twice as natural. But they parody themselves in the
same breath, have an ear permanently cocked for the overdone
phrase, the false note, the bit of romantic excess. They are more
continuously aware than Synge's people of how fluid their identity
is and how precariously dependent on the words they use, on frail
and treacherous language that is liable to die on them at any
minute. So Dan Rooney, in that most Irish of Beckett's plays, *All*

That Fall, tells his wife: 'Do you know, Maddy, sometimes one would think you were struggling with a dead language', and when she agrees, 'Yes, indeed, Dan, I know full well what you mean, I often have that feeling, it is unspeakably excruciating', offers her the comically cold comfort: 'Well, you know, it will be dead in time, just like our own poor dear Gaelic, there is that to be said.'

The joke has a rough edge to it. It hints at an ambivalent attitude in Beckett towards English, as well as a more general feeling about the troubling frailty and power of language. Balancing on a knife-edge between spontaneous and self-conscious, romantic and satirical, is an art he practises with great virtuosity. Perhaps he needed to master it partly because he had inherited such a strange language, so prone to histrionic exaggeration, so 'made', and yet so well adapted to an easy, natural colloquialism and to humour.

Beckett's exceptionally sensitive ear, which has enabled him to play such complex variations on the Synge speech tunes, must also have made for difficulties in his first grapplings as a writer with Anglo-Irish English. Given such a context it isn't hard to envisage French appealing as a language free of tone, a distancing device, a means to a different perspective on English. His move in that direction began with his studies at Trinity College, Dublin (where he also taught French for a short time), and continued when he chose Paris as a resting-place in the thirties, after a period of short stays in places which included London and Germany. At that time he could have been thought of as another Irish writer in exile in Paris. He moved in the Joyce circle, was close to Joyce, and was still writing in English. Paris and London divided the honours of publication, but it was the slighter works on the whole that came out in Paris, the poetry, and such critical *jeux d'esprit* as the essay on Joyce in *Our Exagmination round his Factification for Incamination of Work in Progress* (1929). The full-length study of Proust was published in London in 1931 and so were the collection of short stories set in Dublin, *More Pricks Than Kicks* (1934) and the London novel, *Murphy* (1938).

But for Beckett 'exile' was not exactly the word. When the war came and the Germans occupied Paris, he did not leave for Switzerland (where Joyce went) nor return, as he so easily could have done, to neutral Eire, but threw in his lot with the French and joined a Resistance group: after narrowly escaping arrest by the Gestapo, we are told, he took refuge with his wife in unoccupied France, living and working under an assumed name as a French farm labourer. So his life may have depended, as Alec Reid suggests,[3] on his being able to act the Frenchman; a harrowing way of having one's second language become the 'natural' one. Still he kept to English for writing. *Watt* was the unlikely, endearing fruit of that bleak time. It wasn't published till 1953, however, and by then its Englishness made it something of a sport, for Beckett had moved right over to French. In that same year *L'Innommable* came out, to complete the trilogy begun with *Molloy* and *Malone meurt* in 1951. From then on, all the published fiction, with the notable exception of *From an Abandoned Work* (1958), has been written in French and then translated into English. The collection of shorter fiction, *Nouvelles et textes pour rien*, appeared in 1955, the major work, *Comment c'est* in 1961, and since then there has been a fairly continuous flood of shorter fiction, and fragments including *Imagination morte imaginez* (1965), *Sans* (1969), and *Le Dépeupleur* (1970). There have been French poems and criticism too, and the plays which made him internationally known were also in French, though *En attendant Godot* (produced 1953) and *Fin de partie* (produced 1957) have had to give pride of place, so far as frequency of production and quotation goes, to their English cousins, *Waiting for Godot* (produced 1955) and *Endgame* (produced 1958).

The plays in fact tell a different story from the fiction. Since the first two they have mostly been written in English; this is true of all the radio plays except *Cascando*. That could no doubt be explained in practical terms of their success with English-speaking audiences and of commissions received, particularly from the BBC. But it would take a less simple explanation to account for Beckett's extraordinary practice of preserving equality for his two languages by translating all his own works (either alone or in collaboration) from French into English, and English into French. Well before he went back to English as first language, with *Krapp's Last Tape* in 1958, he had taken pains to give the English *Molloy*, *Malone Dies* and *The Unnamable* equal status with their French originals by being his own translator. He has done the same for French, though perhaps English has a very slight edge here: there have been English versions of all the French works published in book form, usually soon after the originals – the gap between *Nouvelles et textes pour rien* (1955) and *Stories and Texts for Nothing* (1967) is exceptional – whereas French-speaking readers had to wait till 1947 for *Murphy* (1938) and 1968 for *Watt* (1953), and have not yet had translations of *Proust* (1931) or *More Pricks Than Kicks* (1934).

More Pricks Than Kicks could well seem a book to defy translation. Its highly self-conscious, almost aggressive Anglo-Irishness
is a reminder of the linguistic strains Beckett has suffered under –
and profited from. This collection of short stories, given unity by
the linking presence of the central character, Belacqua, is Beckett's
Dublin book; his *Portrait of the Artist as a Young Man*, some have
said, though so far as tone of voice goes, St John Gogarty's
allusive and anecdotal *As I was Going Down Sackville Street* might
be nearer the mark. The narrator in *More Pricks Than Kicks* has
some difficulty in finding a natural voice. He is good on other
people's – like the lady's in 'Ding-Dong', selling tickets for heaven
at tuppence apiece, four fer a tanner – and there are times when
he hits exactly the right note for himself too, as in the sombre
throw-away at the close of 'Dante and the Lobster'. But he is
rather inhibited by his hypersensitive ear: his cool self seems to be
always listening for histrionics from the other self, the Irish one,
perhaps; he sets up mocking defences; parodies, masks and
distances himself till it's sometimes hard to know what the
experience really is that he is telling: the story of Lucy's accident
in 'Walking Out', and the voyeuristic episode so cryptically connected with it, is one such curiously screened event.

The experience of writing in French does seem to have had a
great releasing effect. In the later English works, that intermittent
linguistic uneasiness and evasiveness of the earlier fiction has
either disappeared or been brought into the open and made the
central subject of the piece, as it is in *Words and Music*.

There are still narrators of a kind in these pieces – *Happy Days*
is almost pure monologue – but they no longer have trouble with
their tone of voice. Winnie's marvellous gift of the gab, the racy
ease of her musing and dreaming, makes her seem a true descendant
of the Playboy, and Beckett very completely Synge's heir: in those
subtly shifting tones, that highly suggestive balance between
spontaneity and self-consciousness, Synge's technique for theatric-
alising the inner workings of the imagination is given a great
modern extension.

He can be seen in this way, but of course there are a hundred
ways of seeing him: take a slightly different angle, and other facets
dazzlingly come into view; according to whether we read him in
English or French (however close the texts are, their tone colour
can't be quite the same), or approach him through his fiction
or his drama, come in at a late or early point in the *œuvre*, and so
on. He has been claimed by practically every modern literary
movement, placed as a Proustian, a Joycean, a founder of the

nouveau roman, a Sartrean existentialist, a Christian existentialist, an absurdist, a Jungian: the list goes on, and will do, no doubt, to the crack of doom.

Any of these views can be persuasive; any of them claiming to be exclusive must be off the mark. Beckett can only be surely placed as a man of many facets, the writer above all who has sensed the deep movements of the modern imagination and found spellbinding images to express them. He draws out contradictions in his critics because his art is a place where opposites are continually juggled with and held in tension. He makes them look back at his predecessors (and see them differently through his prism) because so many lines from the past run together in his work, to be given startlingly unexpected extensions. Coming in at the tail-end, one might say, of the literary tradition of self-consciousness, he gathers up from sources as opposite-looking as the satirical Augustan novelists and the Romantic poets, as frail-looking as the symbolist drama of Maeterlinck and Yeats, and projects his brilliant new synthesis right into the centre of communal imagination; his capture of the popular theatre is the seal of this achievement. In his multifariousness, he calls to mind Coleridge's saying on Shakespeare, '[he] darts himself forth, and passes into all the forms of human character and passion, the one Proteus of the fire and the flood.' Perhaps one might hesitate to take the whole of this for Beckett (though a case could be made for its appropriateness), but the last phrase could well have been invented for him.

His Proteanism shows in his command of genres and media as well as of languages. There is the astonishing variety within single genres; the easy movement between fiction and drama; the total changes of form involved in the changes of media. Stage, radio, film, television; in all, or almost all (for one contributor enters a serious reservation here), the adaptation is uncannily complete. Each play is a theatre machine, in Peter Brook's phrase; each work of fiction could have no other than the form it has, is perfectly self-contained. And yet self-containment co-exists with a powerful sense of fluidity and interpenetration of forms. There is quotation and reference from one work to another, most obviously in the trilogy, as when the voice in *The Unnamable* unnervingly wonders if the figure he thinks he sees is Molloy wearing Malone's hat. And there are the times when the fiction almost turns itself into drama or the drama seems barely to have detached itself from narrative, as if Beckett were seeing how far one could be pushed in the direction of the other without losing its essential shape. *The*

9

Unnamable is an especially fascinating illustration of this process. Like a great Catherine-wheel, it circles round, throwing off sparks and spurts of dramatic energy that seem sometimes, as the voice gets more and more agitated, on the very point of igniting a play:[4]

> But it's not I, it's not I, where am I, what am I doing, all this time, as if that mattered, but there it is, that takes the heart out of you, your heart isn't in it any more, your heart that was, among the brambles, cradled by the shadows (p. 403).

How close, this, to the spasms of Mouth in *Not I*, the play that most looks like a fiery offshoot from that dark matrix: 'Just the mouth . . . like maddened . . . and can't stop . . . no stopping it . . . something she, . . . something she had to . . . what? . . . who? . . . no! . . . she! . . .'

So near and so far. The effect of these attempts in the fiction to get free of soliloquy, break out into other characters, other stories, get a free-wheeling action going, is, after all, to make us more intensely aware of the narrative envelope that holds the voice in, makes breakaway impossible. The Unnamable communicates to us, partly through the nervous energy of those abortive attempts at drama, something about the nature of the fiction he is engaged in, controls, and is at the mercy of. We are made to register in our pulses both the closeness of the different forms or modes of being and their distinctness.

To register the form, and along with it the ever-shifting tone and mood of Beckett's fiction and drama, is a chief concern of the present writers. John Chalker takes a close look at the tricky form of a funny and difficult early novel, teasing out its layers of satire. Charles Peake is also interested in the early fiction but more particularly in the changes of form that occur between *Murphy* and the novels in the trilogy, showing how these reflect different stages of Beckett's exploration into self-consciousness.

Two of the essays are concerned mainly with the shape of things in the later and in the shorter fiction. Brian Finney traces patterns of connection and change among the stories, *nouvelles*, texts, and 'residua' (he supplies Beckett's own explanation of this term): he emphasises the constant reference back and forwards, the retrospects and anticipations, the formal variety. Victor Sage is especially interested in the widely held idea (nourished by terms like 'residua') that Beckett's is a dwindling art, ever thinning and shrinking, getting closer to the goal of silence that so obsesses his characters. In his analysis of *How It Is*, he sets out to combat the notion, to show the fullness that lies behind the contractions, the new dimensions that are being opened up for readers, however closed and constricted the characters may feel themselves to be.

The argument against the reductive view of Beckett gets powerful, implicit support from Barbara Hardy. Hers is an essay in concreteness, a large-scale demonstration of the lifelike diversity and vivacity of Beckett's world: its strange forms, she shows, are dense with familiar associations and feelings; its witty self-consciousness is a dynamic part of the narrative process as well as a means of stimulating reflection on it. She draws her illustrations from the whole canon, bringing the late fiction under the same light as the trilogy, and finding throughout the same impressively exact, fine relationships of form and feeling.

That oddest aspect of Beckett's Proteanism, his total bilingualism, is Harry Cockerham's subject. The contributors have written, on the whole, without reference to the French texts (even when they came first); it seems reasonable to do this when Beckett himself is the guarantor for the accuracy of the translations, if, indeed, translation is the word. Still, one is apt to be haunted by those shadow-twins, knowing that they are not exactly identical. Harry Cockerham takes up the questions the rest of us don't ask: about how close, in fact, they are; the nature of the differences; what changes of tone and mood come in with the change of language.

He explores these questions through a comparison of the French and English versions of some of the stage plays. The other essay on the drama takes in the radio plays too, though here there is something of a problem. My subject is the physicality of Beckett's drama, and as things are at present it is rather difficult to assess this in the radio plays; so few recordings are available. Ideally we should listen to these plays with a stock of tapes at hand and a number of different productions to go by. We are a long way yet from that happy situation. However, so far as listening experience allows, I try to gauge the dramatic value of sound and music in the radio plays, as of space and light in the stage plays.

Beckett's isolated incursions into film and television draw out a note of dissent from the general view of his masterful versatility. Martin Dodsworth sees both *Film* and *Eh Joe* as failures: *Film* especially, he thinks, shows the limits set on Beckett's adaptability. He argues that this is not just a failure of execution (though his account of what went wrong in that respect might make one wonder), but the symptom of a flaw in Beckett's genius, and this he seeks to define by analysing *Film* (and *Eh Joe*) in the light of the critical writings and by analogy with works such as John Cage's 'Lecture on Nothing'.

11

The contributors have all been stirred by Beckett and feel they have something to say about him: usual reasons for writing which might hardly need elaboration were it not for that vast bulk of existing criticism. It can induce an uneasy sense that one should make out a special case for adding to it, though in fact there must surely be plenty of room for comment on a major author of such influence and intricacy who is still producing new works, works as different from each other and from what has gone before as *Lessness, The Lost Ones*, and *Not I*. If a case had to be made, however, I suppose ours would be based on the need in Beckett studies for approaches that aim to bring out the great range of his human understanding and sympathy, his approachability.

Readers of the fiction especially could sometimes feel doubtful about this. There are difficulties in the way; notably the general aura of erudition and more particularly the emphasis placed on it by some of the esoteric commentaries. It might well seem to the diffident reader that before daring to approach Beckett he would need to acquire a formidable amount of knowledge; enrol for a course in philosophy, maybe, or learn another language. Is this author a closed book, he might well ask, to those who can't instantly pick up references to Dante or Descartes, play a good game of chess, enjoy mathematical problems?

The answer from the plays is obviously 'No'. It was the ordinary audiences in the ordinary public theatres who made Beckett a household word (even if the process took some time). It was not until *Waiting for Godot* that the thin trickle of criticism turned to a flood and the art began to show its extraordinary power to reach out to all kinds and conditions of men, if only through distant reverberations from its magical images; the long wait for Godot, the dustbins, the tape playback, the voice chatting to itself in the darkness. As John Fletcher and John Spurling remind us in their study of the plays,[5] the political cartoonists and advertisers know they can count on that subliminal recognition; that their ordinary reader will get the joke of Sir Alec Douglas-Home and Selwyn Lloyd bobbing up in their dustbins over the caption, 'Finished, it's finished, . . . it must be nearly finished'; Macmillan and Macleod pondering gloomily under the tree on Budget Day, 'We'll hang ourselves tomorrow – unless Godot comes.'

One function of Beckett criticism must surely be, then, to encourage a sense of that openness, to show there are ways in, even to the more difficult reaches of the fiction, that do not depend on our having specialised knowledge, or being familiar with the commentaries. The fiction, indeed, invites us to recognise the limitations of the 'knowing' mind. The characters know their passion for knowledge is a bit of a joke against them: more often than not they view it wryly; the Unnamable, for instance, reflecting '. . . full of general knowledge we are this evening, we have even piano-tuners up our sleeve, they strike A and hear G, two minutes later . . . ' or: 'I should mention before going any further, any further on, that I say aporia without knowing what it means.'

The process of the fiction, as Charles Peake illustrates, is a quest for the self that lies far below and beyond the self that consciously amasses knowledge. Highly organised Moran, with his impeccable memory, drifts irresistibly towards anarchic, intuitive Molloy: the Unnamable, who can't stop speculating, broods on the felicity of being resigned, unspeculative Worm: '. . . no, if I were Worm I wouldn't know it, I wouldn't say it, I wouldn't say anything, I'd be Worm.' If we want to get right into their experience, we have to move with the characters beyond rational speculation, bring our ignorant intuitions with us as well as our knowledge, our passivity as well as our curiosity. We are encouraged not to be over-censorious, to face ourselves and respond from the whole being: that is one of the great blessings he offers. Indolence, confusion, blank spots, failures of memory – all the things we may not care to admit – are taken up into the fiction and brilliantly redeemed, made part of the imaginative process.

The best commentary on Beckett's work, Brian Finney suggests, is the work itself, and this must surely be true so long as responses stay free and open. But there are hazards here too: familiarity with the *œuvre* can be mechanical, no more than a recognition of recurring motifs and ideas. The effect may be to blur and blunt. One reviewer guessing the reaction of the audience to the first London performance of *Not I* might have included[6]

> a sense of comfortable familiarity. The Voice, unable to stop . . . is the voice of the Unnamable; the narrative, such as it is, might be one of those glimpses of the life up there which occur in *How It Is*; such ironies as 'tender mercies . . . new every morning' could have been spoken by Winnie.

Anyone who could feel comfortable during Billie Whitelaw's performance in *Not I* would have been better off coming to the theatre in total ignorance of Beckett; then he might have been able to receive the unnervingly discomforting real experience. Of course there are echoes from other works, but what they draw attention to is surely not sameness but the stunning diversity Beckett contrives from his closely restricted materials.

Not I is by no means the only play anticipated in *The Unnamable*. All the plays, practically, seem to be in it, waiting to
form, hovering in incidents, images, and refrains (like the insistently recurring 'Not I'). *Waiting for Godot* is hinted at in the rhyme
about the dog that steals the loaf of bread; *Endgame* in the
imagined business of changing the sawdust in Mahood's jar; *Play*
and *Cascando* in the vision of the lights 'rearing up in a blaze and
sweeping down upon me, blinding, to devour me'; and all the radio
plays in those pervasive voices the Unnamable hears panting to
be given bodily shape. But even at the points where they are
closest, fictional and dramatic are far apart: we can't ever forget
the Unnamable controlling the dramatic process; however real
Mahood, Worm, and the rest become, they always refer us back
to him, come over as his 'project'.

'How physical this all is', the Unnamable says at one point.
Yes, but how far still from the awesome physicality of the drama,
the terrible reality it acquires from the bodies, the heads, the livid
mouth that can't get away, be shuffled off, dispensed with, like
the Macmanns, Molloys, Mahoods. The Unnamable can view his
shifts from first into third person and back again with a certain
cool amusement: 'I shall not say I again, ever again, it's too
farcical.' He gets agitated and desperate too, but he has some
power over his moods. What a world away from the fixity of
Mouth, condemned to babble in the third person, always refusing
the first person in those harrowing shrieks, 'Who? . . . No! . . .
She! . . .' No play of fiction in this, it comes over as only too painfully real, human and (perhaps) unchangeable.

Criticism has to aim at keeping the writings open in this way
too, by sharpening distinctions, and focusing on the particular,
making our experience of reading Beckett and the expectations
we derive from it work constructively. Beckett relies on this
happening, Victor Sage suggests, but there is a danger of abstract
ideas fouling up the process: although Beckett criticism has such
a relatively short history, there has been plenty of time for myths
to form and ideas to harden. He examines one such myth in his
analysis of *How It Is*, showing both how Beckett himself makes
use of it and how it can backfire and make it harder for readers
to see what is really there. Similarly, John Chalker's examination
of form in *Watt* is an argument against the 'philosophical' reading
of the novel. Martin Dodsworth's close scrutiny of *Film* leads
mainly into censure of Beckett himself (with his critic's hat on),
but there are implications for those critics – and Beckett attracts
them – who deal in ideas more readily than processes and can

14

rather easily lose sight of the thing as it is (admittedly, as he says, *Film* is a special problem, being so hard to see at all, in the most literal sense).

It should not be too difficult to make adjustments to one's view of Beckett, since happily new works keep appearing to stimulate flexibility. *Not I*, *First Love* (written in French in 1946), and *The Lost Ones* have all come out since 1970. And it seems that a new radio play is now being written. So there are still pioneering tasks for criticism, first assessments as well as reassessments, explorations into relatively uncharted territory such as Brian Finney offers in his survey of the shorter fiction and Harry Cockerham in his study of textual changes and French literary sources.

It would be an irony to look for a common point of view in a collection of essays on Beckett, the writer above all who makes us more completely ourselves. 'What doesn't come to me from me has come to the wrong address', says the Unnamable. Beckett always brings this home. And yet although he speaks to us so privately, he can, remarkably, put us in touch with each other too. So it seems to have happened with the contributors to this volume: we have our own interests, valuations, and reservations, but we come close when we speak of what matters most to us in Beckett's writings and how we have found it best to approach him. There is a general feeling, for instance, that philosophical interpretation has loomed rather too large in Beckett criticism up to now. This is understandable, of course: his characters give the lead with their non-stop speculating and relish for hypotheses, games of logic, ideas of all kinds. It must obviously be helpful to have critical light thrown on all that frenetic mental activity, but it is disconcerting when the ideas that are toyed with in the fiction are built into models by which to read the fiction; when the novels are taken, as Charles Peake implies they sometimes are, as illustrations of a philosophical system. It is all too easy for the absurd to turn into the 'Absurd' and the wrong kind of seriousness to get into the commentary.

Philosophy is, after all, only one of the things that keep Beckett's people going, one of their dubious consolations, in Barbara Hardy's phrase. Perhaps it is more dubious than any other, a source of acuter self-mockery, irritation, and even anguish. Bantering notes regularly come in when the characters catch themselves theorising: Malone, for instance, jokes: 'But it is gone clean out of my head, my little private idea. No matter, I have just had another. Perhaps it is the same one back again, ideas are so alike when you get to know them.' The self-mockery is amused there, but it can

15

get very edgy, as it does in *Words and Music*: although the form of this piece is grotesquely comic, it is a real frustration that comes through when Croak groans over the meaningless abstractions offered up to him by Words: an arid pedantry has got ludicrously out of hand and could go on for ever, one suspects, elaborating on any given theme, always shying away from anything personal or real. A state of mind Beckett evidently knows well and is as wary of as critics must try to be.

Literature in its turn is no more than a dubious consolation for Beckett's characters, but there is a rich abundance of literary allusion and quotation which the present writers have found a sensitive guide to complexities of tone and mood.

John Chalker's line out to Sterne and Swift helps him to place the equivocal relation of narrator and reader which is for him the pivot of the fiction; while for Barbara Hardy the same comparisons bring out the pain and self-laceration in Beckett's satire: echoes of Keats are called up and in turn help to identify Beckett's distinctive voice; its extraordinary balance of dry and lyrical, satirical and romantic, and the new note of comic theatricality that gives the self-consciousness such an astonishingly full projection. Keatsian reference too enters into my interpretation of *Happy Days*; the line from 'Ode to a Nightingale' which is among Winnie's treasured memories is one of the keys needed to unlock the mood of this most ambiguous play.

When there is no literary context, as in *Film*, the work suffers badly, so Martin Dodsworth argues. Beckett's fatal Cleopatra takes possession: the schematist in him comes to the fore and instead of a living body of art we get a thin ghost called anti-art, that would like, if it could, to extinguish itself altogether. A real case of philosophy clipping an angel's wings.

Whether or not we are persuaded by the argument,[7] we may well share his disappointment at the thinness of the comedy in *Film*. A film that has Buster Keaton in it (even in old age) and doesn't draw out his comic genius, must surely have gone wrong somewhere. In the high value all the contributors put on Beckett's humour, perhaps, in the end, a common point of view does emerge. For us all, I think, the humour is something more than the wit, brilliant and satisfying though that is; more pervasive, not to be pinned down in the virtuoso set pieces, puns, parodies, and intellectual acrobatics: it is held throughout in the tone. Small, droll comments and asides – 'Mr Hackett called in his arms'; Molloy reflects, 'Tears and laughter, they are so much Gaelic to me' – bring us close to the characters, keep us in sympathy with them as

16

people even when the quests they are engaged on, their attempts to see into themselves and the meaning of things, are being devastatingly mocked. A reassuringly human perspective is kept throughout all the fantastic, taxing and often dark vicissitudes their fictions involve us in.

Beckett changes the shape of things in so many ways. He makes us see the scene around us with his eyes: we all run into 'Beckettian' situations now, keep noticing ourselves or other people behaving like Molloy or Winnie or Krapp, hear clichés, 'little words', turns of speech with new sharpness. Language, syntax, punctuation are lifted out of the dullness of habit; we are required to think about semi-colons, be aware how our vocabulary expresses us and our rhetoric gives us away. The shape of his writings is often so strange and lovely, it can seem enough in itself; something to be totally absorbed in. *Lessness*, for instance; easy to enjoy it simply as an exquisitely skilful structure, its paragraphs arranged like a string of widely spaced beads, each bead a cluster of sentences, a new arrangement of words drawn from an austerely limited vocabulary and set in an austerely compressed syntax: 'Little body ash grey locked rigid heart beating face to endlessness.' A concrete poem, one might think, to be heard like music. And yet it is still prose fiction; a narrator can be sensed there, though so attenuated, patiently shifting the words into new patterns, trying to get past and future into the right shape; distilling the experience of the little body he watches so intently, is so concerned for. The shape as he structures it tells the experience. Disconnection is part of it; incompleteness, a sense of something missing – the word 'issueless' sounds throughout like a knell – but there is calm too, and a serenity that has something to do with the achievement of this pure, uncluttered vision: 'Figment dawn dispeller of figments and the other called dusk.'

In this oblique austerity, as in his droll, endearing humour, Beckett's is still a human tone. Of course he is formidable; he takes us into such odd, dark, unacknowledged corners of human personality; it is disturbing to recognise the workings of our own minds among the strange forms of his visionary and vividly actual world. But the recognition is releasing and inspiriting too, coming about as it does in the humane context of his tone of voice; in being given the courage to face ourselves, we can experience a great access of feeling for others. We have to hold on hard to this Proteus, to follow him through his fine changes; read hard, listen and look hard, go in and out of the dark with him. The truth he offers is in the process of change itself: a movement of the mind towards heightened perception, freer and fuller sympathies. How that process works is what the contributors to this volume have been attempting to register.

Finally, I should like to record my gratitude: to our first audience for their interest and encouragement; to Barbara Hardy for helpful advice on additional material; and to Winifred Bamforth for her always efficient and good-humoured organisation of the original lecture series. Her calm and resourcefulness, qualities well known to those who have worked with her, were a special boon on that occasion. She aided and abetted our attempts to get something of Beckett's concreteness into the course; small visual reminders (a programme in lower-case and the punctuation of *How It Is* proved strangely inflammatory in some quarters); bits of theatrical performance and sound recordings of the radio plays. Although she wasn't able to fish up from the BBC archives the recording of *Words and Music* we had hoped for, she did succeed in borrowing the score of John Beckett's music, and this was a first step towards the new production which has been made by the University of London Audio-visual Centre (with music by Humphrey Searle, Patrick Magee as Words and Denis Hawthorne as Croak). The University Audio-visual Centre has recently made a recording of another inaccessible play, *Eh Joe* (with Patrick Magee and Elvi Hale).[8] I am glad of this opportunity to acknowledge the invaluable aid they are giving to Beckett studies and to thank the University of London for supporting and encouraging this creative activity.

NOTES

1 'Can we go back into our mother's womb? – a letter to the Gaelic League', in J. M. Synge, *Collected Works*, vol. 2, ed. A. Price, OUP, 1966, p. 399.

2 See account of the programme of Shaw Centenary celebrations (June 1956) in *Samuel Beckett: An Exhibition* (Catalogue of the Beckett exhibition at Reading University Library, May to July 1971), Turret Books, London, 1971, p. 23.

3 A. Reid, *All I Can Manage, More Than I Could: An Approach to the Plays of Samuel Beckett*, Dolmen Press, Dublin, 1969 rev. ed., p. 14.

4 References to *The Unnamable* are to the one-volume edition of the trilogy, 1959 (John Calder).

5 J. Fletcher and J. Spurling, *Beckett: A Study of His Plays*, Eyre Methuen, London, 1972. The caricatures referred to are on pp. 46 and 146.

6 *Times Literary Supplement*, 12 October 1973.

7 I myself value *Eh Joe* much more highly and interpret its ambiguities as a painful exploration in the region between memory and fiction.

8 *Eh Joe* was produced by Sandra Clark with Katharine Worth and directed by David Clark. *Words and Music* was produced by Katharine Worth and directed by David Clark.

Chapter 2

The satiric shape of *Watt*

John Chalker

To write on the shape of *Watt* is an exercise in absurdity. The novel has no shape in the conventional sense; its development is arbitrary and unpredictable, its manner wildly digressive, and its end offers an apparent conclusion which takes place at a mid-point in the story. It combines, moreover, sections of comic realism in which the characters and situations are related, even if only tenuously, to the life of Dublin and its surroundings, with passages of abstract allegory, of ebullient farce and of mock-scholastic reflections on events. These disconcerting shifts in the nature of the fictional world occur with an apparent spontaneity which mocks attempts at definition in terms of normal narrative shape. Yet it is through its very shapelessness, its resistance to definition, that its mode is made clear. Analogues to *Watt* are found, not in the narrative of events, but in satiric fictions, and the purpose of this essay is to look at some of the ways in which the satiric form is established and the effects of that form on the reader's relationship to the narrator and his story.

In its opening section *Watt* offers a grotesque but highly stylised comedy set in a recognisable world. Turning a corner, Mr Hackett sees a seat, which he often sits on, occupied by a man and a woman who, Mr Hackett supposes, are perhaps 'waiting for the tram . . . for many trams stopped here, when requested, from without or within, to do so' (p. 8):[1]

Mr Hackett decided, after some moments, that if they were
waiting for a tram they had been doing so for some time.
For the lady held the gentleman by the ears, and the
gentleman's hand was on the lady's thigh, and the lady's
tongue was in the gentleman's mouth. Tired of waiting for the
tram, said Mr Hackett, they strike up an acquaintance. The
lady now removing her tongue from the gentleman's mouth,
he put his into hers. Fair do, said Mr Hackett. Taking a pace
forward, to satisfy himself that the gentleman's other hand
was not going to waste, Mr Hackett was shocked to find it
limply dangling over the back of the seat, with between its
fingers the spent three quarters of a cigarette.

I see no indecency, said the policeman.

We arrive too late, said Mr Hackett. What a shame.

The passage is characteristic of Beckett's manner in the opening section of the novel. There is first the observation of a commonplace situation and set of attitudes which depends on the assumption of scientific objectivity and precision. Perhaps no writer since Sterne has recorded bodily contortions with this combination of attention to detail and detached seriousness. The comedy here arises, indeed, primarily from the play of objectivity with which Beckett presents commonplace activities so that, as in Sterne, the normal is revealed as bordering on the grotesque once it is accurately seen. In a different sphere there is a similar emphasis on the inherent comedy of bodily attitudes in Sterne's picture of Mr Shandy trying to put his left hand into his right-hand pocket[2] or in the measurement of the exact inclination at which Corporal Trim stood to deliver the sermon, 'bent forwards just so as to make an angle of 85 degrees'.[3] At times of crisis Sterne's characters are often left with no direct means of expression except through extravagant theatrical gesture of the kind that Mr Shandy so memorably affects when he learns that Tristram's nose has been crushed by Dr Slop's clumsy delivery, 'prostrate across the bed . . . in the most lamentable attitude', an emblem of rhetorical despair.[4] He appears dehumanised, an automaton. Beckett's interest in the automatism of gesture and attitude in the opening of *Watt* is similar to Sterne's and the interest is a continuing one. It is found again, for example, in the description of Watt's extraordinary manner of walking (p. 32) or in the physical effects produced by words on the characters of both novels. Sam, the narrator of Beckett's story, says that one of Watt's sentences caused him 'more alarm, more pain than a charge of small shot in the ravine' (p. 174), and Tristram that 'had ten dozen of hornets stung my father behind in so many different places all at one time, he could not have exerted more mechanical functions in few seconds' than one single question 'popping in full upon him in his hobbyhorsical career'.[5]

In both Beckett and Sterne the observation of gesture and attitude is precise, but the tone ensures that physical reactions are seen as essentially bizarre and comic. The tone of the passage from *Watt* is partly established by the nervous, half-parodic, semi-official yet mocking exactitude of 'many trams stopped . . . when requested, from without or within, to do so', a sentence which by its parenthetical slowness and its play with formal language invites a sceptical attention to what is being presented. Mr Hackett's understated explanation of the scene he witnesses ('tired of waiting for the tram . . . they strike up an acquaintance') and his frustrated voyeurism ('[he] was shocked to find . . .') contribute to the tone of surprised detachment and speculation. And the dislocation of temporal expectations in the interval between paragraphs, leaving the reader to supply Mr Hackett's summoning of the policeman, further suggests that the writing must be approached analytically, with the kind of co-operation that Sterne demands when he scolds his reader for not being sufficiently active: 'How could you, Madam, be so inattentive in reading the last chapter?'[6] This demand is reinforced in *Watt*, as early as the opening episode, by a footnote which claims that 'much space has been saved, in this work, that would otherwise have been lost by avoidance of the plethoric reflexive pronoun after say'. The note reveals the narrator's pedantic and self-regarding character, but it also invites attention to the mechanics of the story and at the same time mocks the reader's participation by inevitably raising the impossible question of whether space can, in this sense, be said to be 'saved' or 'lost'. The rhetorical effect of the scene is to establish that the fiction will not be transparent, in the sense that it might be if the fictional world could be accepted passively or undiscriminatingly; it must be constantly scrutinised and interpreted by a sceptical and active reader.

The assumption that there is a close yet equivocal relationship between author and reader continues in the opening section of *Watt* to support a comedy which is Sternean in mood. After giving up his seat, Mr Hackett meets a lady and gentleman who, after seeing a pregnant woman whose 'belly could be dimly seen, sticking out like a balloon', recall the sudden birth of their son with an excitement that is undercut by earnest comments and painstaking inquiries from Mr Hackett which have a Shandean combination of speculative and impractical absurdity (p. 15):

That is a thing I often wondered, said Mr Hackett, what it feels like to have the string cut.

For the mother or the child? said Goff.

For the mother, said Mr Hackett, I was not found under a cabbage, I believe.

For the mother, said Tetty, the feeling is one of relief, of great relief, as when the guests depart. All my subsequent strings were severed by Professor Cooper, but the feeling was always the same, one of riddance.

Then you dressed and came downstairs, said Mr Hackett, leading the infant by the hand.

At this point in the story it can be suggested that the tone of the comedy, its preoccupations, the linguistic play, narrative disjunctions, involvement of the reader, are close enough to Sterne to make it appropriate to respond to *Watt* in the light of one's experience of *Tristram Shandy*, despite the fact that the narrative voice is objective and the speaker is not apparently, like Tristram, involved in the action. But there are already features in the narrative method which, while Sternean, point beyond Sterne to Swift, and especially to *A Tale of a Tub*.[7]

Some narrative devices which link *Tristram Shandy*, *A Tale of a Tub* and *Watt* are clear in the very typography and layout of the book. Footnotes, for example, are common, sometimes providing elementary information, sometimes supplementing the narrative, sometimes calling attention to its inadequacies, or sympathising with the perplexities of 'the attentive reader'. There are lacunae in the text indicated either by question-marks or, towards the end, by statements that there is a 'Hiatus in MS' or 'MS illegible'. And these indications of authorial inadequacy are reinforced by the concluding 'Addenda', a collection of enigmatic snippets, described in a footnote as 'precious and illuminating' which, it is said, were omitted only because of 'fatigue and disgust'. The effect is to call into question the reliability of the fictional world by stressing the arbitrariness of what is presented and its incompleteness. The sense of formlessness is emphasised when the narrator corrects himself in mid-sentence – 'This refusal, by Knott, I beg your pardon, by Watt . . .' (p. 126) – or pauses to observe: 'How hideous is the semi-colon' (p. 172).

These features of the narrative are obvious on the page and the links that they suggest between Beckett and the tradition of learned wit have a most significant bearing on the structure of *Watt* as a satiric work. The most important function of the narrative peculiarities is that they validate doubts that we are bound to have about Sam, the teller of the tale. Sam's status, indeed his existence, is realised only gradually by the reader of *Watt*. The first section appears to be told by an omniscient third-person narrator. It is only in the second section, some 130 pages through the work, that the narrator reveals himself as an acquaintance of Watt who is recounting a story that he had himself been told.

'For all that I know on the subject of Mr Knott, and of all that
touched Mr Knott, and on the subject of Watt, and of all that
touched Watt, came from Watt, and from Watt alone' (pp. 137–8).
And Sam asserts a little later that when the impossibility of his
knowledge seems 'absolute and insurmountable, and undeniable
and uncoercible', yet his information comes direct from Watt who
knew 'because someone told him, or because he found out for
himself' (p. 140). As readers, however, we are bound to be suspi-
cious of this claim because there are many things in the first section
of the novel that Sam could not possibly have learned from Watt –
the scenes with Mr Hackett, for example, in which Watt plays no
part and about which he could have had no information, or the
reactions of Mr Hackett and Tetty to Watt's first, dehumanised
appearance as he gets off the tram (p. 17):

> a solitary figure, lit less and less by the receding lights,
> until it was scarcely to be distinguished from the dim wall
> behind it. Tetty was not sure whether it was a man or a
> woman. Mr Hackett was not sure that it was not a parcel,
> a carpet for example, or a roll of tarpaulin, wrapped up in
> dark paper and tied about the middle with a cord.

His knowledge of these scenes is not accounted for by Sam, except
perhaps indirectly, by an admission which in its comprehensiveness
nullifies his entire claim to special knowledge. Everything he
knows he knows from Watt, but this (pp. 138–9)

> does not mean that Watt may not have left out some of the
> things that happened, or that were, or that he may not have
> foisted in other things that never happened, or never
> were. . . . And this does not mean either that I may not
> have left out some of the things that Watt told me, or foisted
> in others that Watt never told me, though I was most
> careful to note down all at the time, in my little notebook.

The fact is that Sam's assertion that he has special knowledge is
shown, by this later admission, to be completely valueless to the
reader. It is not necessarily that nothing he says is true, but that
there is no longer any way of distinguishing between the true and
the false, between events which could be authenticated and those
which have been 'foisted in'. Nor, even if a way could be found
of distinguishing the insertions, would it be possible to say whether
Watt or Sam had played false with the evidence. There is no base
within the work from which the action or events can be viewed.
It is the combination of a plausible but completely unreliable
narrator with a lack of any apparent normative standpoint in the

fiction that relates the experience of reading *Watt* to that of reading Swift, and especially *A Tale of a Tub*, a work which in important formal respects stands as a forerunner of *Tristram Shandy*.[8] Indeed, one way of suggesting the structure of the work would be to say that what happens as one moves in *Watt* from the basically realistic setting of the first section in Dublin to the central sections which deal with Watt's experiences in Mr Knott's house, is that Swiftian features in the narrative method become dominant and must be taken fully into account if one is to read the work appropriately.

Swift's narrator is a busy, progressive modernist, a figure who is built up through parody as a representative satiric object who embodies the complacency, the aimless bustling energy and misdirected zeal that Swift wished to attack. He is 'a most devoted servant of all modern forms' who believes that contemporary writers have completely 'eclipsed the weak glimmering lights of the ancients' and who laments that 'no famous modern hath ever yet attempted an universal system, in a small portable volume, of all things that are to be known, or believed, or imagined, or practised in life.'[9] In this situation he finds it an ease to his conscience that he has 'writ so useful a discourse without one grain of satire intermixed', and he lays claim to 'an absolute authority in right as the freshest modern' to a despotic power over all writers that preceded him.[10] Like Sam he is assured and complacent about his competence and it is from this standpoint of satisfaction that he moves by devious ways to his celebrated examination, in the 'Digression Concerning . . . Madness', of delusion as the great source of all human happiness:[11]

> How fading and insipid do all objects accost us, that are not
> conveyed in the vehicle of delusion! How shrunk is
> everything, as it appears in the glass of nature! So that
> if it were not for the assistance of artificial mediums,
> false lights, refracted angles, varnish, and tinsel, there
> would be a mighty level in the felicity and enjoyments of
> mortal men.

Happiness involves the maintenance of delusion, it is 'a perpetual possession of being well-deceived', an ability to be content with 'the films and images that fly off upon his senses from the superfices of things'. Because of this definition of happiness the narrator believes that the 'flaws and imperfections of nature' should be kept hidden: the truth about man is best left uninvestigated.

The argument is plausible and indeed partially correct in its diagnosis of the human condition. Any investigation that probes below the surface will show that man is corrupt. The modernist narrator of *A Tale of a Tub* is wrong only in the treatment that he prescribes, that is that it is good to 'sodder and patch up' human nature rather than to expose its faults. And because the argument is both plausible in its development and correct up to a point in its conclusions, there is a great weight of responsibility on the reader to interpret the *Tale* correctly. He is tempted in two directions, either to reject the diagnosis (which is a correct one) or to accept the proposed treatment (which is wrong-headed), and he can reach an appropriate interpretation only by bringing the right assumptions with him to the work, the assumption that human nature is fallen and therefore corrupt, and that it must always be right to face the truth rather than hide it.

But the fact that this is nowhere stated in the work and that the reader is responsible to himself for interpreting the *Tale* leads to a curious effect of alienation which is shown in the first place by a total absence of pressure. The reader is in the hands of a narrator who is unpredictable and unhurryable. It is no good expecting forward or measurable movement, and a mood of patient contemplation becomes the only possible one. Because the relationship with the narrator is equivocal, despite his marked affability, the reader lacks the sort of commitment that would normally be given even in a discursive work (a commitment at least to the mode of discourse itself) and there is a sense of total detachment as the narrator exposes his absurdity in a complete unawareness of what is happening.

The total detachment between narrator and reader which is an essential part of Swift's strategy in the *Tale* is a condition of the effect in the major satirical passages, most notably in the 'Digression Concerning . . . Madness' where, in the famous passage, the narrator's scientific busyness becomes most alarming:

in most corporeal beings, which have fallen under my cognizance, the outside hath been infinitely preferable to the in; whereof I have been further convinced from some late experiments. Last week I saw a woman flayed, and you will hardly believe how much it altered her person for the worse. Yesterday I ordered the carcass of a beau to be stripped in my presence, when we were all amazed to find so many unsuspected faults under one suit of clothes. Then I laid open his brain, his heart, and his spleen; but I plainly perceived at every operation that the farther we proceeded, we found the defects to increase upon us in number and bulk.

The passage gains its effect by a startling combination of experimental curiosity and moral insensitivity which leads very soon to the absurd praise of the 'serene peaceful state of being a fool among knaves'. The reader's reaction is one of increasing unease and disturbance as the impossible yet apparently unqualifiable argument moves forward.

In *Watt*, Sam has an equally bland insensitivity, both to his subject-matter and to his possible audience, in a passage on the innocent garden diversions that he enjoyed with Watt during their time in the asylum, and the reader experiences an equal consternation (p. 170):

> But our particular friends were the rats, that dwelt by the stream. They were long and black. We brought them such titbits from our ordinary as rinds of cheese, and morsels of gristle, and we brought them also birds' eggs, and frogs, and fledgelings. Sensible of these attentions, they would come flocking round us at our approach, with every sign of confidence and affection, and glide up our trouserlegs, and hang upon our breasts. And then we would sit down in the midst of them, and give them to eat, out of our hands, of a nice fat frog, or a baby thrush. Or seizing suddenly a plump young rat, resting in our bosom after its repast, we would feed it to its mother, or its father, or its brother, or its sister, or to some less fortunate relative.
>
> It was on these occasions, we agreed, after an exchange of views, that we came nearest to God.

The reader's shocked sense of alienation from this passage, and anything other than alienation would surely be unthinkable, is enforced in various ways. There is the grotesque humour of the language in its use of Biblical echoes ('then we would sit down in the midst of them, and give them to eat') and elegant formality ('sensible of these attentions'); the absurdly anthropocentric systematising of the family relationships ('its mother, or its father, or its brother, or its sister'); the disturbing unintended irony of 'or some less fortunate relative' and, above all, the cool theological nihilism of the final comment. Confronted by these things the reader must inevitably dissociate himself from Sam and judge what is being presented. Even if he accepts the implications of the final comment on the nature of God, he is unlikely to accept Sam's complacent mimicry of divine attributes. Again, as in Swift, he has the responsibility for establishing a just position in relation to elaborately indirect material, and this must involve a rejection of the narrator's position.

The unreliability of the narrator, the lack of any clear authorial guidance within the fiction, and the necessity for a special kind of responsibility in the reader links *Watt* and *A Tale of a Tub*. And this analogy, if accepted, carries implications which are central not only to one's response to the narrator, but also to the form of the novel and, finally, to Watt himself and his experiences.

The formal implications have to do with the collapse of structure which makes the experience of reading *Watt* so strange and even at times unnerving. At the beginning of Section IV Sam suggests that he has a clear plan in mind: 'As Watt told the beginning of his story, not first, but second, so not fourth, but third, now he told its end. Two, one, four, three, that was the order in which Watt told his story' (p. 237). Yet, as has often been pointed out, this clearly proclaimed order is not the order of the book, which proceeds rather: one, two, four, three. But in the context of the story this inconsistency is a trivial one because as it is written the line of development is at best a tenuous one, continually deflected or overlaid with digressive material so that the form itself becomes a satiric representation of a failure of authorial control. Here again the parallel with *A Tale of a Tub* and *Tristram Shandy* is close. In these works the thin line of plot is submerged in arabesques of apparent irrelevance which demonstrate in one case the inadequacies of the narrator and in the other the dangers of memory. What the books show is a collapse of form which undercuts all the assumptions that the narrators make about the 'illustrious moderns' or the possibility of autobiography. As, in Pope's *Dunciad*, a key idea is contained in the word *spawning* ('Hints, like spawn, scarce quick in embryo lie' . . . 'Maggots, half-formed, in rhyme exactly meet'),[12] and we see the pattern of the epic collapse under the pressure of duncical material so that the failure of the form mimes the pessimistic prophecy that Pope is making, so, in *A Tale of a Tub*, the digressive convolutions of the form enact inadequacies in the mind of the modernist narrator. Similarly in *Tristram Shandy*, the elephantine series of digressions always threatens to submerge events and in a sense does so since, because of them, Tristram, instead of getting nearer the end of his story as he goes on finds that, on the contrary, he is continually receding from it: '. . . was every day of my life to be as busy as this . . . I should live 364 times faster than I should write. It must follow . . . that the more I write, the more I shall have to write.'[13]

The tone is bemused, humorous, and this is what we expect in

Sterne, but objectively considered, the situation is one of horror with a surrealistic, Ionesco kind of quality about it which shows man at the mercy of something that grows beyond his control, something that spawns. 'Matter grows under our hands', says Tristram. 'Let no man say, – "Come – I'll write a duodecimo".'[14]

The growth of matter in the hands of Sam is the most disconcerting feature of *Watt*. In its major phases this is seen in Arsène's 'short statement' on his experiences in Mr Knott's house, which covers nearly thirty pages, the story of Louit's adventures with Mr Nackyball or the elaborate account of the Lynch family and its ambitions. The characteristic note is one of absurdity bordering on the grotesque, the grotesque arising from the element which Tristram commented on in his own story, the apparently self-generating power of the narrative. This is experienced very strongly in Sam's treatment of the Lynch family whose members look after the dog which has to be available to eat any left-overs from Mr Knott's dinner. Each member of the family, twenty-eight of them, all meticulously described, is smitten by paralysis, pox or some other disease, but none the less they have an ambition with which Watt can entirely sympathise. Their combined ages amount to 980 years: 'Five generations, twenty-eight souls, nine hundred and eighty years, such was the proud record of the Lynch family . . .' (p. 113), and their ambition is to reach a communal millennium. Since they are naturally all growing older all the time, they can expect to reach their goal in eight months and a half. But it is here that the material begins to spawn. The situation is not static. There can be deaths and births, as there are, and with each one the calculations have to be done afresh. But apart from the calculations, Sam finds it necessary to consider the reasons for the various accidents that befall the family. At a critical point, after the Lynch family has been cast into gloom by a sudden death and unexpectedly made hopeful again when Ann retired to her room and 'gave birth, first to a fine bouncing baby boy, and then to an almost equally fine bouncing baby girl', the 'question that began on all hands openly to be asked was this, who had done or whom had Ann persuaded to do, this thing to Ann?' (pp. 116–17):

> Some said it was her cousin Sam, whose amorous disposition was notorious, not only among the members of his immediate family, but throughout the neighbourhood, and who made no secret of his having committed adultery locally on a large scale, moving from place to place in his self-propelling invalid's chair, with widow women, with married women and

with single women of whom some were young and attractive,
and others young but not attractive, and others attractive
but not young, and others neither young nor attractive, and
of whom some as a result of Sam's intervention conceived and
brought forth a son or a daughter or two sons or two
daughters or a son and a daughter, for Sam had never
managed triplets, and this was a sore point with Sam, that
he had never managed triplets, and others conceived but
did not bring forth, and others did not conceive at all,
though this was exceptional, that they did not conceive at
all, when Sam intervened. And when reproached with this
Sam with ready wit replied that paralysed as he was, from
the waist up, and from the knees down, he had no purpose,
interest or joy in life other than this, to set out after a
good dinner of meat and vegetables in his wheel-chair and
stay out committing adultery until it was time to go home
to his supper, after which he was at his wife's disposal.

In passages of this kind the narrative develops a comic life of its
own, expanding and burgeoning in apparently arbitrary directions
and demonstrating through its evident fictionality, the hollowness
of Sam's claim to be giving a merely verbatim report. Here, as in
the Louit-Nackyball section, or the splendid account of Watt's
amours with Mrs Gorman, Sam gains the freedom of fiction, but
he does so only by destroying the form of the narrative that he
purports to be telling, and by showing again, this time through
his fertile invention, his own unreliability as a witness. And this
erosion of credibility produces a situation where all the assertions
of the speaker become suspect.

The most radical suspicion arises when we consider the relationship between Sam and Watt, the man whose story he is supposedly
telling. As we saw, Sam does not explicitly come forward as the
narrator before page 137, and until that point Watt appears to
have an objective reality. His first appearance, looking like a 'roll
of tarpaulin, wrapped up in dark paper and tied about the middle
with a cord' (p. 17), his arrival at Mr Knott's house where he
enters through a door which is 'on the latch' (p. 39), his encounter
with Arsène and the early adventures with the routines of Mr
Knott's mysterious household – all these build up a figure whom
we come to accept as having a strange but recognisable reality, a
man engaged in a dogged and in some ways admirable attempt to
find an explanation for the experiences that beset him. With the
introduction of Sam, however, the reader's response to Watt

becomes far more problematic. The difficulty is that it is soon impossible to maintain any clear distinction between Sam and the subject of his story. The characteristically patient search for an explanation of his experiences had seemed to be the distinguishing feature of Watt's mind. 'For to explain had always been to exorcise, for Watt' (p. 85), and in order to explain he is prepared to entertain an unlimited number of hypotheses concerning an experience, to select, modify and change them 'as often as might be found necessary'. But his explanations suffer from the limitation that they are entirely speculative and private, owing as little as possible to tradition or verifiable opinion, for Watt does not care to ask for information. He believes that 'all will be revealed in due time' (p. 130) and meanwhile surrounds himself with a wall of hypotheses. When we meet Sam, however, it is clear that Watt's habits of thought and language, though strange, are by no means unique. They are shared by Sam to a remarkable degree. When, for example, in Section III, Sam recounts his meeting with Watt in the grounds of the 'asylum' in which they live, he speculates on the cause of holes in the fence which give them access to each other, and he concludes that the hole must have been made by the weather rather than by a boar or a bull (p. 175):

> For where was the boar, where the bull, capable, after
> bursting a hole in the first fence, of bursting a second,
> exactly similar, in the second? But would not the bursting
> of the first hole so reduce the infuriated mass as to render
> impossible, in the course of the same charge, the bursting of
> the second? Add to this that a bare yard separated the
> fences, at this point, so that the snout would be, of necessity,
> in contact with the second fence, before the hind-quarters
> were clear of the first, and consequently the space be
> lacking in which, after the bursting of the first hole, the
> fresh impetus might be developed necessary to the bursting
> of the second.

The manner of the argument – its fancifulness, its fertility and its gratuitousness – are entirely Wattian. Arguments of this kind by Sam enable us to see, retrospectively, the extent to which his presentation has dictated our understanding of Watt. At first, for instance, Sam's mid-point comment on the episode of the Galls, father and son, seems to express the Wattian anxiety for completeness (pp. 82–3):

For the incident of the Galls father and son was the first
and type of many. And the little that is known about it has
not yet all been said. Much has been said but not all.

Not that many things remain to be said, on the subject of
the Galls father and son, for they do not. For only three
or four things remain to be said, in this connexion. And
three or four things are not really many, in comparison with
the number of things that might have been known, and said,
on this subject, and now never shall.

Retrospectively, however, passages of this kind seem equally or
even more centrally to reflect Sam's neurotic narrative compulsion
to 'tell all', and one has increasingly the impression that Watt is
either concealed by the elaborations of Sam's narrative method,
a method which inevitably reflects Sam's mind, or alternatively
that he exists only as a fictional image of Sam himself. The second
possibility is most clearly suggested by episodes in Section III
which bring the two figures close to identity. Immediately after
the passage on the fence discussed above, Sam sees Watt in an
adjacent part of the garden, and as he looks across the garden he
comments: 'I suddenly felt as though I was standing before a great
mirror in which my garden was reflected, and my fence, and I and
the very birds tossing in the wind.' And when he moves into the
apparent mirror and joins Watt they come together in a kind of
ritualistic dance which is a demonstration of their closeness to
each other (p. 178):

> Then I placed his hands, on my shoulders, his left hand on
> my right shoulder, and his right hand on my left shoulder.
> Then I placed my hands, on his shoulders, on his left
> shoulder my right hand, and on his right shoulder my left
> hand. Then I took a single pace forward, with my left leg,
> and he a single pace back, with his right leg (he could
> scarcely do otherwise). . . . And so we paced together between
> the fences, I forwards, he backwards, until we came to where
> the fences diverged again.

The symbolic identity of the couple, or pseudo-couple, supports
more abstractedly an earlier moment in the garden when Sam and
Watt had embraced on the bridge: 'I touched Watt's left cheek
with my lips, and then Watt touched my left cheek with his (he
could scarcely do less), the whole coolly, and above us tossed the
overarching boughs' (p. 169). Such a scene makes it clear that
Watt, despite his apparent autonomy early in the story, can never

be more than Sam's creature. Watt has sometimes been seen as a heroic and more often as a questing figure whose search for understanding, though hopeless, is to be regarded seriously.[15] But it seems doubtful whether the satiric structure of the book allows this interpretation: rather that structure deliberately mocks the reader who attempts to make it by inviting false interpretations.

The early adventures in the house, for example, do seem to offer Watt as an Everyman, perhaps a heroic one, and the reader is clearly invited to see the action as an allegory of life itself, a chain of arbitrary events in which the individual participates without having the slightest power to alter them, only, in the end, to be supplanted by the next comer. On another level there are times when the house becomes an ironical parallel to conventional religious conceptions of the universe. We are told that (p. 144)

> Watt had more and more the impression, as time passed,
> that nothing could be added to Mr Knott's establishment,
> and from it nothing taken away, but that as it was now, so
> it had been in the beginning, and so it would remain to the
> end, in all essential respects, any significant presence . . .
> proving that presence at all times

where the house, the description reinforced by strong religious echoes, has the plenitude, the completeness of the universe seen through the eyes of an eighteenth-century deist, and Mr Knott figures as an inaccessible prime mover. But the reader who is tempted to take Mr Knott as a conventional godlike figure is eventually mocked. He is so, notably, in a passage which discusses Mr Knott's strange habits as regards the clothes he wears, which always have a complete inappropriateness (p. 222):[16]

> So that (Mr Knott) was not seldom to be seen, in his room,
> in his house, in his grounds, in strange and unseasonable
> costume, as though he were unaware of the weather, or of the
> time of year. And to see him sometimes thus, barefoot and
> for boating dressed, in the snow, in the slush, in the icy
> winter wind, or, when summer came again, by his fire,
> charged with furs, was to wonder, does he seek to know
> again, what is cold, what is heat? But this was an
> anthropomorphic insolence of short duration.
>
> For except, one, not to need, and, two, a witness to his
> not needing Knott needed nothing, so far as Watt could
> see.

It is anthropomorphic insolence for Watt to question Mr Knott's ways, yet at the same time he is the exact opposite of God as traditionally conceived. Far from being a divine sustaining consciousness whose constant presence gives life to all created things, Mr Knott is the incarnation of the irrational who needs a witness to sustain him. Here the house is working allegorically to provide satire of systematic interpretations of life and to focus not so much upon the situation in which Watt finds himself as the explanations which Sam, and through him the reader, have been inventing.

And it seems that there is equal satiric force in the presentation of Watt's early existentialist problems and particularly the long discussion that arises from the incident of the Galls, piano-tuners who visit Mr Knott's house 'all the way from town, to choon the piano' and whose visit ends in an absurd dialogue which Watt cannot understand but which he is unable to ignore or forget (p. 81):

> He did not know what had happened. . . . But he felt the
> need to think that such and such a thing had happened
> then, the need to be able to say, when the scene began to
> unroll its sequences, Yes, I remember, that is what happened
> then.

And because this need is insistent the 'fragility of the outer meaning had a bad effect on Watt, for it caused him to seek for another' (p. 79) until the literal meaning of the words disappears altogether, and he is left only with his anxious and frenetic attempts at imposing a significance. More and more Watt now found himself 'in the midst of things which, if they consented to be named, did so as it were with reluctance'. This applies not only to events, but to objects as in the celebrated case of the comfortless pot (p. 89):

> Looking at a pot, for example, or thinking of a pot, at one
> of Mr Knott's pots, or of one of Mr Knott's pots, it was in
> vain that Watt said, Pot, pot. Well, perhaps not quite in
> vain, but very nearly. For it was not a pot . . . it resembled
> a pot, it was almost a pot, but it was not a pot of which
> one could say, Pot, pot, and be comforted.

There is some pathos in Watt's consternation, but if one compares his experience with the anguish produced by similar doubts in the hero of Sartre's *Nausea*, then the extent to which Watt's response is being satirised is very clear. Sartre's Antoine Roquentin puts his hand on the back of a seat in a tram, names it to himself, but discovers that surrealistically, the seat is no longer contained by its name:[17]

> I murmur: 'It's a seat,' rather like an exorcism. But the
> word remains on my lips, it refuses to settle on the thing.
> It stays what it is, with its red plush, thousands of little
> red paws in the air, all stiff, little dead paws. This huge
> belly turns upwards, bleeding, puffed up – bloated with
> all its dead paws, this belly floating in this box, in this grey
> sky, is not a seat. It could just as well be a dead donkey,
> for example, swollen by the water and drifting along,
> belly up on a great grey river . . . things have broken free
> from their names. They are there grotesque, gigantic, stubborn
> . . . I am in the midst of Things which cannot be given
> names. . . .

Roquentin acknowledges the unique reality and horror of the individual experience. But Watt, through his reasoning (or at least through Sam's account of it) denies the individual experience. He never loses his sense that the defining word is superior to the object itself, that the explanation and the generic relationship is more important than the event. Watt is at the farthest possible remove from the mode of perception described by Beckett in *Proust*:[18]

> when the object is perceived as particular and unique
> and not merely the member of a family, when it appears
> independent of any general notion and detached from the
> sanity of a cause, isolated and inexplicable in the light
> of ignorance, then and then only may it be a source of
> enchantment.

Watt escapes always away from the particular and unique so as to organise the enchantment of his experiences according to 'the propositions of his team of syntheses'.

To accept the object or the moment as isolated and inexplicable is impossible for him, though there is one point when he seems close to doing so. During his departure from Mr Knott's house 'he contemplated with wonder . . . the ample recession of the plain, its flow so free and simple to the mountains, the crumpled umbers of its verge' (p. 247), and as, from the station, he looks back over the road he has travelled and sees what appears to be a figure moving along it, he recognises that 'it was greatly to be deplored that he cared what it was, coming along the road, profoundly to be deplored' (pp. 249–50). But the caring, the anxiety, is inescapable for Watt, or at least for Sam. But neither can he reach the point of understanding achieved by Arsène during his monologue when he says (p. 48):

The glutton castaway, the drunkard in the desert, the lecher in prison, they are the happy ones. To hunger, thirst, lust, every day afresh and every day in vain, after the old prog, the old booze, the old whores, that's the nearest we'll ever get to felicity, the new porch and the very latest garden. I pass on the tip for what it is worth.

Metaphorically Sam's creature, Watt, hungers, thirsts and lusts while remaining anxious always to find the explaining formula which will lead to escape from these things. These contradictions make him at once a very human figure, and a fitting subject for the complex satirical shape of the book.

NOTES

1 Page references are to the Olympia Press ('Traveller's Companion') edition, Paris, 1958.
2 *The Life and Opinions of Tristram Shandy, Gentleman*, ed. Ian Watt, Riverside Edition, Riverside Press, Cambridge, 1965, vol. III, ch. 2.
3 Ibid., vol. II, ch. 17.
4 Ibid., vol. III, ch. 29.
5 Ibid., vol. III, ch. 41.
6 Ibid., vol. I, ch. 20.
7 For studies of the relationship between Swift and Beckett see John Fletcher, 'Beckett et Swift: vers une étude comparée', *Littératures* (Toulouse), vol. X, 1962, pp. 81–117, and *Samuel Beckett's Art*, Chatto & Windus, London, 1967, ch. V.
8 See Melvyn New, *Laurence Sterne as Satirist: A Reading of 'Tristram Shandy'*, Gainesville, Florida, 1969.
9 *A Tale of a Tub*, 'The Author's Preface' and 'A Digression in the Modern Kind'. Passages are modernised. See the edition by A. C. Guthkelch and D. Nicol Smith, Oxford University Press, 2nd ed., 1958.
10 Ibid., 'The Author's Preface' and 'A Digression in the Modern Kind'.
11 Ibid., 'A Digression Concerning . . . Madness . . .'.
12 Pope, *Dunciad*, 1743, bk. I, ll. 59–61.
13 *Tristram Shandy*, vol. IV, ch. 13.
14 Ibid., vol. V, ch. 16.
15 Cf. R. Federman, *Journey to Chaos*, Berkeley and Los Angeles, 1965, ch. IV.
16 It is incidentally interesting to compare Swift's account of Jack in section XI of *A Tale of a Tub*: 'In winter he went always loose and unbuttoned, and clad as thin as possible, to let *in* the ambient heat; and in summer lapped himself close and thick to keep it *out*.'
17 Jean-Paul Sartre, *Nausea*, Penguin Modern Classics edition, Harmondsworth, 1965, p. 180. I am grateful to Michael Mason for suggesting a comparison of *Watt* and *Nausea*.
18 Samuel Beckett, *Proust*, 1931, reprinted London, 1965, pp. 22–3.

Chapter 3

'The labours of poetical excavation'

Charles Peake

It may be irritating for Beckett to have his work repeatedly interpreted in the light of a critical study published over forty years ago, but nothing has appeared since his *Proust* (1931) which provides a better discursive terminology for what the subsequent fictions are about. Not that the critical language is clearer or more precise than the later images – on the contrary, much of it is fully intelligible only because the fictions show what Beckett had in mind – but it approximates to the familiar abstractions of psychology or philosophy and suggests in general terms the direction of Beckett's interests as an artist. He rejected realism and naturalism as 'worshipping the offal of experience . . . and content to transcribe the surface, the façade behind which the Idea is prisoner':

> The only fertile research is excavatory, immersive, a
> contraction of the spirit, a descent. The artist is active,
> but negatively, shrinking from the nullity of extra-
> circumferential phenomena, drawn into the core of the eddy.

The 'extracircumferential phenomena' from which the artist shrinks are those of ordinary consciousness, of the so-called 'reality' outside the circumference of the self; his true task is to explore what he is: 'The heart of the cauliflower or the ideal core of the onion would represent a more appropriate tribute to the labours of poetical excavation than the crown of bay.'

The image borrowed from Ibsen has been transformed in the borrowing. When Peer Gynt stripped away the layers of his onion, identifying each with one of the false selves he had assumed, he found nothing at the centre; it was an emblem of the loss or destruction of his true self. But Beckett's centre is 'the ideal core', the idea of a self, imprisoned beneath the surface of appearances: it is 'nothing' only in the sense that it belongs to a different order of existence from ordinary 'reality', which without it would not exist. It resembles the stock image of 'the still centre of the turning wheel', the mathematical point, implicit in the nature of the wheel but not expressible in terms of the physical substance of the wheel. If reality is defined as the wheel, the still centre is unreal, a nothing, an Idea, and yet it is the point around which and in relation to which the wheel turns. Beckett's excavations have been towards such an ideal centre, towards 'the only world that has reality and significance, the world of our own latent consciousness'. Yet this latent consciousness can neither be described nor imaged, because words and images belong and refer to 'extracircumferential phenomena'; if they are used, they must be used with an awareness of their falseness, and repeatedly contradicted or negated. Every fiction must be exposed as fictitious, and, consequently, since *Murphy* (1938) each novel has penetrated beneath and undermined its predecessors.

Murphy, itself, does not go very deep: it is more concerned with ridiculing the absurd insubstantiality of surface reality than with representing the inner life to which Murphy endeavours to escape and which is honoured by a whole chapter given to an account of 'what it felt and pictured itself to be', a world 'hermetically closed to the universe without' (p. 107).[1] Murphy is not interested in Cartesian explanations of the apparent intercourse between body and 'bodytight' mind; he is concerned only with being as often and as long as possible in his three mental zones, the light, half light, and dark. In the first, 'the elements of physical experience' are present but capable of rearrangement or reversal, so that a kick received by the physical Murphy can be delivered by the mental Murphy; in this daydream world 'the whole physical fiasco became a howling success'. The forms of the second zone have no parallel in the physical world: here Murphy chooses and contemplates forms created by his imagination. However, it is the 'dark', where there are no stable forms or states but only 'a flux of forms, a perpetual coming together and falling asunder of forms', which increasingly attracts Murphy. Whereas in the first two zones he feels himself to be 'sovereign and free', in this third trancelike state, he is 'not free, but a mote in the dark of absolute freedom'; and this perpetual flux 'without love or hate or any intelligible principle of change', this condition of 'will-lessness', is his ideal centre where the self is freed from space and time (pp. 108–13). The core is described, but in terms hardly less abstract than those used in *Proust*; all the fictional inventiveness has gone into the comic representation of the incompatibility of Murphy's inner and outer lives.

The dark zone may be without 'any intelligible principle of change', but the physical world, though a fiasco, seems governed by laws as rigid as those of mechanics. According to Wylie, the character most adapted to the ways of the world, 'the syndrome known as life is too diffuse to admit of palliation. For every symptom that is eased, another is made worse.' A man's wants and desires form 'a closed system' – the 'quantum of wantum cannot vary' (p. 57). In this closed system the characters of the novel flounder about. Murphy is pursued by four grotesques, each seeking him for some private end which, if achieved, would cease to be desired, while he himself is distracted from his true course by wanting Celia, the prostitute. He wants Celia to be with him and therefore to give up the nightly pursuit of her profession, but Celia, who wants Murphy even more than he wants her, sees the continuance of their union as conditional on Murphy's becoming a wage-earner – a role for which he has an absolute repulsion ('For what was all working for a living but a procuring and a pimping for the money-bags' – p. 76) and an almost total inadequacy. Murphy, better able to see others' delusions than his own, tries in vain to persuade Celia that her plan is self-defeating (p. 36):

> 'What do you love?' said Murphy. 'Me as I am. You can want what does not exist, you can't love it.' This came well from Murphy. 'Then why are you all out to change me? So that you won't have to love me. . . .'

The repeated frustration of everyone's desires and schemes articulates in farcical narrative what had been theoretically asserted in the book on Proust. The physical world is not hostile to man, but indifferent to him. There is no President of the Immortals sporting with Murphy and the rest: their frustrations and disappointments are self-induced, because they cannot accept the situation for what it is: 'Humanity is a well with two buckets,' said Wylie, 'one going down to be filled, the other coming up to be emptied' (p. 58).

Murphy's superiority over those who pursue him lies in his realisation that nothing can prosper in the outer confusion. He prefers torpor or escape into his mental world, but Celia disrupts his cultivated apathy and his mind is only an occasional and temporary refuge. Whenever he tries to palliate or improve his situation, he, like the rest, comes up against the closed system. On the small scale, he tries to introduce a little variety into his daily lunch, a packet of assorted biscuits, by working out the possible permutations in the order of consumption; the result is that, while he cogitates, a dog eats all the biscuits except the ginger ones, and he cannot bring himself to eat 'a rutting cur's rejectamenta' (p. 102). More importantly, he solves his work-problem by becoming a mental nurse in an asylum, where he envies the patients' condition because his experience 'obliged him to call sanctuary what the psychiatrists called exile and to think of the patients not as banished from a system of benefits but as escaped from a colossal fiasco' (pp. 177-8).

Yet even the relief he finds in his work has to be paid for; he finds himself no longer able to escape into the mental world, partly through fatigue and partly through 'the vicarious autology' (p. 189) he enjoys with the patients. Moreover, his dream of sharing the schizophrenics' freedom, like all other dreams, leads only to bitter disappointment. He becomes particularly fascinated by one patient, Mr Endon (*Greek* 'within'), who seems utterly and contentedly absorbed in his own inner life. Murphy's ultimate frustration is figured in a remarkable game of chess with Mr Endon, printed in full in chess notation and supplied with analytic commentary. Since Mr Endon will initiate nothing, Murphy has to take the white pieces, and opens with the commonest of opening moves, Pawn to King's fourth. At once there is a note: 'The primary cause of all White's subsequent difficulties' (p. 244). This is precisely true, for it is Murphy's plan to enter and share Mr Endon's abstracted state by imitating each move that he makes; but, after four moves, Mr Endon moves a Knight to King's fourth, which Murphy cannot imitate because of his unfortunate opening move. He has to introduce another move of his own, and so falls farther and farther behind in his imitation, until in despair he tries to make Mr Endon acknowledge his presence by placing pieces where they may be taken. The attempt is vain; Mr Endon's chess, like his mind, is entirely self-contained. His pieces execute a ritual dance across the board, change places with each other, and after forty-three moves all, except for two pawns necessarily advanced a square, have returned to their starting-points. Murphy, unable to penetrate Mr Endon's blissful self-absorption, collapses over the board, and later the same night is burnt to death in a ludicrous accident with a gas-fire.

Murphy's envy of the schizophrenics is also foreshadowed in *Proust*, which suggests that the only way in which 'the essence of ourselves' can escape the oppression of the physical world is by moving 'into the spacious annexe of mental alienation, in sleep or the rare dispensation of waking madness'. Murphy's mistake is in thinking that he can, of choice, enter the world of the mentally alienated; he does not recognise that it is 'a rare dispensation'. The initial move which is the origin of all his troubles on the chessboard symbolises his sin, 'the sin of having been born' – at least, of having been born sane.

The ironic discrepancy between the inner and outer worlds brushes aside man's own feeble attempts at irony. Posthumously

Murphy tries to have his own little joke against life by leaving a letter requesting that his ashes be disposed of in a lavatory in the Abbey Theatre 'where their happiest hours have been spent' (p. 269), but the man entrusted to carry the parcel of ashes back to Dublin becomes involved in an argument in a pub and the parcel is kicked and thrown about in the mêlée (p. 275):

> By closing time the body, mind and soul of Murphy were freely distributed over the floor of the saloon; and before another dayspring greyened the earth had been swept away with the sand, the beer, the butts, the glass, the matches, the spits, the vomit.

Murphy is the most accessible of Beckett's novels, but its contribution to the excavation of the hidden self is limited to breaking up the surface by presenting the ludicrous incompatibility of the two worlds in which men live, and the futility of attempts to palliate or escape the consequent pains. *Watt* (1953)[2] goes deeper, and tries to create a fictional image of what lies beneath the surface. In many respects it is complementary to *Murphy*, since the first novel is chiefly concerned with the absurd bafflement and distress of man in the indifferent world of external events, while *Watt* represents him as equally absurd, baffled and distressed in the inner world which to Murphy had seemed an unattainable sanctuary.

Watt, one of Beckett's barely mobile incompetents, enters the service of a Mr Knott, a mysterious gentleman who cannot be described because he is without any constant form, appearance, dress, manner, behaviour or gait: he never seems the same, yet never really changes. Nor, apparently, does he have any needs. Why then, Watt asks himself, does he have servants? His conclusion is that (p. 223)

> Mr Knott, needing nothing if not, one, not to need, and, two, a witness to his not needing, of himself knew nothing. And so he needed to be witnessed. Not that he might know, no, but that he might not cease.

Through the clumsy words of Watt (or attributed to Watt by the author) one can perceive the first shadowy image of the Self as mere existence. Mr Knott exists apart from time and space; he does not change, but, because he has no external qualities of his own, to the observer his qualities seem different every time he is observed; and he can have no ordinary needs since they are meaningless in a non-physical, timeless world. He is integral Self, and therefore is not conscious of himself, because that would imply a division into a self, and another self conscious of the first. His need to be witnessed is an application of the Berkeleyan dictum *esse est percipi*, used later as the structural principle of Beckett's *Film*. All that can be predicted of the ideal core of the human onion is that it has no needs and that it needs to be perceived, since that is the condition of all existence.

In Mr Knott's house, Watt finds the absolute freedom to which Murphy aspired and which he experienced in his 'dark' mental zone. It is a still point, a resting-place, a refuge from the world (p. 43):

> All the old ways led to this, all the old windings, the
> stairs with never a landing that you screw yourself up,
> clutching the rail, counting the steps, the fever of shortest
> ways under the long lids of sky, the wild country roads
> where your dead walk beside you, on the dark shingle the
> turning for the last time again to the lights of the little town,
> the appointments kept and the appointments broken, all
> the delights of urban and rural change of place, all the
> exitus and redditus, closed and ended.

These words are spoken by Arsène, a servant who is about to leave the house as Watt arrives. Arsène describes for Watt's benefit the feelings of a newcomer to Mr Knott's house (pp. 43–4):

> He is well pleased. For he knows he is in the right place,
> at last. And he knows he is the right man, at last. . . .
> The sensations, the premonitions of harmony are irrefragable,
> of imminent harmony, when all outside him will be he, the
> flowers the flowers that he is among him, the sky the sky
> that he is above him, the earth trodden the earth treading,
> and all sound his echo. When in a word he will be in his
> midst at last, after so many tedious years spent clinging
> to the perimeter.

Here the old painful division of outer and inner, body and mind, seems dispelled; man 'is in the right place, at last'.

Why, then, is Arsène leaving? That he finds 'hard to say' (p. 46). All he knows is that each man who enters Mr Knott's service eventually leaves it and is replaced by another; only Mr Knott himself 'neither comes nor goes . . . but seems to abide in his place' (p. 63). For Arsène, after his initial bliss, a day came when there was a change – he cannot say whether internal or external because in Mr Knott's house the distinction between the two cannot be drawn. 'Something slipped' (p. 46); there was a 'reversed metamorphosis' (p. 48):

> The Laurel into Daphne. The old thing where it always
> was, back again. As when a man, having found at last
> what he sought, a woman, for example, or a friend, loses
> it, or realises what it is. And yet it is useless not to seek,
> not to want, for when you cease to seek you start to find,
> and when you cease to want, then life begins to ram her
> fish and chips down your gullet until you puke, and then
> the puke down your gullet until you puke the puke, and
> then the puked puke until you begin to like it. The
> glutton castaway, the drunkard in the desert, the lecher
> in prison, they are the happy ones. To hunger, thirst, lust,
> every day afresh and every day in vain, after the old
> prog, the old booze, the old whores, that's the nearest
> we'll ever get to felicity, the new porch and the very
> latest garden.

Murphy's notion of 'felicity' was of a 'self-immersed indifference to the contingencies of the contingent world' (*Murphy*, p. 168), but Arsène, having achieved such self-immersion, cannot endure it indefinitely. Like Johnson's Rasselas, but unlike Mr Knott, he and the other servants need to have needs. Murphy found it impossible to escape, except briefly and occasionally, from the torments of needing and wanting: Arsène's experience suggests that, even when freed from them, a need for them at length asserts itself. A nostalgia for change and transience develops in Mr Knott's house which, as Watt discovers, admits of no significant change (p. 144):

> Watt had more and more the impression, as time passed,
> that nothing could be added to Mr Knott's establishment,
> and from it nothing taken away, but that as it was now,
> so it had been in the beginning, and so it would remain
> to the end, in all essential respects.

Thus the first penetration below the surface unearths a new impasse, more fundamental than any in *Murphy*: what Murphy dreamed of as a final goal turns out to be yet another dilemma. Man's duality is so radical and chronic that he cannot settle either in the external world, which goes its ways indifferent to him, or in the self-immersed internal world indifferent to what lies outside it.

But this is only Arsène's account, who is counted among the 'small fat shabby seedy juicy bandylegged potbellied potbottomed men', and may not tally with the experience of Watt, who belongs to the category of 'big bony seedy shabby haggard knockkneed rottentoothed rednosed men' (p. 65). Certainly the two men seem different in every way (apart from a common seediness and shabbiness). Arsène speaks poetically, nostalgically, even sentimentally of the natural world and the seasonal cycle; Watt seems devoid of poetry and is more mechanical than natural. His walk, if it can be called a walk, is a kind of rationalised progression, and even his smile is manufactured (p. 26):

> Watt had watched people smile and thought he understood
> how it was done. . . . But there was something wanting to
> Watt's smile, some little thing was lacking, and people
> who saw it for the first time, and most people who saw
> it saw it for the first time, were sometimes in doubt as
> to what expression exactly was intended. To many it
> seemed a simple sucking of the teeth.

Watt, in his blundering way, is rational, needing to analyse and understand a smile before he can attempt one. Consequently, it is not the same kind of nostalgia as troubled Arsène that begins to trouble Watt; it is an equally incurable human compulsion, the compulsion to understand. He is not looking for profound or symbolic meanings; on the contrary, we are told that he had been satisfied with face-values all his adult life. But, at Mr Knott's, events occur – in particular, the arrival and behaviour of two piano-tuners – which leave Watt baffled. In this unchanging world, there is no necessary concatenation of cause and effect (or, as it is put in *Murphy*, no 'intelligible principle of change'), and Watt, trying to explain to himself what is taking place, engages in long and fruitless permutations of conceivable explanations. The occurrences disturb him because he is unable to (pp. 81–2)

> accept them for what they perhaps were, the simple games
> that time plays with space, now with these toys, and now
> with those, but was obliged, because of his peculiar character,
> to enquire into what they meant, oh not into what they
> really meant, his character was not so peculiar as all that,
> but into what they might be induced to mean, with the
> help of a little patience, a little ingenuity.

This introduces another characteristically Beckettian theme – the notion of 'meaning' as that ordering of experience which man compulsively needs and, not finding (since it exists only as his need), imposes or seeks to impose. The resulting explanations, never wholly satisfactory and always temporary, give an illusion of security in the welter of experience. Men are like Watt who (p. 85)

> considered, with reason, that he was successful, in this enterprise, when he could evolve, from the meticulous phantoms that beset him, a hypothesis proper to disperse them, as often as this might be found necessary. . . . For to explain had always been to exorcize, for Watt.

This same compulsion to discover order and meaning rules the scientist and the artist, the novelist and the critic, and is prominent among the self-defeating principles of Beckett's works.

Consider its treatment in *Waiting for Godot*. The situation is simple enough; here are two men at a place, hardly chosen, where they seem to have been before the play began and where they remain when it is over. It is merely a situation, but, for them to endure it, it must be endowed with meaning. If they are there, it must be for a reason – they must be waiting. But for whom? For Godot. It soon appears that they have never seen Godot, never spoken to him, know nothing of him, don't know what he can do for them, don't know what they are going to ask him to do for them. Questions as to who he is or what he is are unanswerable. There is nothing to show that the word 'Godot' like the word 'waiting' is any more than part of the explanation they have evolved to account for their situation and thus to make it a little less unendurable.

Yet Beckett, in order to present this vision of meaninglessness, has to order and arrange words and dramatic action, has to impose a meaning on his own experience; and the critic, in order to talk about the play, is similarly compelled to impose a meaning on what he experiences in the theatre. Yet to do so, as I have just done, is to exorcise the play, because, whatever the significance of a work of art, it is not reducible to discursive statement. The only excuse is the human obligation to impose meanings. As, in terms of the physical world, the 'latent consciousness' is nothing, so, in the terms available to criticism, the work of art is nothing. Both are human 'meanings', both are fictions, but they belong to different worlds: one cannot 'mean' the same as the other. Yet, according to Beckett's scheme, the reader (and a critic is only a special kind of reader) has no more choice than the artist: as Beckett says in *Watt*, 'the only way one can speak of nothing is to speak of it as though it were something' (p. 84). I have referred to the Ideal core as the Self: Beckett refers to it as Mr Knott; both are fictions; like Arsène (p. 69),

> what we know partakes in no small measure of the nature of what has so happily been called the unutterable or ineffable, so that any attempt to utter or eff it is doomed to fail, doomed, doomed to fail.

This sounds like the end of excavation, the acceptance of defeat, yet, in expressing Mr Knott's inexpressibility, Beckett has got nearer to the core than he had in the abstract terms of *Murphy*, and other kinds of failure may articulate more precisely the nature of the unutterability, expressed and exemplified in the nature of the failure. This is presumably why, in *Three Dialogues* (written 1949), Beckett stated his preference for 'the expression that there is nothing to express, nothing with which to express, nothing from which to express, no power to express, no desire to express, together with the obligation to express'.

In *Murphy*, he had made an image of man increasingly distressed by his inability to achieve a lasting retreat into his mental world, and, in *Watt*, the counter-image of man increasingly distressed by prolonged self-immersion. Yet if the real task was not to express the inexpressible but to express its inexpressibility, a different approach was possible – one which created an image not of the obstacles to self-excavation nor of the resulting state, but of the process of excavation, 'doomed to fail' – and this seems to be what he undertook in the trilogy, *Molloy* (1951), *Malone Dies* (1951) and *The Unnamable* (1953).[3]

Implicit in the initial metaphor of excavation was the difficulty – 'If the ideal self, the latent consciousness, is the object of the search, who or what is doing the digging?' Ask 'What am I?', and the first-person pronoun at once appears to suffer a fission into one 'I' which is being investigated and one which is investigating. Moreover, there are many modes of investigation – one uncertain, intermitting, with little sense of motivation or direction, another severely rational, systematic and analytic – and each will have its own characteristic 'I'. If what is sought is the true self, 'the only world that has reality and significance', then these seekers must be convenient fictions, personified projections of the various modes of operation. What they will have in common will be inevitable eventual failure, and as the investigating procedures break down so the separate fictitious identities projected by them will collapse and become progressively inert.

In *Molloy*, there are two such investigating fictions, two first-person narrators, each separately writing an account of his journey. First, there is Molloy himself, decrepit, crippled, decaying, gradually losing mobility, and yet constrained to keep moving: 'For in me there have always been two fools, among others, one asking nothing better than to stay where he is and the other imagining that life might be slightly less horrible a little further on' (p. 48). Yet his journey, such as it is, for it never passes beyond the limits of a region to which he is mysteriously confined, is not dependent on decisions: 'my resolutions were remarkable in this, that they were no sooner formed than something always happened to prevent their execution' (p. 32). He drifts in and out of town, in and out of the hands of the police, in and out of the clutches of a woman who wants him as a household pet, driven by what he calls his 'imperatives', to which he submits without knowing why: 'For they never led me anywhere, but tore me from places where, if all was not well, all was no worse than anywhere else' (p. 86). He recognises, however, that all these imperatives bear on a common matter (p. 86):

> my relations with my mother, and on the importance of
> bringing as soon as possible some light to bear on these
> and even on the kind of light that should be brought to
> bear and the most effective means of doing so.

Whatever he does, wherever he goes, what prevents him from resting still and gives a vague direction to his wanderings is the compulsion to return to his mother, whom he describes as a blind, deaf, dumb, stinking, shrivelled, immobile, senile hag, whose head is for ever 'veiled with hair, wrinkles, filth, slobber' (p. 19). No purpose or desire is involved, merely the imperative to return to his point of origin, as though this would throw some light on what he is and why he is engaged in his aimless and painful journeys. He does not find his mother, but, after being reduced to crawling and thence to immobility, is transported, he doesn't know how or when, to her room where he finds himself occupying her bed: 'I have taken her place. I must resemble her more and more' (p. 8). There, in her bed, he writes his report, the pages of which are collected from him by a weekly visitor. So much for the search (if it can be called a search) of the incoherent, involuntary, disorganised Molloy, who fails to find what he seeks but comes to resemble what he had imagined himself to be seeking.

The second narrator, Moran, is a very different figure – a pillar of the community, house-owner, church-goer, and a severe father, briskly efficient, systematic, and self-confident (p. 93):

> Seeing something done which I could have done better
> myself, if I had wished, and which I did do better whenever
> I put my mind to it, I had the impression of discharging
> a function to which no form of activity could have exalted
> me.

Moran, unlike Molloy, is a professional searcher, the agent of a chief, Youdi, but he is angered to receive instructions via Gaber, Youdi's messenger, that he must find Molloy. Although he has never seen or heard of Molloy, it seems that he already knows something about the vagrant, as though he has invented him as his polar opposite. But Moran is, as he declares, 'a solid in the midst of other solids' (p. 108), and he cannot conceive why a man like himself 'so patiently turned towards the outer world as towards the lesser evil' (p. 114) should be commissioned to seek out such a chimera as Molloy.

In the past, he has been similarly employed to track down and report on various other moribund figures – among them Murphy and Watt – and this suggests that he represents Beckett's alert, practical, critical, efficient pseudo-self, undertaking for the author (or for his messenger, Gaber, for it turns out that it is also Gaber who collects Molloy's weekly instalments) the unearthing of the more inaccessible and disorderly aspects of his being. But this time, Moran's report is not about Molloy; it is about the accelerating failure of his mission. Even before setting out, he unaccountably fails to make his usual scrupulous plans and estimates, and as the journey proceeds he is gradually incapacitated, losing his son, his bicycle, becoming crippled and unpredictable, and 'ageing as swiftly as a day-fly' (p. 149). There is (p. 149)

> a crumbling, a frenzied collapsing of all that had always
> protected me from all I was condemned to be. Or
> it was like a kind of clawing towards a light and
> countenance I could not name, that I had once known and
> long denied.

When at last, alone, sick, abandoned, he receives orders to return home, he does so to find his bees and chicken dead, his house empty, and himself radically changed. As Molloy became like the mother towards whom he was impelled, so Moran has come to resemble the object of his search, the aimless and crippled Molloy – despite which he now has 'a sharper and clearer sense of my identity than ever before, in spite of its deep lesions and the wounds with which it was covered' (pp. 170–1). At the end of the book, he is planning to set out again, this time not in search of Molloy but of a different self: 'I have been a man long enough, I shall not put up with it any more, I shall not try any more' (p. 176).

In terms of the descent towards the centre, Beckett has begun the trilogy with the paired images of two pseudo-selves, vainly seeking, and slowly disintegrating into approximations to what they seek. He shows only two, but there is reason to believe that they are representative: Moran speaks of belonging to an army of agents, all seeking. Both reporters, Molloy and Moran, are at pains to inform us that their reports are fictitious, written, as Molloy says, in compliance 'with the convention that demands you either lie or hold your peace. For what really happened was quite different. . . . Simply somewhere something had changed' (pp. 87–8).

The second novel of the trilogy, *Malone Dies*, at once claims to operate on a deeper level than the preceding works. Since all the stories of Murphy, Watt, Molloy, and Moran are confessedly fictitious, perhaps all their heroes are not selves or aspects of the self or seekers for the self, but merely fictions projected by the true self, an authorial figure, inventing stories, none of them his, but all bearing his mark. Life and the novels are equally tales told by the Self to himself, as he lies alone, unmoving, awaiting death.

This is Malone's condition, alone, in a bed, in a room, but where he does not know, nor how he got there; in a body of sorts but so detached from him that he can control only the arms and hands. He claims to have written all the earlier stories, and can no longer be certain whether the places and events he remembers were in his life or invented in his stories. He sometimes feels that he was always in his room, born there, never out of it, but now he believes he has not long to wait for death and sets out to tell a new story, this time pure play, a story of someone quite unlike him, whose life cannot be confused with his. He begins the story of the boy, Saposcat, interrupting it with observations and comments on his condition and situation, and congratulating himself (p. 193):

Nothing is less like me than this patient, reasonable
child, struggling all alone for years to shed a little light
upon himself, avid of the least gleam, a stranger to the
joys of darkness. Here truly is the air I needed, a lively
tenuous air, far from the nourishing murk that is killing me.

But, from the beginning, the story of Saposcat, a precociously dull boy, acquires darker tones. The boy has a characteristic open-mouthed gawp, which his teacher ascribes to besottedness, and his father to the first faint stirrings of sex. Despite his intentions, Malone cannot resist presenting his own view: 'his dream was less of girls than of himself, his own life, his life to be. That is more than enough to stop up the nose of a lucid and sensitive boy, and cause his jaw temporarily to sag' (p. 192). Saposcat's childhood and youth become progressively darker, more attended with brutality, until, suddenly, the story is dropped, and when it is taken up again the boy is so altered that even his name has to be changed – to Macmann, a creature distinguished from the earlier protagonists of Beckett's (and Malone's) novels only by being still more helpless and incompetent than they.

Macmann is a subhuman, despairing reflection of his creator, Malone – a mere mortal animal, unlike other men in that he is able to accept life as a state of suffering without trying to find explanations for it. Macmann can lie in the mud, soaked to the skin, without attributing his suffering to the rain (p. 243):

> For people are never content to suffer, but they must have
> heat and cold, rain and its contrary which is fine weather,
> and with that love, friendship, black skin and sexual and
> peptic deficiency for example, in short the furies and
> frenzies happily too numerous to be numbered of the
> body including the skull and its annexes, whatever that
> means, such as the club-foot, in order that they may know
> very precisely what exactly it is that dares prevent their
> happiness from being unalloyed.

Thus Beckett relates the human compulsion to seek explanations to what, in *Proust*, he called 'our pernicious and incurable optimism'.

Beckett has now got down to the image of a single creative self, isolated, practically without physical needs, and impotent save for the ability to write, inventing lives for a series of creatures who conclude with the helpless and crazy Macmann, 'of the earth earthy and ill-fitted for pure reason' (p. 244): as Malone says, 'The forms are many in which the unchanging seeks relief from its formlessness' (p. 198). The growing resemblance of pursuer to pursued, in *Molloy*, now seems to be due to the projection, into both figures, of the nature of their inventor. The physical world, which in *Murphy* had been an obstruction to the life of the mental world, now seems to be no more than a figment devised to relieve

54

the Self's isolation, immobility and unchanging formlessness. Malone's life is what he has written (p. 276):

This exercise-book is my life, this big child's exercise-book, it has taken me a long time to resign myself to that. And yet I shall not throw it away. For I want to put down in it, for the last time, those I have called to my help, but ill, so that they did not understand, so that they may cease with me. Now rest.

It is a plausible and convincing image, seeming to explain and underlie all that has gone before, and to suggest a way in which the physical and mental lives may be related, but *The Unnamable* almost at once reveals what should have been obvious – that Malone is only one more in the series of pseudo-selves, one more attempt to foist on to the unknown centre, which lies beneath all phenomena, an existence in the world of phenomena. The voice which now speaks denies all that has been said before: 'I have been here, ever since I began to be, my appearances elsewhere having been put in by other parties' (p. 296). As Murphy was puzzled by the apparent intercourse between the world of his body and the world of his body-tight mind, the Voice cannot understand how, never having been out of his dark place (wherever it may be), he can know anything of the outer world. Such knowledge as he does have of it must have come to him through the pseudo-selves, but he cannot explain how he can be 'indebted for this information to persons with whom I can never have been in contact' (p. 300).

In this voice, without form, location or place in time, Beckett's excavation seems to have reached its goal. This must be a representation of the central core, the Idea, the nothing, mere being without qualities or attributes: 'these creatures have never been, only I and this black void have ever been. . . . Nothing then but me, of which I know nothing, except that I have never uttered' (p. 306). But, in that case, what is the source of the words we read? The words, the Voice says, are not his. They come from the surrounding darkness, are uttered through him. Sometimes they seem to originate in a single hated figure, Basil or Mahood, who has been responsible for all the false stories and false creatures attributed in the past, and continues to offer new ones, each more depleted of resources than its predecessor. The Voice is temporarily almost persuaded that he is a grotesque figure with one arm and one leg, moving round the globe in a vast spiral, until his course slowly brings him back to his home and family, who are all dead and rotten by the time he reaches them, and whose bodies he tramples over in his spirallings, until, having reached his centre, he begins to move outwards again. When that figure, reduced to mere geometry, is rejected, another representative is offered – an armless, legless trunk and head stuck in a jar in a Paris street, observed by no one save a woman who attends to his basic needs. To press acceptance, as these stories are told, the words change from third to first person, so that once again the Voice appears to be telling his own story. But, after some doubts and hesitations, he asserts the falseness of these new pseudo-selves: he is Worm, a mere blur in the darkness of a pit (p. 349):

> Worm, to say he does not know what he is, where he is,
> what is happening, is to underestimate him. What he does
> not know is that there is anything to know. His senses
> tell him nothing, nothing about himself, nothing about the
> rest, and this distinction is beyond him.

For a time Worm seems an adequate reduction, but the more the words say about Worm, the more evident is it that he is just another fiction. In his attempt to find some way of speaking of himself, the Voice descends from the animate, from even the barely animate; since words pass into him, through him, and from him, perhaps he is no more than a partition (p. 386):

> perhaps that's what I feel, an outside and an inside and
> me in the middle, perhaps that's what I am, the thing
> that divides the world in two, on the one side the outside,
> on the other the inside, that can be as thin as foil, I'm
> neither one side nor the other, I'm in the middle, I'm the
> partition, I've two surfaces and no thickness, perhaps that's
> what I feel, myself vibrating, I'm the tympanum, on the
> one hand the mind, on the other the world, I don't belong
> to either, it's not to me they're talking, it's not of me
> they're talking.

In such an inanimate image (at once rejected), Beckett seems to have come to the end of his resources. He has penetrated beneath the outer world, beneath his own fictions, beneath, now, any animate image. Nothing will serve, because one thing remains impenetrable – language. Words belong to the world of phenomena and 'meaning', while 'the one to be sought, the one to be, the one to be spoken of' is 'in the silence', is 'made of silence', can never speak or be spoken of. The Voice itself is a fiction, not the Unnamable. The Unnamable's is the story to be told, but 'he has no story' or 'he's in his own story, unimaginable, unspeakable' (p. 417). Yet the impossible attempt must be made, the Voice is obliged to continue (p. 417):

> the attempt must be made, in the old stories
> incomprehensibly mine, to find his, it must be there
> somewhere, it must have been mine, before being his,
> I'll recognize it, in the end I'll recognize it, the story
> of the silence that he never left, that I should never
> have left, that I may never find again, that I may
> find again, then it will be he, it will be I, it will be
> the place, the silence, the end, the beginning, the
> beginning again.

Excavation can go no further, because words, the instrument of excavation, have become an impenetrable barrier. The words have to go on, but can never do more than circle round the silence of the Unnamable. Yet, as the passage just quoted suggests, perhaps in some way the Unnamable was in all the stories, as Malone was in all the stories he invented, or as the presence and nature of the still centre is implicitly manifested in every part of the turning wheel.

Not surprisingly, after *The Unnamable*, Beckett said 'There's no way to go on', and the *Textes pour rien* which followed, though beautifully conceived and written, were hardly more than elaborations on the last volume of the trilogy. They carried no hint of the fresh resource discovered, after eight years, in *How It Is*, and even that extraordinary fiction penetrates no deeper than *The Unnamable*, but creates an even more savagely painful image of the endless and self-tormenting search to discover and express the inexpressible. The subsequent pieces seem like gropings towards a new method of investigation but do not match the sustained penetration of the trilogy, and would, I think, hardly be intelligible without the reader's experience of the long process of excavation which preceded them.

In following the course of that process, I have ignored much and brushed aside complexities in order to suggest the continuity of Beckett's work in the novels from *Murphy* to *The Unnamable*. Consequently I have made the novels sound like allegories, which they are certainly not, if by allegory one means the fictional representation of what may be adequately stated in abstract terms. But just as Beckett in order to explore the only reality had to employ fictions and then to correct false implications by exposing their fictitiousness, so there seems to be no way of considering the relationship of these novels to our experience other than by treating them as though they were in some sense allegorical, and then repudiating the method. To talk of the Self, of pseudo-selves, of inner and outer worlds is not to explain but to invent a parallel fiction, just as a psychologist may people his account of the mind with plainly fictitious characters like the Id, Ego, Subconscious or Collective Unconscious. The fictions of abstract terms (such as Beckett himself was sometimes forced to use) are less precise, less significant than the fictions of the novelist: their chief recommendation is that, through their comparative familiarity, they point vaguely towards the area of experience which the novelist tries to articulate in his fictions. The phrase, 'the world of our own latent consciousness' served a similarly vague purpose for Beckett in 1931. For this reason I have made no reference to the philosophers to whom Beckett sometimes referred and in the light of whose writings the novels are often discussed – Descartes, the Occasionalists, the Existentialists. The novels are not derived from nor illustrative of any philosophical system: they derive, like other novels, from the author's insights into his own nature and his sense of the nature of human existence; references to philosophers occur, as literary allusions often occur, to supply a comment or a convenient phrasing and to acknowledge the creators of earlier fictions relating to approximately similar territory.

Beckett's attempt to dig down to the ideal core of the human creature failed as it was bound to fail: it was undertaken in the knowledge of the certainty of failure. Beckett had no interest in doing what he knew could be done, still less in doing what he knew he could do. Yet given his conviction that the only significance and reality in man lay in the inexpressible, the only proper pursuit for an artist was to dig in that direction; there was nothing else worth doing. He was uninterested in art which limited itself to 'the plane of the feasible', content with 'doing a little better the same old thing, of going a little further along the dreary road': he declared, in *Three Dialogues*, that 'to be an artist is to fail, as no other dare fail, that failure is his world, and the shrink from it desertion, art and craft, good housekeeping, living', and he demonstrated that to fail in attempting the impossible might, at the same time, be to succeed in creating genuinely original works of art which could illuminate, through the process of their vain search, what it is to be a man.

NOTES

1 Page-references to the novels are to the following editions: *Murphy* (Grove Press, 1957); *Watt* (Olympia Press, 1958); *Molloy, Malone Dies, The Unnamable* (one-volume edition, Calder, 1959).
2 *Watt* was written in 1941–2.
3 The dates given here are those of the French texts. English versions appeared in 1955, 1956 and 1958 respectively.

Chapter 4

Assumption to *Lessness:* Beckett's shorter fiction

Brian Finney

The reader of Beckett's writing finds himself in a similar position to Gulliver in the land of the Houyhnhnms. Confronted with a series of Yahoo-like tramps, his instinctual reaction is to deny any resemblances between himself and these repulsive creatures. Like Gulliver, however, he cannot remain aloof for long. Beckett's derelicts are no fools; they have thought a great deal more about their seemingly meaningless predicament than has the average reader. Any certainties he may have entertained about his superiority to them are quickly undermined by these professional sceptics, to whom man's reasoning powers are a subject of particular ridicule. 'We may reason on to our heart's content', as the protagonist of 'The Expelled' observes, 'the fog won't lift.' Man only uses his reason to deceive himself into thinking that life will yield some kind of sense and purpose. But the uncertainties of death and beyond annul the rational certainties of life and leave everything in a terrifying state of confusion. 'The confusion is not my invention,' Beckett protested to Tom Driver. 'It is all around us and our only chance is to let it in.'[1]

Beckett lets into his art both the confusion and man's even more confusing flight from it. The inhabitants of his world fluctuate between rational illusion and the despairing cries of the living damned. Tragi-comedy is his natural mode. The laughable effects of man's attempts to create a semblance of order (Belacqua's lunch ritual, Watt's endless lists, Winnie's stocktaking, the searchers' elaborate rules of conduct in *The Lost Ones*) alternate with terrifying glimpses of man's suffering in the face of unending uncertainty ('But whom can I have offended so grievously,' asks the voice in *Texts for Nothing*, 'to be punished in this inexplicable way.'). The greatest uncertainty of all arises from the subjective bias of our method of perceiving both others and ourselves. The final insult for Beckett is man's inability to know even himself, especially as, like so many writers of this century, he sees the artist's function as 'excavatory, immersive', an exploration of the self. Because the self is unknowable, he told John Gruen in 1970, 'when man faces himself, he is looking into the abyss'.[2]

Beckett's world has remained remarkably consistent. His first published work in 1929 ('Dante ... Bruno, Vico ... Joyce') already

63

talks of 'this earth that is Purgatory'. His most recent work to date, *Not I*, makes a similar identification. There is no better commentary on a work of Beckett's than the rest of his writings. Each successive piece of writing amplifies, comments on, progresses from, and negates, its predecessor. Belacqua sought refuge in motion, Murphy in stasis. Watt acknowledges his prior existence as Murphy and so on through to the last of the first-person narrators, 'Bom', who is still Belacqua crouched up in the familiar foetal position, but 'fallen over on his side tired of waiting forgotten of the hearts where grace abides asleep'.

The fiction that has appeared since 1961 is what Beckett calls 'residua', what remains, as he explained to me, both from larger original wholes and from the whole body of his previous work. As such it is connected with the earlier fiction in precisely the same fashion, pursuing problems of self-perception while demolishing previous models ('All that goes before forget', *Enough* begins) or exploring their antitheses (like 'the unthinkable end' in section 15 of *The Lost Ones*).

Beckett's shorter fiction has inevitably received less attention than the longer works owing to its early inferiority and its later difficulty. Yet it has its own distinctive contribution to make to our knowledge of his world. It is a form uniquely suited to Beckett's stark and deliberately simplified vision of man's predicament. For over a decade now it has constituted his only fictional output. Even where it fails artistically, it can throw fascinating light on subsequent works. All the uncollected shorter fiction up to *More Pricks Than Kicks* comes into this category.[3] There are the two early stories 'Assumption' (1929) and 'A Case in a Thousand' (1934), besides two self-contained extracts from his suppressed first novel 'Dream of Fair to Middling Women' published as 'Sedendo et Quiescendo' and 'Text' in 1932.[4] Despite their obscurity in both language and meaning they contain nuggets Beckett was to mine later.

In 'Assumption' the male protagonist is locked in an unnatural 'humanity of silence'. Contact with a woman leads to nightly crucifixion ('each night he died and was God') from which he longs to be released into 'the light of eternity'. Finally love breaks down his dam of silence and with 'a great storm of sound' he dies. Beckett still had to discover the imprisoning effects of time-bound speech on those desiring dissolution into a timeless void. But the story is potent with themes that continue to obsess him. The collapse of a lifetime's silence that leaves the suffering victim 'fused with the cosmic discord' is a situation he has recently reverted to with great effect in *Not I*. The concept of man as a suffering God, crucified by the world and sexuality in particular, anticipates numerous parallels between successive heroes and Christ: the stoning of the hero of 'The End'; Molloy making his entry to his Jerusalem on a bicycle; Macmann and 'Bom' stretched out on the ground in the attitude of the cross: the list is endless.

In particular the association Beckett makes between women and death in 'Assumption' is developed more fully in his subsequent fiction. In 'Assumption' the woman contemplates the hero's 'face that she had overlaid with death'. In the chapter 'Love and Lethe' from *More Pricks Than Kicks* Belacqua sets out on a suicide pact with his latest girl, Ruby, only to end up making love instead. Beckett claims sardonically that 'at least on this occasion, if never before nor since, he achieved what he set out to do'. Love means exile from the self; for Beckett this is a little death in a less playful sense than that punned on by his Elizabethan predecessors. It constantly distracts Belacqua in both 'Dream of Fair to Middling Women' and *More Pricks Than Kicks* from seeking refuge in his mind, which both he and Murphy saw 'as the last ditch when all was said and done'. Murphy goes one better than Belacqua in managing to turn his back on Celia, the first of many prostitutes that feature as the heroines of his subsequent fiction.

Behind Beckett's paradoxical attitude to love and sexuality lies his vision of man's suffering condition. The illusory joys of sex lead to the all-too-real suffering of a new life. His opening remark to John Gruen in 1970 was: 'The major sin is the sin of being born.' He went on to claim that he has a clear memory of his own foetal existence, one of agony and darkness. This could well explain the enigma inherent in Beckett's other early short story, 'A Case in a Thousand', where Dr Nye, the protagonist, refuses to accept man's universal sadness as anything but a personal disorder. Only after his nurse has related to him 'a matter connected with his earliest years' too trivial to 'be enlarged on here' can one make any sense of his earlier proposition: 'Myself I cannot save.' He has already undergone the trauma of birth, but can at least avoid bequeathing it to a further generation. To Beckett midwife and gravedigger are indistinguishable.

Dr Nye anticipates Belacqua's wish 'to be back in the caul, on (his) back in the dark for ever', which would at least avoid the 'night-sweats' of his sexuality. *More Pricks Than Kicks* (1934) has been given more attention than Beckett would have liked (to judge from the blurb on the Calder & Boyars reissue of 1970), primarily because Belacqua stands first in his long line of fictional derelicts. He shares with them many of the distinctive features which instantly set Beckett's protagonists apart from so-called normal experience. His physical disabilities and his associated love for bicycles, his sloth, his abhorrence of clocks and other reminders of his temporal condition, his distinction between mind and body, his 'faculty for acting with insufficient motivation', and his penchant for lunatic asylums all find parallels in the heroes of the subsequent novels.

What is distinctive about this first book of short stories is its concentration on Belacqua's sexual misadventures. During the course of the book Belacqua is paired off in turn with Winnie Coates, Alba Perdue, Ruby Tough, Lucy, Thelma née bboggs, and the Smeraldina. In each relationship Belacqua's conduct reverses the norms of gallantry. A moment of tenderness for him on Winnie's part strikes Belacqua as 'a drink of water to drink in a dungeon'. Love at the least is an imprisonment – with minor privileges for good conduct. Belacqua appears to be seeking a wife or mistress who is so uninterested in him sexually that he is freed of his bodily compulsions, able to seek slothful peace in an extended 'Beethoven pause' of the mind. Only that bluestocking, the Alba, seems capable of such selflessness; yet their platonic night together ends with the comment in German 'Not possible . . .'. Ruby lets him down badly, depriving him of his 'temporarily sane' determination to commit suicide with the 'ignis fatuus' of her sex appeal. Much to his disappointment Lucy stubbornly refuses 'to establish their married life on [the] solid basis of a cuckoldry'. Belacqua's idea of marital happiness is only achieved when she has been 'crippled for life and her beauty dreadfully marred'.

Belacqua seeks to escape from the bondage of his sexuality by playing the peeping Tom. It is an inadequate solution to a problem which is solved in more solipsist style by his successors in the *Nouvelles* and the trilogy (*Molloy, Malone Dies*, and *The Unnamable*), who resort to onanism. But at least it detaches him one remove from the evil of procreation, besides saving him the physical effort in the spirit of Dante's original, 'sloth's own brother'. Lucy does not survive her accident long, and only after his own death is Belacqua finally able to enjoy the prospect of his third wife, the Smeraldina, taking Hairy as her cicisbeo because 'this is what darling Bel would wish'. Simultaneous detachment from, and satisfaction in, the sexual act is only permissible to the dead. The living are already in Purgatory. Belacqua's lifelong endeavour to attain a god-like omniscience from sex ('I am what I am' he claims, like St Paul, to whom the title also refers) is doomed to failure in a godless world. There are more pricks than kicks to life in every sense.

Belacqua's fictional successors learn faster the bitter connection between their sexuality and the curse of their own conception. Molloy even admits to sometimes confusing his mother's image with that of his old lover, Ruth, an experience that he finds 'unendurable, like being crucified'. Rather than inflict the pain of existence on another generation, the French heroes set out to reverse the pattern of growth, to return to the tomb of the womb, to spend their last days, like Mahood, in their mother's entrails. Their efforts to effect the impossible are comic, their failure tragic. Conception is irreversible and these heroes are constantly being ejected from their womb-like refuges and thrown back violently on to the stage of life, like the Player in *Act Without Words*.

This image of repeated expulsion first surfaces as a dominant motif in the four *Nouvelles* (*Premier amour*, 'L'Expulsé', 'La Fin', and 'Le Calmant' respectively translated as *First Love*, 'The Expelled', 'The End', and 'The Calmative'), Beckett's earliest French fiction, written in 1945 before both *Mercier and Camier* and the trilogy. In all but one story ('The Calmative') the hero makes his fictional entrée on being expelled from a womb-like room, which in the case of *First Love* has been bequeathed him by his father. In all three stories the exiled anti-hero spends his time wandering in search of a substitute refuge, which when found proves hopelessly inadequate. In the initial room the hero, like the foetus, was at least fed and evacuated regularly. But the coffin-shaped cab of 'The Expelled' (the title speaks for itself), the sitting room emptied of its furniture in *First Love*, the hut in 'The Calmative', and the basement room, cave and shed in 'The End' all fail to reproduce even the substitute convenience of the initial room. In 'The End', for example, the hero is only saved from starvation by the chance arrival of a cow; and where previously he had had his chamber pot emptied daily, in his shed he dirties his own nest. As he sardonically says of his tragi-comic predicament: 'To contrive a little kingdom, in the midst of the universal muck, then shit on it, ah that was me all over.' Interestingly, there is less comic detachment in the earlier version of this story which reads in place of the last phrase 'ah the pity of it'.

Far the most interesting of the *Nouvelles* in this context is *Premier amour* (*First Love*), which Beckett withheld from publication until 1970 and which only appeared in English translation in 1973. Beckett wrote to me saying he withheld *Premier amour* because he found it 'even less satisfactory than the others', and now regrets having released it for publication. I must confess that I still find it the most fascinating of the four *Nouvelles*. From the beginning the first-person narrator links marriage with death, his own marriage to Anna with the death of his father. Marriage can only bring mortality to the child born from it into sorrow. Considering that the narrator remembers the trauma of his own birth, the date of which lies graven in his memory 'in figures that life will not easily erase', it is surprising – even to him – that he should so quickly be involved in inflicting the same agony on another. What emerges from his account of his first love affair is that yet again he is only seeking in this woman a return to the womb. Expelled from the room in his father's house, his clothes dumped outside it like an afterbirth, he re-creates the image of his initial room in the house of Anna, the prostitute he meets and goes to live with. Although she undertakes all the maternal functions of feeding him and emptying his pot, he is driven to desert her by the birth-cries of what she alleges is his child, cries which continue to haunt his memory for the rest of his life.

Crudely summarised in this way, the story sounds like the neurotic outpourings of a sick mind. What above all saves it from this charge is Beckett's comic detachment. As Nell says in *Endgame*, 'nothing is funnier than unhappiness'. The narrator is life's victim, doing his best to avoid the gross errors of his fellow creatures, but finally and hilariously proving just as vulnerable. Fleeing from Anna, his first love, he takes refuge in an abandoned cow-shed. There

> for the first time in my life, and I would not hesitate to
> say the last if I had not to husband my cyanide, I had to
> contend with a feeling which gradually assumed, to my
> dismay, the dread name of love.

Above all what convinces him that he must be in love is finding himself tracing the word 'Anna' on 'time's forgotten cowplats'. By this Augustinian juxtaposition of love and excrement, as of sublime language and banal action, Beckett induces us to laugh at the essential tragedy of existence. For existence is not all suffering. As the narrator has come to realise: 'Catch-cony life! To be nothing but pain, how that would simplify matters! Omnidolent! Impious dream!' Such temporary wisdom and detachment fails to prevent him being ricocheted between the extremes of love's tortures and relative happiness. He even finds himself pulling up nettles under the evil influence of love, instead of manuring them as was his usual custom, Beckett informs us, tongue in cheek, with

68

all malevolent weeds. Weeds remind him of the reality of things which is only concealed by the ephemeral beauty of flowers. Repeatedly the hero of the *Nouvelles* obtains hyacinths or crocuses as *memento mori* over whose decay and promise of oblivion he perversely rejoices.

Apart from the unforgivable association between love and birth, the narrator also finds love a distraction from what he sees as his only hope in life, 'supineness in the mind, the dulling of the self and of that residue of execrable frippery known as the non-self and even the world, for short'. This search for the oblivion of womb or grave that obsesses the heroes of all his subsequent fiction can only be conducted by being oneself: 'For when one is [oneself] one knows what to do to be less so', he claims, little appreciating the epistemological complications awaiting his fictional successors pursuing this programme. Whereas love on the other hand means exile from the self, 'and it is painful to be no longer oneself, even more painful if possible than when one is'. Paradoxically true as this may be, the narrator of *First Love* is unable to use this theoretical insight to extricate himself from Anna. His expulsion from her refuge is ironically forced on him by the unforgivable reproduction of life, in which he may have played an unwilling part.

First Love contains so many of the major themes of the French fiction in embryonic form that it deserves greater attention than it has received to date. The narrator experiences all the problems of perception that are to torture his successors. The outside world, other people, even his own memory are not to be trusted, since, as Beckett said in *Proust*, 'the individual is a succession of individuals, the world being a projection of the individual's consciousness'. Words like 'love' and 'beauty' remain enigmas to this lover, qualities he has read about but is liable to apply to the wrong situations, owing to the subjective nature of his perception. Despite her age and permanent squint, Anna could well be beautiful, he claims, if he had some data on beauty – which none of us has, Beckett implies. Constantly the certainties of daily living are being undermined by the narrator's painfully honest scepticism. For example, he returns to the bench for the fourth or fifth time, 'at roughly the same hour, I mean roughly the same sky, no, I don't mean that either, for it's always the same sky and never the same sky, what words are there for that, none I know, period'. The incomprehensible nothingness of reality can only be approximated to by the writer's use of such mutually annihilating antitheses.

In fact the entire story is constructed in this manner. The narrator loves death and hates love, that death of the self. He seeks out the self to escape it. He tells his story so as to reach 'là où le verbe s'arrête', as Beckett wrote in the French version but omitted from his English translation ('the point where speech ceases'). For, like the heroes of the other *Nouvelles* and the trilogy, he is a writer whose writings 'are no sooner dry than they revolt me'. As a writer he is particularly aware of the vulnerability of language: 'I heard the word fibrome, or brone, I don't know which, never knew, never knew what it meant and never had the curiosity to find out. The things one recalls! And records!' Words are as arbitrary as life and as meaningless. How can one person ever be sure that the meaning of what he says is not understood wholly differently by the recipient? How can we ever get outside our own heads? If we can't, then all life becomes a fiction, and, like the narrator of *First Love*, we can decide to alter someone else's name from Lulu to Anna without more than our usual inconsistency.

Like his contemporaries, Nabokov and Barth, Beckett never lets his reader forget the deceptive nature of the form he is using. He plays linguistic games throughout the *Nouvelles*. The narrator of 'The Expelled' ends up unable to explain why he told this story rather than another: 'Perhaps some other time I'll be able to tell another. Living souls, you will see how alike they are' – alike because they emanate from the same brain. In all the *Nouvelles*, as the narrator of 'The Calmative' explains, 'we are needless to say in a skull'. Like his successors in the trilogy he tells himself 'this story which aspires to be the last' to calm himself in the terrifying face of death. Repeatedly Beckett reminds us that life is a fiction of our own invention: 'So much for that description' he will make his hero exclaim with satisfaction, or 'No reason for this to end or go on. Then let it end.' In parodying fictional conventions he is mocking the artificiality of the life we have invented for ourselves: aesthetic and metaphysical considerations become indistinguishable in his work.

The remaining three *Nouvelles* anticipate the structure and major themes of the trilogy quite closely at times. Both sets of works present the same protagonist, exiled from the oblivion of the womb in a world of his own invention, seeking to end his suffering existence by coming to know his unknowable self. Like Belacqua, Murphy and Watt before him, and Molloy, Moran, Macmann and Mahood after him, the hero of 'The Expelled' finds his body a very imperfect instrument of locomotion. Whenever he attempts mentally to correct the clumsiness of his gait he 'managed a few steps of creditable execution and then fell'. Mind and body are related to each other too precariously to withstand any conscious interference by mind alone. It is appropriate that the dualist philosopher Geulincz's *Ethics* should be mentioned by name in the same story. The hero of the *Nouvelles*, like those of the trilogy, wears his father's hat and greatcoat, suffers from similar sores of the scalp, and tramps across the same landscape with its fortified town, hills, bogs and coastline.

The links between the two trilogies of stories and novels are of two kinds: similarities in situation, and references in the novels to events in the stories. There are a number of striking parallels between 'The Expelled' and *Molloy*, 'The End' and *Malone Dies*, and 'The Calmative' and *The Unnamable*. In the first pair both heroes begin their wanderings in the prime of life, have a contretemps with policemen, knock down old women or their dogs and confess to being the author of their own stories. In the second pair both heroes seek to create their own fictional death; both seek out rooms in which their food is fetched and their pot emptied regularly, only to lose these conveniences; both slowly degenerate into tramps, now sitting on the bench by the river first introduced in *First Love*, now exposed to the elements; both end drifting out to the open sea in a boat to meet their imagined end. The final pair, 'The Calmative' and *The Unnamable*, both imagine the continuation of mind and voice after the body has died. Both heroes are tortured by fictional assassins or tyrants of their own invention in a place of terror that both identify with the inside of their distant skulls. Both attempt to escape into the silence of their true self by telling their own story rather than one about a fictional counterpart, and both in effect conclude: 'All I say cancels out, I'll have said nothing' – and go on.

If these parallels suggest repetition, the way in which each subsequent work demolishes its predecessors suggests progression of a kind. Not only does each of the four *Nouvelles* trace the roughly chronological career of the same protagonist (twenty-five years old in *First Love*, ninety years old when he died according to 'The Calmative', but all three novels that follow draw on the *Nouvelles* for incidents in their characters' past history. Molloy remembers his past incarnation as the hero of 'The End' who put out to sea in a boat and wonders if he ever returned from that journey. This memory of his is promptly undermined by speculating whether any relationship is possible between past and present selves, the one setting out and the one returning. Likewise Malone has a photograph of the ass by the shore that carried him to his cave in 'The End', a cave that Malone now remembers with pleasure, where in the earlier story he had felt compelled to abandon it. Once again memory is playing tricks on its victim. Even the Unnamable acknowledges his past origins in the *Nouvelles* by quoting the opening sentence of 'The End', 'They clothed me and gave me money.' He sees all his predecessors from Belacqua to Malone in orbit around him and disowns them all as fabrications of a self that still remains inaccessible, because unnamable. Each protagonist acknowledges his fictional predecessors in order to demolish them, another example of Beckett's use of mutually destructive antitheses.

Beckett's gallery of moribunds extends beyond the *Trilogy* to *Textes pour rien* (1955), translated as *Texts for Nothing* and *Comment c'est* (1961), translated as *How It Is*. In both cases previous incarnations are evoked only to be dismissed as illusions seen from the perspective of the present. In *Texts for Nothing* the voice tries to free itself of its author by treating him 'like a vulgar Molloy, a common Malone, those mere mortals'. In *How It Is* Bom recalls an image from his past life in 'The End' where he was growing a crocus in a basement area, only to dismiss this and other memories as 'rags of life in the light', too concrete to be of relevance to his present more realistic state of darkness and confusion. In both 'The Calmative' and *Texts for Nothing* the voice recollects the story of Breen or Breem that his father told him as a child. With its happy ending it had acted on him as a calmative in his youth and he still hopes to repeat its soothing effect on him in the *Nouvelle*. But by *Texts for Nothing* he has learnt to see it as 'a comedy, for children' that he could never believe, partly because of its impossibly happy ending, partly because in his memory he had usurped his father's function, having told and listened to his own story, trapped in the solipsistic prison of his own head.

Beckett's *Texts for Nothing* cannot properly be labelled either shorter fiction or a novel. Other commentators have already pointed out that it is modelled on a musical form. Beckett himself calls the last section, XIII, a coda. Viewed in a wider context the whole work is a coda to the trilogy. The voice in *Texts for Nothing* is the same voice as in *The Unnamable*. But instead of the Unnamable's gradual breakdown in punctuation before a growing torrent of words, each of the Texts represents an 'evening's' worth of fiction. The voice now finds it harder to find subjects for self-narration and anticipates the far more frequent pauses for breath that subdivide *How It Is* into its numerous short phrases and paragraphs.

Texts for Nothing represent Beckett's penultimate attempt in fiction to explore his own existence in the first person in a world 'where to be is to be guilty'. Because life is for him a fiction, the writer shares his predicament with the rest of mankind. All the texts are almost wholly occupied with the writer and his creations. His principal creation in *Texts for Nothing* is the voice that is forced to assume responsibility for actions in the writer's past, but which the writer has foisted off on to an invented character because of the fictitious nature of his own memory. Just as Pim is to be tortured into speech by Bom, so the victimised voice (I) is given a pseudo-existence independent of its author (he): 'If at least he would dignify me with the third person, like his other figments, not he, he'll be satisfied with nothing less than me, for his me.' The protagonists from Belacqua to Watt were overtly paraded as fictions in the third person. From the *Nouvelles* through to *How It Is* Beckett deliberately exploits the use of the first person to demonstrate the more forcefully his complete inability to reach any satisfactory understanding of himself.

'It is impossible for me to talk about my writing,' he told John Gruen. 'It is impossible because I am constantly working in the dark. It would be like an insect leaving his cocoon.' Instead Beckett has enlarged the dimensions of his interior life to let us glimpse into the abyss, however obliquely. The difference between *The Unnamable* and *Texts for Nothing* is formal, not thematic. Both voices share a similar predicament, 'knowing none, known of none'. But the futility of their effort is shaped differently. If each quest for the self is doomed to failure then the shape of the fiction must be made to reflect the antithetical forces that constantly dispatch new search parties and as constantly thwart them from reaching their goal.

Beckett applies the principles of progression and circularity that were present as themes in his earlier work to the form of *Texts for Nothing*. There is an appearance of progression from text to text that frequently surfaces in the opening sentences. New questions are asked that offer the illusory possibility of a final solution ('Where would I go . . .?' or 'How are the intervals filled . . . ?' or 'Did I try everything . . . ?'). Or the previous section is curtly dismissed ('Leave, I was going to say leave all that' or 'Give up'). Yet many of the texts prove circular by the conclusion, the final lines mockingly echoing the opening lines as in Text IX or XIII. Or the question asked in the opening sentence is negated by the answer in the final sentence as in Text IV.

Equally within each text Beckett elaborately constructs a whole series of grammatical equations whose answer is nought, as in Text XI which starts 'When I think no that won't work', or as at the end of Text XIII which imagines a time when it will be 'all said, it says, it murmurs'. Often these circular sentences are imbued with all the beauty of the transient world from which the author through his invented voice is seeking to escape:

> Ah, says I, punctually, if only I could say, There's a way out there, there's a way out somewhere, then all would be said, it would be the first step on the long travelable road, destination tomb, to be trod without a word, tramp tramp, little irrevocable steps, down the long tunnels at first, then under the mortal skies, through days and nights, faster and faster, no, slower and slower, for obvious reasons, and at the same time faster and faster, for other obvious reasons, or the same, obvious in a different way, or in the same way, but at a different moment of time, a moment earlier, a moment later, or at the same moment, there is no such thing, there would be no such thing, I recapitulate, impossible.

The illusion of progression in the first half of this sentence is quickly dispelled in the second half in a maze of self-negating phrases: faster . . . slower, different way . . . same way, earlier . . . later – they all reduce themselves to the same nothingness by the end. Progression in time becomes stasis (or unending progression) in a context of timelessness, which is why recapitulation is impossible. The voice is at the mercy of an author who 'protests he doesn't reason and does nothing but reason'. The structure of the thirteen texts is an elaborate demonstration of this flaw in man's search for a meaning to life.

This self-annihilating quest for certainty by a first-person narrator ends with *How It Is*, a novel whose tripartite form parallels this theme of apparent progression and actual circularity with immense skill. Bom's journey through space and time turns out to be both circular and infinitely repeatable, and the concluding pages ruthlessly demolish the whole fragile, illusionistic fable. Since 1961 Beckett has only written shorter fiction or what he calls 'capita mortua': *Imagination morte imaginez*, translated as *Imagination Dead Imagine, Assez*, translated as *Enough, Le Dépeupleur*, translated as *The Lost Ones, Bing*, translated as *Ping*, and *Sans*, translated as *Lessness* (in that order of composition, except for the final section of *Le Dépeupleur* which was written immediately prior to its first publication in 1970). Apart from *Enough*, the first person gives way to the third person in all of these pieces and the voice telling itself stories from its past life is now reduced to a murmur, the 'murmur of memory and dream' as the voice calls it in *Texts for Nothing*. John Fletcher was told by Beckett that *Enough* 'is out of place in the series'. Beckett added, 'I don't know what came over me'.[5] It must represent a throw-back to his previous phase of writing, not just because it uses the first person, but because, as I shall show, it concentrates on the delusive dream, where the other works strive (vainly) for an image of unpalatable reality.

It is as if Beckett as narrator has abandoned his earlier pretensions of discovering the self when he paraded his own involvement in his fiction with the first person singular. Instead he offers us a series of narrative ideograms in the familiar convention of the third person. In all of them man is close to unconsciousness, inanimate but for breathing and blinking in *Imagination Dead Imagine*, 'entering night' in *Enough*, 'languishing . . . imperceptibly' in *The Lost Ones*, 'a nature only just' in *Ping*, 'face to endlessness' in *Lessness*.

With the exception of *Enough*, these works are more closely interrelated than might be realised. *Imagination Dead Imagine* shares with *The Lost Ones* a similar fluctuation of heat and light, to the confusion of the bodies suffering between these extremes. *Bing*, as Beckett informed me, 'is a separate work written after and in reaction to *Le Dépeupleur* abandoned because of its complexity getting beyond control'. If one examines the earlier drafts of *Bing* published in Federman and Fletcher's bibliography, the first text shows similar atmospheric variations, and the little body rests his hands on a ladder leaning against a niche in the wall, features identical to those in *The Lost Ones*. By the tenth and final draft of *Bing* light and heat have become static, ladder and niches have disappeared, and the body is left in its coffin-like box in silence and stasis. *Lessness* is written in direct reaction to *Ping*'s image of 'ruins true refuge'. Within the first paragraph the body is deprived of its latest shelter to confront the reality of infinitude: 'Blacked out fallen open four walls over backwards true refuge issueless.' *Lessness* is to date the last in a series that began with *Imagination Dead Imagine*, just as *How It Is* can be traced back to *More Pricks Than Kicks*. The later series constitutes the residual distillation of the earlier line of fiction. The little body that faces endlessness in *Lessness* confronts Beckett's first hero Belacqua with the predicament he sought to evade so resourcefully, but without success.

What Beckett calls 'the art and craft' in *Enough* assumes major importance in these last works. Both form and language are bent to his purposes in increasingly radical ways between *Imagination Dead Imagine* and *Lessness*. *Imagination Dead Imagine* begins with the predicament in which many of the heroes of the French novels found themselves: 'No trace anywhere of life, you say.' With immense confidence the unseen narrator dismisses their solipsistic defeatism with: 'pah, no difficulty there, imagination not dead.' Once again there is the expectation of making real progress, of winning so much ground from infinity. All that is needed, claims the narrator, is a more rigorous form of imagination, one that can construct its image of human existence in the head with the exactitude of a mathematician. Embryonic man and woman are plotted geometrically, their dimensions are measured, phenomena are timed to the second, variations in temperature are calculated and scientific tests executed. To buttress further the solidity of his image Beckett borrows the language of science and technology: diameters, right angles, semi-circles, numbers and letters proliferate.

And yet from the start another language, that of the supposedly dead subjective imagination, disconcertingly intrudes amidst the pseudo-scientific jargon. So between the rise and fall of light and heat there may intervene 'pauses of varying length, from the fraction of a second to what would have seemed, in other times, other places, an eternity'. Measured time falters before experienced time. The certainties of mathematics are used to construct the impossible, a 'world still proof against enduring tumult'. The yearning poetic language betrays the hopelessly subjective bias underlying the sham knowledge. As doubt grows, Beckett places his use of scientific method and terminology in ever more absurd contexts: 'Neither fat nor thin, big nor small, the bodies seem whole and in fairly good condition, to judge by the surfaces exposed to view.' What starts out as an objective statement ends up as self-parody.

The theory of relativity is not so new to philosophy as to science. All perception is relative to the perceiver. It is this form of relativity which begins to interfere with the image of the rotunda as time passes. The fluctuations in light and heat (those manifestations of eternity and infinity) begin to affect the perceiver. Inspection is no longer easy as memory begins to distort his reactions. The contrast between stasis and movement becomes 'striking, in the beginning, for one who still remembers having been struck by the contrary'. Habit, our 'guarantee of a dull inviolability', erases the past. Finally the image of suffering humanity proves too much for the observer. The rotunda and its occupants that at first seemed so solid vanish in the last sentence in language of haunting but transient beauty. Poetry has replaced logic and doubt has dispelled scientific certainty. The perceiver has vetoed his perception of reality and fallen victim to his own shortcomings. The promise of progress so confidently predicted in the opening lines has proved circular once again. Like its title it returns to its beginnings.

Illusion proves too attractive to be resisted not just in *Imagination Dead Imagine* but in *The Lost Ones* and *Enough*. Even the end of *Ping* is no end seen from the perspective of *Lessness*. Rather than face the intolerable reality of his condition man prefers to go on believing in the possibility of a way out in *The Lost Ones* or deliberately falsifies and idealises his past life in *Enough*. In *The Lost Ones* an impersonal narrator, like Gulliver, observes Lilliputian man closing his eyes to the inferno which he inhabits. In *Enough* the last of the many 'I's' eliminates his remaining memories of unpleasantness in order to imagine himself in a paradise of flowers. Dante continues to hold Beckett's imagination. If the *Purgatorio* is Belacqua's natural habitat, *The Lost Ones* owes more to the *Inferno* and *Enough* to the *Paradiso*.

Dante is the only proper name to figure in *The Lost Ones*. But even without his appearance in person the connotations are unmistakable: 'What first impresses in this gloom is the sensation of yellow it imparts not to say of sulphur in view of the associations.' The black humour suggests that man's life on earth is hell, a fact he would recognise if only he could be granted the omniscient viewpoint of the narrator. But he is himself suspect with his eternal 'ifs' and 'would be's'. If where we are is hell, then the narrator is no exception and can only achieve his Mephistophelian clarity of vision by postulating a probability ('if this notion is maintained' he keeps saying) that remains outside the scope of proof. As *Ping* shows, man is liable to lapse into the illusion that the search may reach an end. Even *The Lost Ones* has an apocalyptic vision of, not the end, but 'the unthinkable end'.

Rather than face the pointlessness of their search, Beckett's little population of bodies prefers to construct rules governing the conduct of their search so labyrinthine that no one is able to foresee the complete inaccessibility of their goal. Not even the vanquished searchers manage to discover 'the all of nothing'. The passion to search has simply died in them – or rather, almost died, as they are still liable to recommence their search in accordance with the laws of relativity governing this microcosmic world. As in *Imagination Dead Imagine* and the earlier drafts of *Bing*, conditions are such that no certainty is possible. The regular variations in light and heat are subject to random interruptions when 'the questing eyes . . . fix their stare on the void' to their intense discomfort. Far better to search than suffer such agony, even if the search leads to growing blindness and defeat. Man prefers to fill the void of existence with an assumed purposiveness which he pursues with rationally devised codes for his better deception.

Life on earth, divided as it is into days and nights, summers and winters, birth and death, marvellously disguises from man its real timelessness. Far from enlightening him, the repetition of days, weeks, months and years only serves to blind him with the illusion of finitude and an end to his suffering existence. Even the rules he constructs for himself are skilfully devised to give the monotony of a meaningless existence a semblance of variety and purpose. As the voice in *Texts for Nothing* exclaims in sardonic wonder: 'What agitation and at the same time what calm, what vicissitudes within what changelessness.' It is the same malignant 'harmony that reigns in the cylinder between order and licence'. Man can only look for an escape to 'the unthinkable end' of Section XV. Like 'the unthinkable past' the end is a chimera of the rational mind of the narrator. The reality is the unending search for an end. In giving *The Lost Ones* an ostensibly fictitious end, Beckett is mocking those Aristotelian norms of art (and life, itself a fiction), the beginning, the middle and the end. It is all middle. Any termination is unthinkable.

Enough is closer to *The Lost Ones* than might appear at first. Beckett is again concentrating on man's unwillingness to face the horror of his meaningless existence. But the viewpoint is different; in place of an omniscient narrator conducting a pseudo-socio-historical survey we enter the mind of a first-person narrator. Like his predecessors in the novels he is an artist seeking a 'way out'. His solution is to tell himself more and more congenial stories about his past life. He revels in his memory's natural deficiencies and seeks to escape from himself into a world of dream and fantasy. The narrator has already parted company with his earlier, older self (in the sense that the child is father to the man). His youthful self had some remaining links with the world around him: 'Of the wind that was no more. Of the storms he had ridden out.' But even these vestigial reminders of life's unpleasantness are excluded from the self's latest fiction, a pastoral world in which 'the very flowers were stemless', 'as if the earth had come to rest in spring'.

78

To convert a hell of suffering into a dream of heaven, the self has been driven to extremes of inventiveness, finally erasing everything from his memory but the flowers through which he had dragged with his youthful counterpart. Expelled from paradise into the hell of life on earth, he seeks to reverse his fate and return to an Eden of his own creation. *Enough* begins and ends with an ostentatious display of the 'art and craft' used by the narrator to reconstruct his past life in a fiction that fulfils his fondest wishes. Even the earlier self suffered from the natural distortions of perception (he only viewed the sky in a mirror); the present self adds to these the distortions of memory. The fiction he invents is based on falsity. His idyll has all the beauty and transience of a mirage, but the 'stony ground' of the desert of existence can only be denied for the duration of the story he tells himself.

The language in *Enough* is reminiscent of those poetic passages in *Imagination Dead Imagine* in which the old illusory imagination of 'islands, waters, azure, verdure' reasserts itself. Beckett consciously summons language of haunting beauty to convey his narrator's wish-fulfilment: 'Night. As long as day in this endless equinox. It falls and we go on. Before dawn we are gone.' In all his mature work lyricism of this kind is invariably associated with self-deception, with what 'Bom' calls 'last little scenes' of 'life in the light'. The problem for a writer like Beckett, who is constantly trying to penetrate deceptive appearances so as to see into the heart of things, is that language itself is subjective and reflects the deceptions practised by its users. Like Mrs Rooney, we are all struggling with a dead language. Beckett's reaction, as he told John Gruen in 1970, has been to turn 'toward an abstract language', one which approximates to the purity of mathematics. As Watt discovered, even logic and arithmetic are incapable of defining nothingness, but they can better indicate its inescapability than the emotionally charged language of the very early works like 'Text' or 'Sedendo et Quiescendo': 'I won't kiss your playful hand, dass heisst spielen, my dolorific nymphae and a tic douleureux in my imperforate hymen, what's the Deutsch for randy, my dirty little hungry bony vulture of a whorehen....'

Both *Ping* and *Lessness* make frontal attacks on what might be termed the Joycean linguistic tradition. In both works 'sentences' embrace a series of linked images. Syntax is minimal, all the verbs being reduced to participles in *Ping*, all the definite and indefinite articles being omitted in both works except for the incursions of past memories and dreams. *Ping* presents the image of a body on the point of reaching unconsciousness by a process of becoming all-conscious. Total knowledge and whiteness are identified with each other, and reality is represented as 'Bare white body fixed white on white invisible'. However, vestigial traces of the old life of imperfect knowledge and perception (which intrude with a 'Ping') still prevent the body from becoming merged with the 'white infinite'. These traces bear the linguistic hallmarks of the old dead language of illusion. 'Only the eyes only just light blue' or 'Ping of old only just perhaps a meaning a nature' contain those give-away definite and indefinite articles that remind the reader of what *Lessness* calls 'the days and nights made of dreams of other nights better days'.

The language of endlessness must be devoid of colour, sound, emotion, and meaning itself. *Ping* claimed to attain this desired end by a process of knowing all. *Lessness* rejects this solution as another fiction. All is unknowable. Infinity cannot be grasped by a finite process. But it can be indicated allusively. In *Lessness* the body is removed from its protective white box of knowledge to confront the endlessness of true existence. But simultaneously it is made to perform the impossible: 'One step in the ruins in the sand on his back in the endlessness he will make it.' Beckett repeatedly uses paradox to reflect the paradoxical nature of man's predicament. Faced with endlessness, how ridiculous to make one step more. But we all do it. In attempting to know all, the body in *Ping* was doing just that. But the white walls screened off the changelessness all around. Outside the white chamber, as Clov reported, all is 'light black', like the 'grey air' of *Lessness*. Night and day, black and white, are perceptual illusions from the vantage point of eternity. Speed up the camera of man's eye and universal greyness covers all: 'Never but this changelessness dream the passing hour.'

In *Lessness* Beckett has devised a form that perfectly reflects the relativity of man's perspective. Order and disorder, symmetry and chaos are reflected in the construction of its 120 sentences. Man's obsessive need for order is given formal expression in the fact that each sentence in the first half is repeated in the last half, and that, as Martin Esslin was told by Beckett, the sixty sentences belong to six groups of images, ten sentences in each. (The Calder & Boyars cover lists these as ruin, exposure, wilderness, mindlessness, and past and future (1) denied and (2) affirmed.) But the random order of endlessness is suggested by the random reappearance of each sentence in the second half, the random sequence of the six images, and the random length of the paragraphs. Unlike *Ping*'s false sense of an ending, *Lessness* could continue to oscillate between these poles to infinity.

80

Beckett has travelled a great distance from the verbal exuberance of his early short fiction. Linguistic acrobatics have given way to the conscious dislocation of language. The puns and scholarly wit of *More Pricks Than Kicks* have no place in his latest work, where a sparse vocabulary is ranged against itself in a series of mutually annihilating paradoxes. Thwarted by the relativity of perception, Beckett has concentrated, increasingly as time has passed, on inventing literary forms that can overcome the subjective limitations of traditional fiction, obsessed as it is with 'figments' like love, beauty, time and memory. In the last phase of his writing he has sought literary structures that admit the chaos of man's meaningless existence while not excluding man's hopeless search for an order and a meaning to life. The result has been a series of prose texts whose difficulty is matched by their originality. The little population of lost ones, the pastoral idyll of *Enough*, and the body face to endlessness join their predecessors in a gallery of unique and compelling images that reflect Beckett's lifelong search for that impossible shape that will capture in its own destruction life's ultimate shapelessness.

NOTES

1 Tom F. Driver, 'Beckett by the Madeleine', *Columbia University Forum*, vol. IV, no. 3, Summer 1961, p. 22.

2 John Gruen, 'Samuel Beckett talks about Beckett', *Vogue* (London), vol. 127, no. 2031, February 1970, p. 108.

3 See R. Federman and J. Fletcher, *Samuel Beckett: His Works and His Critics*, University of California Press, 1970, for full bibliographical sources of these stories.

4 A further extract, 'Jem Higgins' Love-Letter to the Alba', was published in the Durham University magazine, *New Durham*, in June 1965.

5 John Fletcher, *The Novels of Samuel Beckett*, Chatto & Windus, 1970 ed., p. 235.

A SELECTIVE BIBLIOGRAPHY OF BECKETT'S SHORTER FICTION

In view of the confusing and haphazard manner in which Beckett's shorter fiction has been published in France, England, and the USA, I append this special bibliography which attempts to differentiate between approximate dates of composition (or first appearance in periodicals) and publication in collected form. All quotations from Beckett's work in my chapter are from Calder & Boyars' English texts.

1   'Assumption', in *Transition* (Paris), vols XVI–XVII, June 1929, pp. 268–71 (collected in *Transition Workshop*, ed. Eugene Jolas, Vanguard Press, New York, 1949).

2   'Sedendo et Quiescendo' (extract from 'Dream of Fair to Middling Women') in Eugene Jolas, ed. *Transition: An International Workshop for Orphic Creation*, Servire Press, Holland, 1932.

3   'Text' (extract from 'Dream of Fair to Middling Women' (in *New Review*, vol. II, April 1932, p. 57.

4   *More Pricks Than Kicks*, Chatto & Windus, 1934 (collection of ten stories, of which the first, 'Dante and the Lobster', had already appeared in shorter form in *This Quarter*, vol. V, December 1932, pp. 222–36).

5   'A Case in a Thousand', in *The Bookman*, vol. LXXXVI, August 1934, pp. 241–2.

6   *Nouvelles et textes pour rien*, Editions de Minuit, Paris, 1955.
    The three *nouvelles* were written in 1945:
    (a) 'L'Expulsé' (an early version appeared in *Fontaine*, vol. X, December 1946 to January 1947, pp. 685–708).
    'The Expelled' (English translation; first printed in *Evergreen Review*, vol. VI, January–February 1962, pp. 8–20; collected in *Stories and Texts for Nothing*, Grove Press, New York, 1967, and *No's Knife*, Calder & Boyars, London, 1967).
    (b) 'Le Calmant'.
    'The Calmative' (English translation; first printed in *Evergreen Review*, vol. XI, June 1967, pp. 46–9, 93–5; collected in *Stories and Texts for Nothing* and *No's Knife*, 1967, as 6(a)).
    (c) 'La Fin' (an early version entitled 'Suite' appeared in *Temps modernes*, vol. I, July 1946, pp. 107–19).
    'The End' (English translation; first printed in *Merlin*, vol. II, summer–autumn 1954, pp. 144–59, and with variants in *Evergreen Review*, vol. IV, November–December 1960, pp. 22–41; collected with revisions in *Stories and Texts for Nothing* and *No's Knife*, 1967, as 6(a)).
    The thirteen *Textes pour rien* were written about 1950:
    (d) *Textes pour rien* (textes III, VI and X first appeared in *Lettres nouvelles*, vol. I, May 1953, pp. 267–77, texte XI in *Arts-Spectacles*, vol. 418, 3–9 July 1953, p. 5, and textes I and XII in *Monde nouveau* (Paris), vol. X, May–June 1955, pp. 144–9, all except the last with variants).
    Texts for Nothing (English translation; text I first appeared in *Evergreen Review*, vol. III, summer 1959, pp. 21–4, and text III in *Great French Short Stories*, ed. G. Brée, Dell, New York, 1960; collected in *Stories and Texts for Nothing* and *No's Knife*, 1967, as 6(a)).

7   *Premier Amour*, Editions de Minuit, Paris, 1970 (*nouvelle* written in 1946 but withheld from publication longer than its three companion *nouvelles*). *First Love* (English translation), Calder & Boyars, London, 1973.

8   'From an Unabandoned Work' in *Trinity News: A Dublin University Weekly*, vol. III, 7 June 1956, p. 4, and *Evergreen Review*, vol. I, no. 3, 1957, pp. 83–91. Published separately by Faber & Faber, London, 1958, and collected in *No's Knife*, 1967, as 6(a)).

9   'Jem Higgins' Love-Letter to the Alba' (extract from 'Dream of Fair to Middling Women') in *New Durham*, June 1965, pp. 10–11.

10 *Imagination morte imaginez*, Editions de Minuit, Paris, 1965 (collected in *Têtes mortes*, Editions de Minuit, Paris, 1967).
    Imagination Dead Imagine (English translation) in the *Sunday Times*,

7 November 1965, p. 48; Calder & Boyars, London, 1965 (also in *Evergreen Review*, vol. X, February 1966, pp. 48–9, and collected in *No's Knife*, 1967, as 6(a)).

11 *Assez*, Editions de Minuit, Paris, 1966 (collected in *Têtes mortes*, 1967, as 10).
Enough (English translation), in *No's Knife*, 1967, as 6(a)).

12 *Le Dépeupleur*, Editions de Minuit, Paris, 1970 (section 1 first appeared as *Séjour*, Georges Richar, Paris, 1970, section 4 as *L'Issue*, Editions Georges Visat, Paris, 1968, and section 14 as 'Dans le cylindre' in *Livres de France*, vol. XVIII, no. 1, January 1967, pp. 23–4).
The Lost Ones (English translation), Calder & Boyars, London, 1972, and Grove Press, New York, 1972.

13 *Bing*, Editions de Minuit, Paris, 1966 (collected in *Têtes mortes*, 1967, as 10).
Ping (English translation) in *Encounter*, vol. XXVIII, no. 2, February 1967, pp. 25–6, and in *Harper's Bazaar*, no. 3067, June 1967, pp. 120, 140; collected in *No's Knife*, 1967, as 6(a)).

14 *Sans*, Editions de Minuit, Paris, 1969.
Lessness (English translation), in *New Statesman*, 1 May 1970, p. 635, and Calder & Boyars, London, 1970.

Chapter 5

Innovation and continuity in *How It Is*

Victor Sage

I

There is usually a subtle series of connections between the shape
of a writer's career and the reception of his works. The kind of life
the author leads, the sequence of publication, the method of
composition – all these factors can affect the way we make the
apparently pure judgment of the individual work. Through a
mixture of accident and design authors sometimes exercise a
remarkable measure of control over both the critical and uncritical
sectors of public response. Nor is that response simply limited to
the inevitable blindness of a contemporary audience. Death does
not always merely arrest an author's intentions; sometimes it
confirms them.

Take, for example, the careers of Milton and Joyce. In both
cases the early works seem to have been written *as* early works –
as a preparation for later and greater efforts. Even where patently
slight or unfinished the juvenilia of these writers seem to acquire a
natural justification from the fact that the later career contains
major achievements. Development leaves a wake of retrospective
evaluation: we tend to think that Milton's fragment 'The Passion'
in his volume of early poems must have been *significantly* abandoned, if abandoned by the poet of *Paradise Lost*. Though not
unfinished, Joyce's 'slim volume' *Chamber Music* is difficult to
judge for the same sort of reason; even if we have come to the
considered opinion that these poems really are rather undis-
tinguished, there is still a distinct pressure on us to regard them as
literary exercises. No doubt we should view the last lines of
Lycidas or the last words of *Portrait of the Artist* in quite a different
light if either Milton or Joyce had died immediately upon completing them. On the other hand if Sylvia Plath had not died soon
after writing

> Dying
> Is an art, like everything else.
> I do it exceptionally well.

the lines would lose that *frisson* of prophecy which is such an
important part of their power.

The process is inevitably reciprocal; as they are added to the canon, the new works 'prove' (not to say *im*prove) the shape of the career which, in its turn, conditions the way we see the individual works. The shape of Joyce's career is complicated by a barrage of self-consciousness propaganda. He noisily rewrites his own career as he goes along, parodying his former self, producing a better past as it is assimilated to a better present. Like Swift's spider the encyclopedic modern spins his career out of his own belly and keeps up a running commentary on his own progress. Fortunately Richard Ellmann's biography has done a lot to expose the seamy side of the tapestry – now we can at least begin to see where accident meets design, where luck conspires with judgment. Characteristically, on the eve of his fateful departure from Ireland, Joyce cabled Lady Gregory: 'Now I will make my own legend and stick to it.' She replied by sending him an already-legendary fiver. Very much a twentieth-century lower-middle-class version of 'fresh woods, and pastures new'.[1]

Milton and Joyce follow the classic shape – the expansion from lyric through drama to epic. They present themselves with flawless prophetic detachment, demonstrating their mastery of each genre before progressing to a more ambitious one. Beckett's career, if anything, has a stronger predictive logic about it. But part of his distinctiveness lies in the way he has managed to invert this classic literary shape. It is difficult to think about Beckett's development without a series of mental adjustments because the most obvious shape for his career appears to be an arc of diminishing achievement. Traditionally we associate literary development with expansion, but Beckett 'develops' towards inarticulacy and, ultimately, silence.

The rare but not unprecedented paradox that success is failure lurks at the centre of this cobweb; it creates a context of expectation so strong that the act of publication of a Beckett work is almost as important as the work itself. Some of the titles are revealing: *From an Abandoned Work*, *Residua* and, significantly the title of an extract from *How It Is*, 'From an Unabandoned Work'.[2] The intimacy of these allusions is important, I think, because it shows how Beckett himself helps promulgate a myth of continuous regression.

Some of Beckett's later and shorter texts are particularly difficult to judge because of the force of this predictive logic. But the problem is perhaps more urgent in the case of a piece like *How It Is*. Some of the most influential judgments of this work seem needlessly conditioned by a general view of his career; it is often felt to be a substantial piece, but not a separate one. Too much of its significance seems to lie in the fact that Beckett was able to produce it. For Dieter Wellershof, for example, it looks like a miracle:[3]

> The progressive de-mythologisation and dissipation of substances finds its logical end in the *Textes Pour Rien*.
> Nevertheless Beckett, as though it were possible for him to escape fiction and talk directly about his subject matter, has written another book which has the title *How It Is*.

There is, of course, the biographical evidence that Beckett himself felt he had reached an impasse at the end of the *Textes*; but this is not quite how it is being presented. The crisis is a 'logical' one; it derives from a judgment about the nature and sequence of the preceding works. But the logic of this procedure looks a little less inexorable when one considers the order of publication in English. *Comment c'est* (1961), the French original of *How It Is*, occupies a different place in the French canon: it follows the impasse of the *Nouvelles et textes pour rien* (1955). For an English reader the sequence is different: *How It Is* (1964) follows *The Unnamable* (1958) and *No's Knife*, the English translation of the *Nouvelles et textes pour rien*, does not appear until 1967. For the English reader the reference points are different and the sense of continuity is different. The impasse appears more retrospectively. For me, this has the effect of making *How It Is* feel much more like the main line of development.

I am sure that, as things stand at the moment, one could invent many different 'shapes'. My main point is not so much about the inaccuracy of such abstractions as their tendency to condition the judgment of the individual work. Wellershof's response to the logic of reduction is clearly operating in his description of the language of *How It Is*:[4]

> The title is an assertion behind which stands the desire to come to a final halt in this process, even if this final point were no more than that at which the only thing one possessed were the certainty of not possessing anything. This is suggested by the constant use of the word 'yes' which aims at committing language which has been reduced to a stammer of word-fragments to a last remnant of 'factuality'.

The logic of Beckett's artistic commitment is being confused here

with his linguistic performance; the pressure of the idea of reduction is so strong that the language of the books seems to be
literally reduced.

Hugh Kenner on the other hand treats Beckett as if he succeeds
at the outset in making a philosophical statement. Instead of a
linear reduction, Kenner represents Beckett's career as essentially
static – the exploratory element is a merely formal affair. *How It Is*
he claims 'contains no ingredient (unless perhaps mud) which we
have not encountered before. What is new is the absolute sureness
of design.'[5] Again the view of the whole career seems to condition
the view of the book's language. What is the distinction between
the 'ingredients' and the 'design', except a split between form
and doctrine? It is the proportions that are new, not the materials:
'No, what is novel is simply the scale on which this material is
organised, the brilliance no longer local, but gone into the bones
of a work that tends to stay in the memory as a whole.'[6]

This view frees Beckett from failure, but at the price of what
looks like decadence. The loss of the sentence, Kenner argues, is a
gain in the clarity of purely formal relations, a kind of musical
wholeness.

Although virtually opposite in their implications, both of these
views of *How It Is* have something in common; they are essentially
responses to the 'inevitability' of the Beckett canon. As such they
reflect the genuine difficulty of talking about this text in isolation.
But they are exaggerated retrospective versions of continuity
which oversimplify the role of expectation; a reader's expectations
when actually faced with the text are bound to be more delicate
than either of these views can afford to admit. Professor Kenner
gallantly suggests that we jettison the expectation of sentences,
but this would literally make the book nonsensical. Dieter Wellershof on the other hand, in regarding 'yes' as the symptom of a
failure to commit language to certainty, is ignoring the fact that
the Beckett reader is highly trained in responding to certain kinds
of linguistic behaviour. This is not where the newness of the book
lies, because the reader is already acquainted with the miserable
dialectic concealed in such innocent-looking terms. As an earlier
narrator laments in the usual self-contradictory fashion: '. . . ah
if no were content to cut yes's throat and never cut its own. . . .'

How then can we avoid the conditioning pressure of the career?
The short answer is that at the present moment we cannot; we
have no Richard Ellmann to separate the man from the works,
though the Federman and Fletcher bibliography yields a glimpse
of the real complexity and contingency of the career. Professor

Kermode's review of *How It Is* at least avoids the excesses of 'logic'. He treats Beckett as if he were a frustrated Renaissance allegorist to whom we need to grant the right to 'obscure the literal sense':[7]

> The only difference is that his predecessors were sure there was such a sense, and on this bitch of a planet he can no longer have such certainties. The difference does not affect the proposition that Beckett's flirtations with reality are carried on in a dialect which derives from the traditional language of learning and poetry. It is nevertheless true that the more accustomed we become to his formal ambiguity, the more outrageously he can test us with inexplicitness. *How It Is* differs from the earlier work not in its mode of operation but principally in that it can assume greater knowledge of the Beckett world.

This is easier assumed than examined; expectation is difficult, if not impossible, to be certain about. But the assumption at least allows the reader into the picture. It insists, surely rightly, that effects like 'reduction' and 'regression' must be mediated through a reader's responses. If we are to answer the question: in what sense *How It Is* is a new work, it is necessary to examine the nature of our expectations and the role they play in those responses.

II

Any reader of Beckett will know that he has a mania for symmetry. His prose is full of symmetrical patterns; more particularly, the symmetry of affirmation and denial. Any single term seems to call its opposite into play and, in some ultimate sense, to be identified with it. When we put any of the major novels down, our heads are reeling with a dazzling procession of alternative terms: all or nothing, coming or going, on or back, progress or regress, yes or no, up or down, West or East, new or old. Most of these terms are put together in such a way that the distinction between them is effectively removed. Celia's dilemma in *Murphy* (1938), as she sits on the stairs of Murphy's apartment and tries to decide whether to go up and on or down and back, is a classic example: 'How different it had been on the riverside, when the barges had waved, the funnel bowed, the tug and barge sung, yes to her. Or had they meant no? The distinction was so nice' (p. 27).[8] There is a difference, but it is forced into a symmetry: 'The difference between her way of destroying them both, according to him, and his way, according to her' (p. 27). Symmetry, as we know from looking in a mirror, persuades us of identity. Experience is constantly reduced in Beckett's prose to the formula: A is B. This effect is achieved by an enormous variety of rhetorical devices – symbolic use of rhyme, parallelism of clausing, ironic refrain and repetition and so on.

Celia responds to her dilemma by tossing a coin; countering the arbitrary with the arbitrary, or so she thinks. But this only means more of the same thing. The problem is not just a matter of love or personalities or social behaviour – it is a matter of *all* experience, including that of language, reducing to the same invariable pattern. Notice the way, for example, the intimate pain of the following snatch of dialogue is at odds with its acrostic style of presentation (pp. 40–1):

> 'Then is the position unchanged?' said Murphy. 'Either I do what you want or you walk out. Is that it?'
> She made to rise, he pinioned her wrists.
> 'Let me go,' said Celia.
> 'Is it?' said Murphy.
> 'Let me go,' said Celia.
> He let her go. She rose and went to the window. The sky, cool, bright, full of movement, anointed her eyes, reminded her of Ireland.
> 'Yes or no?' said Murphy. The eternal tautology.
> 'Yes,' said Celia. 'Now you hate me.'
> 'No.' said Murphy. 'Look is there a clean shirt.'

Even as a young man Beckett was obviously well-schooled in the delights of domestic solitaire. The tension is extreme here between our sense of a real clash of individuals and the chess-board equation which reduces them to counters: A is B again. The formula can be symbolised at any level. The gestures, for example, enact it: Murphy imprisons her physically, but when he 'frees' her she declares that the position is unchanged. The sky hangs tantalisingly outside the window, the symbol of Absolute Freedom – so near, because so far. If yes or no is the eternal tautology, then their ensuing dialogue acts out that tautology, even though Murphy appears to be capitulating. There is, as the first sentence of the novel damningly declares, 'nothing new'.

The formula A is B is a universal one. Beckett's novels after *Murphy* are littered with manifestations of it. It is a basic expectation of any reader, whether conscious or not. The crucial question is: What is its significance? Is it a formal ambiguity only? A trick of language? Or is it a philosophical dilemma? A problematic 'fact' which language only renders?

There is no simple answer to this question, but whatever answer we do give will tend to define our expectations. It seems to me fruitful to begin by treating it as a persuasive device, but of a special kind. Certainly Beckett's assault on language leaves rationality untouched – it is not directly philosophical in that sense. The great advantage of treating it as a device is that one regards it as the object of expression then, rather than the subject, the end product of our responses, rather than their stimulus.

The formula A is B expresses a relation. Theoretically, it does not matter what terms are used to fill out that relation. Moreover it makes no difference to that relation what literary convention or genre is used to represent it. It can be expressed in an epigram or forty thousand words of narrative. It is a purely abstract relation and as such is prior to the terms in which it is expressed. As Jacques Moran says in *Molloy*: '. . . the falsity of the terms does not necessarily imply that of the relation, so far as I know' (p. 112).[9] Malone even takes a certain satisfaction in his awareness of it: 'And it is a pleasure to find oneself again in the presence of one of those immutable relations between harmoniously perishing terms . . .' (p. 229). Perhaps Malone's greatest delusion is that he thinks of this in the plural.

Implied in Beckett's prose style and his whole manner of writing is a diatribe against certain expectations of language: notably the organic. Time and time again his destructive twisting of proverbs and catchphrases, his constant habit of transposing subject and object and his absurd scrutiny of suffixes and prefixes expose the fallacy of a natural connection between words and meanings. He is fascinated by the mechanical and the systematic; his cadences have the precision of a jewelled watch-movement. The ultimate incapacity of language to be logical and consistent is a major source of frustration and despair. In this sense his prose is mechanistic rather than organic; it woos the abstract paradigm in every situation. Often one has the feeling that another image or character would have done just as well to illustrate the point. Neither Murphy nor Celia, for example, are strictly necessary to the paradigm; in this narrow sense they are arbitrary figures.

This goes for notions of organic form too. There is nothing inevitable about the form of Beckett's novels. Theoretically each one is an arbitrary arrangement of terms which reveals an immutable relation between them. Between *Murphy* (1938) and *How*

It Is (1964) the Beckett reader is intensively trained in this
theoretical expectation. The novels are more like the temporary
assemblages of a Meccano set than uniquely formed growths.

The A is B formula is quite independent of literary convention.
It is highly destructive of point of view, for instance. The novels
involve a progressively explicit erosion of narrative point of view:
they move from the third person into the first. His language acts
like a code: once you have granted the nature of the signal, the
conditions in which it can be given are manifold. It makes no
difference to morse code whether you flash your message on a torch
or a shuttered oil lamp, whether you use a mirror in the sun or a
blanket and bonfire. The methods of transmission are culturally
specific, but the code is an abstraction. For Beckett, literary convention and genre are specific; the paradigm A is B is an
abstraction.

Consider the yeses and noes in the following passage from *How
It Is* (p. 97):[10]

> if he talks to himself no thinks no believes in God yes
> everyday no wishes to die yes but doesn't expect to no he
> expects to stay where he is yes flat as a cowclap on his
> belly yes in the mud yes without motion yes without thought
> yes eternally yes

Thirty years after *Murphy* Beckett is still writing out the 'eternal
tautology'. The style of the passage is different from the conversation between Murphy and Celia, but only superficially. It is in the
form of question and answer – it resembles a questionnaire or a
computer exam. It could be rewritten as dialogue without loss of
effect, if it were not for the indeterminacy of point of view. We
have the illusion (or the possibility) of simultaneous dialogue and
monologue: 'in other words in simple words I quote on either I am
alone and no further problem or else we are innumerable and no
further problem either' (p. 124). For readers of the trilogy this
dilemma is not exactly unexpected. The paradigm is unaltered,
but this particular rhetorical arrangement cuts out all of the
stability of a narrative convention. In *How It Is* the sources and
recipients of speech are not distinguishable.

Yet most readers would agree, I think, that the description I
have just given of our expectations is not the whole picture. The
truth remains that Murphy and Celia are not simply A and B:
Celia, as people are fond of remarking with some surprise, is an
amiable woman and even Murphy is distinguishable from, say,

Vera the waitress. The world of *Murphy* is distinct from the world of *Watt* – only relatively distinct, but distinct.

In other words it matters to us a great deal how the equation is expressed. Our expectations also work at a more concrete instinctive level and they are far from insignificant in our total response. There are, for example, some very concrete features of *How It Is* which make it quite distinct from Beckett's other works. The sentence may have been lost, but there is an artificial restriction on the length of the utterance which makes it much closer to natural breath-pause. This text does not gabble in the same vertiginous way as many of the others; the restriction this device places on sheer impetus is of considerable importance to the reader. The loss of the ubiquitous comma tends to decrease the illusion of a single linear flow. It increases the reader's need to permutate different parts of sentences. Typographical arrangement, though not strictly relevant to meaning in the hard sense, affects pace and mood.

Again, Kenner suggests jokingly that mud is the only new thing in this book. In an abstract sense, it matters not a jot what material Beckett chooses to represent 'this muck where all is identical' (p. 112). It occupies the same role in this work as the other familiar elemental symbolism in the other novels (sand, snow, water, leaves, stones, etc.); it stands for the immutable quantity of matter, the medium of change that is not real change, the vehicle of homogeneity. But it also has all sorts of cultural and psychological associations for us which make it, as a concrete symbol, quite different from sand or snow: mud is basic, repulsive, it readily assimilates to the primitive, if not the primeval. The prominence given to it in this book governs much of its tone and feeling. Whether we feel it is 'new' or not depends on which expectation we bring into play.

This difference in the nature of our expectations is the basis of the endless battles fought in *Watt* between logic on the one hand and usage on the other. Reading Beckett may be a process of scrutinising one's instincts and finding them alien, but he places a crucial reliance on the resistance provided by those instincts. He needs our readiness to attribute continuity to things, in order to collapse continuity so frighteningly.

How It Is begins by assuming a natural order. This is not an unqualified assumption by any means, but the book's intelligibility rests on establishing the idea of a natural sequence of thoughts or events as the opening refrain suggests: 'three parts I say it as I hear it. . . .' This receives a rather disturbing reversal in Part

Three: 'unless recordings on ebonite or suchlike a whole life generations on ebonite one can imagine it nothing to prevent one mix it all up change the natural order play about with that' (p. 107). A good deal of the force of this speculation depends on the fact that the reader has clung to a sense of the 'natural order' through all the doubts and hints of qualification up to this point – indeed this speculation could be part of that order. But the voice is introducing the possibility that the order we have experienced is really random. At this point the Beckett 'voice' is struggling to possess the reader's memory, signalling us to rearrange our reading experience. Our capacity to apprehend 'natural order' (our strongest expectation) is our weakness – it is suddenly treated as evidence that we are not 'free'. The denial uses the weight of our reading experience as a judo expert uses the weight of his opponent. As the natural order reasserts itself the denial is reversed and the reader gains a momentary conceptual leverage.

Throughout the book the texture of the writing varies according to this rhythm. The images in Part One, for example, have a concrete and specific effect. They set up a counterpoint with the mud which perpetually collapses and reasserts itself. The early image of the crocus is a brief example (p. 21):

it dies and I see a crocus in a pot in an area in a basement
a saffron the sun creeps up the wall a hand keeps it in the
sun this yellow flower with a string I see the hand long
image hours long the sun goes the pot goes down lights on
the ground the hand goes the wall goes

This sounds like a memory; our expectation leaps to assert natural continuity. Yet the end of the passage 'uncreates' this experience and fades it out in almost cinematographic fashion. There is no change from the mud, only the pathetic illusion of a change.

Such images have an inviolably concrete and specific effect. They are vital reference points for our anthropomorphic expectations. Take, for example, the 'memory' of Pam Prim. Despite the pressure of a rhetoric that atomises point of view (and therefore individual memory) our expectations are so strong that a natural continuity begins to assert itself (p. 76):

my wife above Pam Prim can't remember can't see her she
shaved her mound never saw that I talk like him I do
we're talking of me like him little blurts midget grammar
past that then plof down the hole.

As we allow this to unfold as a memory the purely abstract lack of a point of view recedes in importance. The concrete detail 'shaved her mound' is an intimacy which is difficult to ignore, even though, from the narrator's point of view, it is qualified by 'never saw that'. The vividness of our expectations makes us override the atomising jokes like 'we're talking of me' and 'I talk like him'. The human continuity of an individual event in time tends to assert itself if only because the image is a memorable one for the reader. For us the story of Pam Prim associates with the earlier tale of the eastern sage who clenched his fists all his life until his finger nails grew through his palms and out the other side. They grew on after he died, just as Pam Prim's 'mound' grows back again after she dies (p. 77):

> in the ward before she went every day all winter she forgave
> me everybody all mankind she grew good God calling her
> home the blue mound strange idea not bad she must have
> been dark on the deathbed it grew again

It is not only mnemonically significant in relation to earlier contradictions about death; it has its own intensification of tone, which again resists the paradigmatic restraint on 'development'. The following passage is a delicate embroidery on the above one (p. 77):

> Outside the road going down lined with trees thousands all
> the same species never knew which miles of hill straight as
> a ribbon never saw that toil in winter to the top of the
> frozen slush the black boughs grey with hoar she at the end
> at the top dying forgiving all white

Like much of Beckett's most impressive prose, this is an ironic exploitation of the Pathetic Fallacy. The choice of details implies a human and seasonal continuity. The visual images, the sounds, the elegiac dignity of vocabulary ('*toil* in winter'. 'grey with *hoar*') invite our response to a traditional area of literary sensibility. The continuity of an individual memory is widening out into a more general context of expectation.

But, at the same time, as readers of Beckett's prose, we have long since learned to question the false security of both these expectations. Memory, as every reader of *Molloy* knows, is only another name for invention. So the inevitable invitation to convert this memory of Pam Prim to a fable eventually arrives: 'dream then that at least certainly not me dream me Pim Bom to be me think pah' (p. 79). Point of view dissolves into indeterminacy again and the concrete sense of an experience in time seems to vanish. Once again we have been seduced into bringing one set of expectations into play, only to have them rudely removed by the appearance of another set which we have been holding in abeyance.

This prose has a subliminal appeal; its allusions and echoes and twisted repetitions flash like a strobe light. The verbal signals are contracted and euphemistic and they grow more so as our range of expectations grows fuller and more sensitive. The vivid images of Part One are withdrawn throughout the other parts, but they are constantly alluded to in passing. This again relies on our sense of continuity. Beckett sometimes baits his reader directly: 'number 81437 may speak misnomer the tormentors being mute as we have seen part two . . .' (p. 119). Do we remember? Consistency is locally important, even though it too is ultimately indistinguishable from invention (p. 111):

> that sack then I did not have on leaving Bem and that I
> had going towards Pim not knowing I have left anyone was
> going towards anyone that sack then that I had I must
> have found it there's reason in me yet that sack without
> which no journey

The apparently cold and timeless refrains which crop up everywhere are also mnemonic signals. They significantly change their meaning when juxtaposed with other phrases: 'an image too of this voice ten words fifteen words long silence ten words fifteen words long silence long solitude once without quaqua on all sides vast stretch of time . . .' (p. 126). This stanza is a solid piece of recapitulation; it is made up of twisted versions of former phrases. Here 'ten words fifteen words' is an echo of the oft-repeated 'ten yards fifteen yards' – the image of someone crawling through the mud has suddenly become a metaphor for a mental (and literary) process. The allusion draws an immediate analogy between consciousness and physical toil. A good deal of the wit of the piece is like this; it looks like a mechanical permutation of motifs, but it is really a continuous series of minute adjustments of expectation.

Many of the motifs of the book are allusions to a problem which has obsessed Beckett for years; their appearance here is only the tip of an iceberg. Take the voice's allusion to the 'free hand'. This is a motif which crops up throughout the novels. Ironically it is present in Celia's dream of Mr Kelly. 'Her cot had a high rail all the way round. Mr Willoughby Kelly came, smelling strongly of drink, knelt, *grasped the bars* [my italics] and looked at her through them.

Then she envied him and he her' (p. 235). Again it is present as an apparently innocent detail in Moran's striking disquisition on the Elsner sisters' dog (p. 106):

> It's a strange thing, I don't like men and I don't like
> animals. As for God, he is beginning to disgust me.
> Crouching down I would stroke his ears, through the
> railings, and utter wheedling words. He did not realise he
> disgusted me. He reared up on his hind legs and pressed
> his chest against the bars. Then I could see his little black
> penis ending in a thin wisp of wetted hair. He felt insecure,
> his hams trembled, his little paws fumbled for purchase,
> one after the other. I too wobbled, squatting on my heels.
> With my free hand I held on to the railings. Perhaps I
> disgusted him too. I found it hard to tear myself away from
> these vain thoughts.

Opposites, as usual, collapse into identity: A is B. This passage depends on a play on words which is never explicitly made. The old joke insists that it is only an arbitrary convention that God is called God and not its anagram Dog. It looks as if Moran is the tyrant, but God and Dog are interchangeable. For one moment, he appears, like Mr Kelly and Celia, to be looking at somebody else's freedom. Read like this, the phrase, 'With my free hand I held on to the railings', looks like an ironic contradiction.

The image seems to mean a great deal to Beckett. Again, when Moran attempts to assert an Old Testament tyranny over his (only begotten) son, the tell-tale 'free' hand is holding the bars again (p. 130):

> Come here! I cried. For on hearing me say we were to go to
> the left he had gone to the left, as if his dearest wish was to
> infuriate me. Slumped over my umbrella, my head sunk as
> beneath a malediction, the fingers of my free hand between
> two slats of the wicket, I no more stirred than if I had been
> of stone.

Here again the would-be tyrant becomes a victim. 'I no more stirred' seems like an insolent reply to his own command: 'Come here!'

All these examples express the same paradoxical relationship between Freedom and Necessity. All of them choose the image of the disembodied 'free' hand clasping the bars of the Universal Cage. There are other examples in almost every one of Beckett's major works: in *Watt* Mr Hackett's hand grasping the rail *permits*

him to strike his stick against the pavement and appease himself
slightly; when Jacques Moran rides on the tandem with his son,
he holds on to him with his free hand; later, almost degenerated
to the condition of his prey, Molloy, he crawls pressing his free
hand against his belly and lets out a roar of triumph and distress;
in *Malone Dies* Molly fingers the canine she has had drilled into
the shape of a crucifix 'with the forefinger of her free hand'. But
although all these examples are the same, there is also an important
sense in which each one of them is 'new': it has a specific context
and specific features of the general proposition which it brings into
prominence.

In *How It Is* the field of our response is different again. The
motif of the hand is linked with the theme of 'the anatomy I had'
– here not just the familiar lament of the Beckett hero for his
ill-remembered academic education, but also a reference to his
waning physical extremities (p. 14):

> I turn to the hand that is free draw it to my face it's a
> resource when all fails images dreams sleep food for thought
> something wrong there
>
> when the great needs fail the need to move on the need to
> shit and vomit and the other great needs all my great
> categories of being
>
> then to my hand that is free rather than some other part
> I say it as I hear it brief movements of the lower face with
> murmur to the mud

The opposition between 'free' and 'need' is threatened here, particularly if we put it in the context of our 'educated' expectations;
it gathers the deposit of other usages. The effect is thus contracted:
it seems no more than a quiet allusion to a paradox that used to be
troublesome, but is now only a paradox.

Other motifs reappear in *How It Is* in an equally contracted
fashion. The theme of witnessing (so important in *Watt*) and the
strange image of the hunter bending over his prey (from *Molloy*)
are combined in the following subdued allusion (p. 133):

> of an ancient voice ill-spoken ill-heard ill some ancient scraps
> from Kram who listens Krim who notes or Kram alone one
> is enough Kram alone witness and scribe his lamps their
> light upon me Kram with me bending over me till the age-
> limit then his son his son's son so on

100

This is strongly reminiscent of the Moran-Gaber-Youdi chain, though the sound-symbolism is more schematic. Vowelling is a well-established means of establishing the A is B relation: Pam Prim, Bom and Pim, Kram and Krim ('one is enough') and, revoltingly parodic, the dog again: Skom Skum. The arbitrariness of these tyrants and victims is familiar. But here the feeling of a new reduction depends on Beckett's explicitness. Simultaneous opposition and identity is an explicit principle of the relationships in this book (p. 140):

> and that linked thus bodily together each one of us is at the
> same time Bom and Pim tormentor and tormented pedant
> and dunce wooer and wooed speechless and reafflicted with
> speech in the dark in the mud nothing to emend there.

This is just like a critic talking; it is a rationalisation of effects which remained implicit through the narrative conventions of the earlier novels. Rationalisation, too, creates the effect of contraction, because one is more familiar with a problem and can state it flatly. Compare this with the narrative of Moran and his son, for example. Have we really 'progressed' or 'regressed'? Isn't it rather a question of using our expectations at a different level?

The final stanzas of the book are very powerful. They rise to a hysterical climax that is quite unique in Beckett's fiction. The immutable relation between A and B, yes and no is as immutable as ever, yet the pace of the writing is climactic (p. 146):

> alone in the mud yes the dark yes sure yes panting yes some
> one hears me no no one hears me no murmuring sometimes
> yes when the panting stops yes not at other times no in the
> mud yes to the mud yes my voice yes mine yes not another's
> no mine alone yes sure yes when the panting stops yes on and
> off yes a few words yes a few scraps yes that no one hears
> no but less and less no answer LESS AND LESS yes

The syntax is a matter of permutation, but not 'free' permutation. The speaker may be separate from the voice which answers him, or he may be confirming or denying his own remarks. Impossibly, he is both, for, as we have seen, the vertebrae of the rhetorical skeleton are A is B. The tormenting yeses and noes, poised tantalisingly between arbitrary tyranny and victimised pleading, seem either to come from the end of a telephone or from deep within the same person. The pacing of the stanza is vitally important: it feels like struggle, a desperation whose violence

101

increases with self-recognition until we can almost hear, behind the last doomed emphasis LESS AND LESS a shadowy whisper: more and more.

III

It is true that Beckett exploits a reductive myth – that of the paradigmatic 'nothing new'. But we tend to forget, I think, that this is an abstraction; if we do respond to the idea of reduction in this way we are likely to get that confused feeling that language itself is reduced. But even outside the specific case of literary style, linguistic 'short-cuts' are notoriously deceptive. To compose a telegram is not simply an activity reduced in complexity because fewer words and grammatical constructions are used; deletion operations may be more complex sometimes than in the case of 'unreduced' English. Some linguisticians argue that speech-contractions in children's language (the omission, for example, of non-referential elements of grammar) are not simply 'economies' due to inadequately developed faculties: contractions may well be relying on a sense of the rules for 'full' expressions.

Much of our response to Beckett's later work will depend on how experienced we are in reading him. Our expectations are complex – they can range from the penumbra of literary tradition at large to the pin-point of a single image. Beckett is an expert at throwing conflicting expectations into prominence at the same time – his wit is a machine for making possibilities look like poverties.

Much of the content in these later works exists not so much on the page as in the reader's mind. What looks like very flat writing suddenly comes alive when we supply the missing links, make the necessary ironic substitutions, etc.

In general perhaps we should make more effort to avoid the domination of abstractions; the themes of the works have a tendency to escape their context and cloud the actual variety of the career of this fascinating writer. *How It Is* is a genuinely new work – it is not at all paradoxical that its newness should rely heavily on a complex set of expectations in the reader.

Indeed recently there have been signs that Beckett has banished introspection and all its Bergsonian problems. He has begun to write in the third person again with a new confidence and a new kind of grace. The prose of *The Lost Ones* (1972) has a Byzantine flatness and finality of perspective which leaves it very close to exposition. The sentence has made a welcome return and the logic of reduction will have a hard time explaining away its syntax.

NOTES

1 Richard Ellmann, *James Joyce*, Oxford University Press, 1966, p. 184.
2 Published in the *Evergreen Review*, vol. IV, September–October 1960, pp. 58–65. Interestingly, published *before* the French original.
3 'Failure at an Attempt at De-mythologisation', in Martin Esslin (ed.), *Samuel Beckett: A Collection of Critical Essays*, Prentice-Hall, New Jersey, 1965, pp. 105–6.
4 Ibid., p. 106.
5 Hugh Kenner, *Samuel Beckett*, Calder & Boyars, London, 1965, p. 199.
6 Ibid., p. 200.
7 Frank Kermode, 'Beckett country', *New York Review of Books*, vol. II, March 1964, reprinted in *Continuities*, London, 1968, p. 175.
8 All quotations from *Murphy* are taken from the Grove Press edition, New York, 1957.
9 All quotations from *Molloy*, *Malone Dies*, and *The Unnamable*, are taken from the Calder edition, London, 1959.
10 All quotations from *How It Is* are taken from the Grove Press edition, New York, 1964.

Chapter 6

The dubious consolations in Beckett's fiction: art, love and nature

Barbara Hardy

Beckett's people are not so unlike the rest of us as to fail to look for solaces of various kinds in art, love and nature. What these solaces may be, and to what extent they sustain the mind, to what extent deepen its suffering, are subjects upon which Beckett is intent. His world is an extraordinary one, but not so remote from other human worlds as to lack these sources of sustenance. Art, love and nature are sources of meaning, and sources of pleasure, though meanings and pleasures are frail, transient, scarred, scotched and annihilated in Beckett's fiction. Even though and even as they disappear or are discredited, these so-called solaces give his strange world a familiar density.

I

There are a few of Beckett's stories where love has virtually diminished to the vanishing-point of dream or remote memory. There are some where the habitable universe has given way to an invented construction, as in *Imagination Dead Imagine*, *Ping*, or *The Lost Ones*. But art is always present, a subject as well as a medium. Beckett's art is an unflaggingly self-reflective activity, and the arts he is chiefly concerned with are theatrical and literary. His plays dramatise and discuss dramatic action, like dialogue, entertainment, scenes, continuous action, performance, exposition, and final curtains. Just as *Waiting for Godot* strangled such theatrical conventions as continuity and conclusion, so some of the novels and stories attack the narrative convention of autonomy, completeness, and steady action. His fiction is concerned with its own genre, of narrative. It illustrates and inspects the need and nature of story-telling, in many forms and guises, as well as the bare possibility of doing and going without. Both plays and stories push their genre as far as possible in the direction of self-destruction, of silence and inactivity, partly, one supposes, out of sheer imaginative zeal and curiosity, partly in admissions of defeat, partly as preparations for dying. They also take a close look not only at forms and conventions, but at language.

Towards the end of *The Unnamable*, Beckett's most taxing long narrative, the narrator is trying hard to do without story, in order to be himself, and to be silent. As he struggles he thinks hard about what fiction can teach us about emotion and reason. After the narrator has for a little while managed to escape narrative and to meditate on silence and on his temporary success in doing without the narrative elements of 'a little nature, and a few names, and the outside of men', he lapses once more into story. He lapses reluctantly, and involuntarily, pushed as usual by forces beyond his control, and it is typical of Beckett that he should in the same breath demonstrate unconscious pressures and most efficiently produce a narrative exemplum. We are presented with a story-lesson.

The story is almost but not quite an anecdote. It is a kind of narrative skeleton, an outline with four unnamed characters, space, time and objects. The history is a sketch, compressed into one long sentence, but allowing for visible improvisation as it develops, prolongs itself, and manages with elasticity and wisdom to contain not only narrative but the analysis of narrative, as Beckett's longer stories always do. Each breathless and rushed narration of event is accompanied by an inference about emotion, and eventually by an inference about rational inference. It moves fast, and also slowly. We are told what happens, then why it happened. We are told what is happening to the characters, what is happening to the narrator/listener, and why events and characters are what they have been seen to become in the course of the narrative (p. 410):[1]

> They love each other, marry, in order to love each other
> better, more conveniently, he goes to the wars, he dies at
> the wars, she weeps, with emotion, at having loved him, at
> having lost him, yep, marries again, in order to love again,
> more conveniently again, they love each other, you love as
> many times as necessary, as necessary in order to be happy,
> he comes back, the other comes back, from the wars, he
> didn't die at the wars after all, she goes to the station, to
> meet him, he dies in the train, of emotion, at the thought of
> seeing her again, having her again, she weeps, weeps again,
> with emotion again, at having lost him again, yep, goes
> back to the house, he's dead, the other is dead, the mother-
> in-law takes him down, he hanged himself, with emotion, at
> the thought of losing her, she weeps, weeps louder, at having
> loved him, at having lost him, there's a story for you, that was
> to teach me the nature of emotion, that's called emotion, what
> emotion can do, given favourable conditions, what love can do,
> well well, so that's emotion. . . .

It is a stunning piece of controlled and compressed lyricism, irony and analysis, a model of slow inching and high speeding. Self-consciousness comes along to shake, scrutinise, and question a story that has appeared out of nowhere, apparently to break the silence, to raise once more, most crucially, the problem of narrative needs and urgencies. The continuous inferences, and the two violently clinching affirmative 'yeps' mark off, underline, structure, frame, punctuate, revise and criticise the happenings. They also mark off, underline, structure, frame, revise and criticise the structures and revisions. The self-analysis is perfectly compatible with a high degree of vivacity, is indeed part of that vivacity, and not a burden it carries. The brutal reduction of story is perhaps intended, so the narrator thinks, to remind him of the old world of fable, though actually it doesn't remind him of anything. But he feels its impact, as he shows in his admissions and explanations of irony and compassion. The story's curtness is not so curt that it doesn't manage to break a rule of emotional writing, as it states and names instead of simply dramatising emotional cause and effect. But feeling is dramatised as well as discussed: the writer's, the listener's and the reader's feelings are breathed out animatedly, pantingly, in namings and inferences and generalisations. My god, yes, it breathes, breathlessly, this is what we do in order to be happy, this is love, yes, it is repeatable, we even do these things over and over again. The little fable about falling between two stools dares us to laugh, forces its irony gaspingly upon us, so that we can't smile or sneer for gasping (pp. 410–11):

> well well, so that's emotion, that's love, and trains, the nature
> of trains, and the meaning of your back to the engine, and
> guards, stations, platforms, wars, love, heart-rending cries,
> that must be the mother-in-law, her cries rend the heart as
> she takes down her son, or her son-in-law, I don't know, it
> must be her son, since she cries, and the door, the house-door
> is bolted, when she got back from the station she found the
> house-door bolted, who bolted it, he the better to hang
> himself, or the mother-in-law the better to take him down,
> or to prevent her daughter-in-law from re-entering the
> premises, there's a story for you, it must be the daughter-
> in-law, it isn't the son-in-law and the daughter, it's the
> daughter-in-law and the son, how I reason to be sure this
> evening, it was to teach me how to reason, it was to tempt
> me to go, to the place where you can come to an end, I must
> have been a good pupil up to a point, I couldn't get beyond

a certain point, I can understand their annoyance, this
evening I begin to understand, oh there's no danger, it's not
I, it wasn't I, the door, it's the door interests me, a wooden
door, who bolted the door, and for what purpose, I'll never
know, there's a story for you, I thought they were over,
perhaps it's a new one, lepping fresh, is it the return to the
world of fable, no, just a reminder, to make me regret what
I have lost, long to be again in the place I was banished
from, unfortunately it doesn't remind me of anything.

This last story, like so many, is being told and also heard,
apparently at the same time, so that the provisional status of the
bolted door and the in-laws speaks of the nature of invention and
the ignorance of the narrator/listener. I'm not sure whether the
'lepping fresh' is a bonus for attentive readers who will, unlike
the narrator, remember a moment in the old world of Beckett's
fables, when Belacqua in 'Dante and the Lobster' (*More Pricks
Than Kicks*) didn't understand the fishmonger's use of the epithet
'lepping' to describe the lobster's freshness (though he came to
understand all too clearly by the end of the story). It would be
rather nice if the naturally unreliable narrator isn't reminded by
his story, but be that as it may, the self-consciousness is witty,
ramifying, and extensive, fulfilling the earlier description, just
before the meditation on silence, of 'just one thing more, just
one space and someone within', which is a laconic but accurate
forecast of the house with only one living someone in it. Its
constant self-checking not only makes the irony, but also draws
attention to the procedures of reasoning, the interest in objects
(especially doors, so important at the very end of *The Unnamable*),
and the refusal to stick with generalisation.

If we learn about emotion we are also learning about 'trains, the
nature of trains, and the meaning of your back to the engine, and
guards, stations, platforms, wars, love, heart-rending cries', in
other and lame words, the meaning of the particulars as well as the
generalisations, of the persons, journeys, objects and emotional
utterances. The self-analysis makes random-seeming survey of the
main narrative elements of symbol, surface, particularity and
themes. The sad and ludicrous self-destructiveness of the passions
is certainly instructively set out in this special piece for a special
occasion, for the occasion of terminus, frustrated silence, minimal
narrative effort. It is a story which is in a hurry to get itself told,
because he wants to get it, and the whole narrative business, over
and done with, yet he knows he has to be patient too. As usual

there is some light in the story, things which are entirely lucid, and some darkness, things which aren't certain and have to be teased out. In an odd and admirable way, it is slightly self-admiring. Odd, because we are put off by what admires itself. Admirable, because the almost throw-away pace and comment make a winning self-deprecation. It is after all a reduced tele-graphic refusal to be sentimental, using that breathless, fast, and laconic style which expresses ruthless salesmanship in Dickens's Jingle and sharp, quick, fond imagination in Joyce's Bloom. The speed not only suggests the narrator's wish to get it over, but also shows the story and its meaning being lapped up, with a wit that proves alacrity, and ensures a further alacrity on the part of the reader outside the novel. Though Beckett's insistence on the narrator as listener, on his provisionalities, dilapidations and reluctance, all make the reader of Beckett probably less outside than he usually is – Beckett blurs the aesthetic borderlines. He ought to make it impossible for critics ever again to use the terms reliable or unreliable narrator, without smiling. Of course all narrators are unreliable. If we didn't know it before, we know it after reading Beckett.

The story is apparently thrown away in order to be more can-didly and startlingly eloquent. But it is a story, wrung from the narrator just as he begins to think he may have got clear of the whole awful business of telling stories, whether to find or lose identity and meaning. An impatience with story betrayed itself in *More Pricks Than Kicks*, most Joycean of Beckett's books, in the uses and criticisms of Dante, Shakespeare and various literary modes of description and narration. Elaborated in *Watt*, it finds its most thoroughgoing expression in the trilogy. Molloy only wants to say goodbye, to 'finish dying' but is forced reluctantly to write his story, even though the writing doesn't work so well any more. He is pretty good-tempered about it, 'I began at the beginning, like an old ballocks, can you imagine that?' Moran is much less good-tempered and open for most of his story, and sulkily remarks that he has to submit to 'petty scrivening'. But he does rather quickly start imagining a time when he may be reconciled to the writing, and may even be helped to endure pain by the 'memory of this work brought scrupulously to a close'. Malone is less passive and more prolific than Molloy or Moran. The reader had to piece together the oddly related, interconfused and ambiguous narratives of Molloy and Moran, but Malone's impatience with steady story is under his own control, shown in his brilliant device of stopping and starting, planning, doing, and undoing, naming, unnaming, and renaming. The problems of all three earlier narrators are included and exacerbated in the situation of the narrator of *The Unnamable*, who pushes even further those problems of meaning and progression, which are at once epistemological and novelistic. Story, plot, action, actions, character, relationships are provided but broken down, by a mind like the one which its owner describes in *From an Abandoned Work* as 'always on the alert against itself'. There is no doubt whatsoever that such breakages convey depression and despair with terrifying success. There is also no doubt that the attacks on art derive from artistic zest and power. There have, after all, been plenty of instances of genuine silence in literature, brought about in many ways. The mind that keeps on attacking literature also loves it, can't stay away from the page and the pencil, must go on. It is necessary to recognise the versatility of Beckett's dilapidations. Story is pitted against story, character against character, word against word, and the result is a virtuoso proliferation of the literary acts. We get more not less, and a new kind of narrative, in which the actual act of writing, failed or successful, becomes action and theme.

Successful narration is brilliantly apparent in the long narratives, particularly *Watt*, the second and third pieces in the trilogy, and *How It Is*. But he does of course offer also failures, stories that haven't developed or exfoliated. *Molloy* seems to be a contribution to the theme of failure. It is essential to see *From an Abandoned Work*, *Imagination Dead Imagine*, and *Ping* as limbs or cell-clusters from ravaged, diseased or deficient longer works. *Imagination Dead Imagine* and *Ping* seem to stop because they are attempting something inhuman, something done from the outside, breaking off or breaking down because humankind can't bear so little story, so little character, so little action, so little time and so little space. The extraordinary, static and careful descriptions of these two fragments seem almost to do what Alain Robbe-Grillet keeps requesting the novel to do, while totally failing to do it himself, namely, to render the visible world without subjectivity. Beckett properly recognises this aim as an imaginative impossibility, which would show imaginative failure, not success. The description of the human pair in *Imagination Dead Imagine* and of the man in *Ping* are so close to being exclusively visual that they eventually convey a painful confinement of the object by and in the medium. But the couple in *Imagination Dead Imagine* are at last allowed to share with the narrator and reader the complicity of 'the infinitesimal shudder instantaneously suppressed' and of the valedictory adjectives 'sweating and icy'. The restriction of sight in *Ping*, associated and conveyed through our own different but similar restriction, is also eloquent of pain. These two pieces seem to confront Robbe-Grillet with the suggestion that to confine narrative to what the eye sees is appropriate only for the description of confinement, and to recognise confinement is, humanly speaking, to express pity. Beckett always speaks humanly.

From an Abandoned Work does not quite imagine the death of imagination. It seems to be an abandonment of something that really could have gone on, or still go on. Its narrative vivacity is a fine instance of Beckett's self-reflection. As usual, he gets there before his critics, and this fragment illustrates not only the painfulness of the reflective process, which shows the medium becoming the message in a way that wonderfully mocks the sterility of MacLuhan's tag, but also the total awareness of process and effect (*No's Knife*, p. 144):

> The questions float up as I go along and leave me very
> confused, breaking up I am. Suddenly they are there, no,
> they float up, out of an old depth, and hover and linger
> before they die away, questions that when I was in my right
> mind would not have survived one second, no, but atomized
> they would have been, before as much as formed, atomized.
> In twos often they came, one hard on the other, thus, How
> shall I go on another day? and then, How did I ever go on another
> day. Or, Did I kill my father? and then, Did I ever kill anyone?
> That kind of way, to the general from the particular I suppose
> you might say, question and answer too in a way, very addling.
> I strive with them as best I can, quickening my step when they
> come on, tossing my head from side to side and up and down,
> staring agonized at this and that, increasing my murmur to a
> scream, these are helps.

Beckett seems at times to be miming the ghastly non-stop analysis found in some pathological states, but he is also the controlled critic, chafing at his victimisation by language. Perhaps he is not always accurate, as when he says he is moving to the general from the particular, when he seems to be also moving in the other direction (from killing his father to killing anyone) or when he speaks of answers where there are only questions. Accurately and inaccurately, he draws attention not only to his figures and forms, but to their effects. The self-conscious narrative is a solace and a pain. Screaming helps, the swaying self-reflection disturbs, the dash from question to answer, or from story to analysis, is like the painful tossing of a head.

Beckett is of course writing in a very old tradition of comic self-consciousness, and his self-analysis is like that of Swift's *A Tale of a Tub*, or of Sterne's *Tristram Shandy*, though these are satiric deflations of literary pretence or pretension. Swift's Grub Street author and the unfortunate, battered Tristram are the disturbed or ineffectual authors of addled narratives, and the 'real' author's irony and travesty set the ideal and structure at a comic remoteness, implying some superiority, some norm of rational discourse or value. In Swift, the dislocations are criticised as irrational and 'modern', in Sterne, the dislocations are defended as imaginative criticisms of simply rational and classical unities. Beckett's self-analysis, like that of these eighteenth-century ancestors, is funny, witty, and extremely clever, but is the language and form of self-laceration, not of satire.

Bergson defines comedy as depending on 'the momentary anaesthesia of the heart' and his metaphor applies to Sterne, at times to Swift, but never to Beckett. Even in Swift, the comic anaesthetic doesn't work perfectly: in *A Tale of a Tub* the aggressive deflations and degradations end by undermining Swift's Anglican middle way as well as the fanatical extremes of Rome and of Dissent. Beckett knows what his anguished comedy is up to; instead of laughing, as Beaumarchais says, so that he may not cry, he laughs and cries at once. The comedy is like an operation without anaesthetic, as in Swift's terrible joke about the flayed woman, where the beau's surprise at the effect of flaying works momentarily like humour but carries such horrified incredulity as to violate irony and give us the thing itself. What is exhilarating or even entertaining in Beckett's wit and literary criticism is also painful, and certainly not without precedent. Donne, for instance, had shown wit as a medium for agony, just as he shared Beckett's impatience with his craft, 'whining poetry'. Beckett's most conspicuous interest in the stories is in narrative form. He manages to toss about agonisedly and alertly, running through all the possible reasons for writing stories. We write them to pass the time, to kill it, to find ourselves, to lose ourselves in others, to get greater clarity and light, or to try for them. We write because there seems to be someone or something urging us or forcing us. Sometimes we write willingly, sometimes hating every minute, sometimes beginning reluctantly but expecting to feel better, especially when we've finished. Our acts of writing and telling are related to all those acts of everyday or every-night life, dreaming, remembering, planning, anticipating, anticipating memory and remembering anticipation. We may go into a story or an act as into a game, play it badly or well, go on, stop short, give up because we forget or are confused, too hard-pressed or too depressed. We may play according to set rules, try to approximate art to science, description to measurement, human relationships or actions to sets and series, quality to quantity. As we play, obey, create, suffer, we may feel addled or desperate. We may even feel enlightened about the nature of feeling and reasoning.

Beckett is interested also in inspecting the word. His self-consciousness about the literary forms that tradition has set up, codified, and analysed extends also to the way language works. He interrupts that interrupting story at the end of *The Unnamable*, and constantly interrupts his sentences, to comment and criticise, looking hard at words, phrases, clichés, metaphors, even punctuation marks. 'How hideous is the semi-colon', comes the observation, mad no doubt (whatever that means), and the reader of *Watt*, exhaustedly alerted to sentences, paragraphs, and larger patterns of event, turns to realise that the page bristles with semi-colons. Beckett calls minute halts, makes us travel as slowly and painfully as his one-legged, crippled and mud-slowed travellers. He divides his characters into travellers and paralytics, and his readers share the experience of both kinds. Like Belacqua, and so many other Beckett people, we are bogged down in the stories and the sentences, can't speed as we usually can through prose fiction, are made to see how difficult it is, are made to feel 'how it is', to meditate bewilderedly on present time, are sent back to read again (more grimly punished by the return than Sterne's lady reader). We emerge, unable to feel the same again about hundreds of well-worn, useful little words and phrases, like 'on my way', 'roughly speaking', 'get off with my life', 'this time', 'that's the way it was', 'my life', 'all (all!)', 'it seemed to me', 'I had the impression', 'go on thinking!'. Molloy says, 'from time to time (what tenderness in these little words, what savagery)'. The end of *The Lost Ones* says: 'So much roughly speaking for the last state of the cylinder and of this little people of searchers one first of whom if a man in some unthinkable past bowed his head if this notion is maintained.' The familiar phrase 'roughly speaking' asserts both its cold glib everyday connotation and a newly learnt precision which strips familiarity, remakes metaphor, and admits provisionality, of speech and fantasy. 'This notion is maintained', proffers its customary dryness but has to be received afresh. Sometimes, of course, the minute halt calls attention to the word and the experience that the word conveys, as when the Unnamable discourses on the eye (p. 378):

> This eye, curious how this eye invites inspection, demands sympathy, solicits attention, implores assistance, to do what, it's not clear, to stop weeping, have a quick look round, goggle an instant and close forever. It's it you see and it alone, it's from it you set out to look for a face, to it you return having found nothing, nothing worth having, nothing but a kind of ashen smear, perhaps it's long grey hair, hanging in a tangle round the mouth, greasy with ancient tears. . . .

The verbal wit alerts us to the deadening acts of language, in the marvellous pun: 'And the face? Balls, all balls, I don't believe in the eye either.' Although it is to the forms of story and drama that he directs attention, he also looks closely at diction with solicitude for familiar and for unfamiliar words, sending us to the dictionary, sometimes severely, sometimes amusedly. His 'gentle skimmer' can't skim, or he will miss the point, not only of fairly accessible jokes like Belacqua feeling 'a sad animal', but smaller essential ones like Malone's 'There I am back at my old aporetics. Is that the word?', followed later by the Unnamable's '. . . how proceed? By aporia pure and simple?' and six sentences later, '. . . I say aporia without knowing what it means.' Dictionary work is soon forgotten, perhaps indeed intended to provide exercises in self-chastening scholarship and amnesia, but here at least is one word that many Beckett readers must have learnt for good from reading Beckett.

I need not labour the entertainment to be derived from such exercises and riddles. We can't skim, we are required to work. Such work is amusing and also exhausting. Readers of fiction expect a certain licence to skim a bit. Beckett doesn't grant it. He knows that literature is a game, but not just a game. It is rewarding but laborious. The reader participates fully in this most precious human solace, works at it and plays with it, understands but is sometimes muddled, loves it, gets fed up, is inspirited but then bored. In this Beckett is not doing anything new, but writing in the old tradition of literary self-consciousness, shared by Shakespeare and Keats as well as the eighteenth-century novelist. Shakespeare broke both comic and tragic tension by dispelling his own figments, admitting that the old mole was in the cellarage and that Cressid had indeed become a type of infidelity. When Theseus in *A Midsummer Night's Dream* reminds the audience, on stage and off, that 'the best in this kind be but shadows' he disturbs more than the dramatic illusion in a *memento mori* for actors, author, and audience. In *The Fall of Hyperion* Keats dispels our belief in artistic unity and our faith in the present by the line 'when this warm scribe my hand is in the grave'. He makes us remember the act of writing in a way very like Beckett's insistence on those pencils and bits of paper. He anticipates Beckett even more precisely and profoundly in 'Ode to a Nightingale', as he attempts to stabilise a vision of art's permanence and joy despite the facts of age, sickness, and death. This imagery is like that of Beckett, though not so minutely particularised:

> Fade far away, dissolve, and quite forget
>   What thou among the leaves hast never known,
> The weariness, the fever, and the fret.
>   Here, where men sit and hear each other groan;
> Where palsy shakes a few, sad, last gray hairs,
>   Where youth grows pale, and spectre-thin, and dies;
>   Where but to think is to be full of sorrow
>   And leaden-eyed despairs;
>   Where Beauty cannot keep her lustrous eyes,
>   Or new Love pine at them beyond to-morrow.

At the end Keats has to admit, with a self-conscious scrutiny both of word and form, that the lyric effort of imagination can't last, hasn't lasted, and has forced him to doubt the enterprise in and of the Ode. He too looks not only at the act of imaginative invention and identification but at language. He repeats his own word 'forlorn', moving it out of the enchantment of faery lands into the more apposite context of his own solitude: 'Forlorn! the very word is like a bell/To toll me back from thee to my sole self!' Keats knows that fancy cheats, that its figments are dispelled in time and space, that we can't always distinguish vision from daydreams. The vision is checked, but also licensed by the act of self-reflection.

II

Keats attempts to find meaning and stability through poetry and also through love. Beckett too is concerned with a world in which Beauty won't keep her lustrous eyes. Beckett's people are mostly extremely ugly, often sick, crippled, impotent. But they still need

and make love, after a fashion. That fashion makes us look hard
at the same facts of mutability and morbidity which Keats faced,
knowing from personal experience that women had cancers and
that consumption was killing. Beckett sets such knowledge down
in detailed imagery. The result is the least romantic treatment of
love offered by English literature, a far cry not only from Keats
but from everyone else.

Beckett's people love things as well as other people, and at times
seem to find them more satisfactory objects of affection. Most of
the things in Beckett are needed for survival, like bicycles, exercise
books, pencils, jars, sawdust, mud, sacks, tin-openers, tins and
biscuits, and this survival is frequently related to love. He also
likes things because they are silent. But things sometimes offer
some sensuous pleasure, as they do for Molloy, who finds that a
pebble in the mouth 'appeases, soothes, makes you forget your
hunger, forget your thirst'. Objects may be substitutes, but their
solace does at times assume surrogate sexuality. Malone sets out
his attempt to understand the human race 'to begin to understand,
how such creatures are possible', plans to write one story about a
stone, but realises that where there are men there are invariably
things too. The thing doesn't get a story to itself after all, but
comes into the human story, sometimes as a love object. Malone is
urgent about his possessions, but makes it clear that the need
isn't simply a need for instruments (p. 249):

> And I loved, I remember, as I walked along, with my hands
> deep in my pockets, for I am trying to speak of the time
> when I could still walk without a stick and a fortiori without
> crutches, I loved to finger and caress the hard shapely objects
> that were there in my deep pockets, it was my way of talking
> to them and reassuring them. And I loved to fall asleep
> holding in my hand a stone, a horse chestnut or a cone. . . .
> And those of which I wearied, or which were ousted by new
> loves, I threw away, that is to say I cast around for a place
> to lay them where they would be at peace forever. . . .

Although Malone feels pity and affection for objects, as for
people, and although they are, like people, eventually ousted, it is
plain that he knows they aren't quite the same as people. He seems
to excuse his attachment to objects by explaining that he hasn't
really 'evolved in the fields of affection and passion'. I think
Beckett sees a love for objects, however sentimental, as an improvement on masturbation, which is pretty severely put in its
place in the stories as an uninteresting satisfaction of appetite,

like eating, and an overrated pleasure, 'the so-called joys of so-called self-abuse'. The love of objects shows the minimal caring for something else. Instead of providing a contrast to the great importance of human relations it rather signals a common and simple need and satisfaction, something like Auden's 'Love requires an object/Almost I imagine/Anything will do'. Sometimes objects, but more usually human beings, of either sex, will do in Beckett.

At moments sexuality, like language, seems to be regarded for the first time, in a way that combines extreme matter-of-factness with sympathetic sense of need ('Enough', *No's Knife*, p. 153):

> I did all he desired. I desired it too. For him. Whenever he desired something so did I. He only had to say what thing. When he didn't desire anything neither did I. In this way I didn't live without desires. If he had desired something for me I would have desired it too. Happiness for example or fame. I only had the desires he manifested. But he must have manifested them all. All his desires and needs. When he was silent he must have been like me. When he told me to lick his penis I hastened to do so. I drew satisfaction from it. We must have had the same satisfactions. The same needs and satisfactions.

There are worse accounts of human connection. Beckett's wit is quietly at work in the pun of 'I drew satisfaction from it'. But the love, if we may call it so, in 'Enough', is not qualified only by the matter-of-factness of style and the cooling reasonability of inference. The relationship itself is restricted, not only by its one-way traffic of desire, which lies within the experience of most of us, one way and another, but by extreme fetishisms and phobias. The older man who leads and instructs the narrator wears gloves, because he dislikes the feel of human skin (though not necessarily of mucous membrane). He leads the narrator, touching him 'where he wished. Up to a certain point'; and the last sentence says, 'Enough my old breasts feel his old hand'. Since the affair began when the narrator was six, it has indeed been a long outing, part walked, part remembered. It seems stupid or indecent to over-analyse this story, compounded as it is of fairly ambitious movements of sexual love, like mutuality, compliance, desire, and the sharing of a past, with the grotesque and comic details that it has in common with dirty jokes, like the gloved lovemaking.[2] Still, as title and last sentence say, it is enough.

We may remember Longinus' strange comment that pity is not

a sublime emotion, in attempting to express an awkwardness about using the term to describe some aspects of loving in Beckett. While his avoidance of pitying tones might be taken as a strong way of invoking pity, I have come to think that pity is the wrong word, carrying with it some complication of superiority, some inclination, however kindly, from high to low. It is as if Beckett refuses to feel compassionate about bestiality or other so-called sexual perversions, recognising them as not only human but compatible with tenderness and fondness, besides signalising common need and gratification. He humanises the dirty joke, or the *graffito*, by giving full particularity, however repugnant this may be or seem to be, then daring us to be disgusted. Joyce shares with Beckett this refusal to outlaw certain modes of sexual connection. Bloom's masturbation, his fetishistic correspondence with Martha Clifford, his rump-licking near-impotence in bed with Molly are all thoroughly understood, and affectionately presented. It is with Joyce and Beckett as though to understand all were to make the word pity redundant or inept. Joyce is good at comprehending impotence, fetishism, various reduced states of sexual connection, but diseased and aging sex lie outside his story. Even the excesses of humiliation are reserved for nighttown. It is as though Beckett brought nighttown into the daylight. Joyce invokes the awful image of a 'grey sunken cunt' to express the uncharacteristic moment of depression in Bloom's day, and it is no wonder that he swiftly invokes the healing counter-image of Molly's warm flesh, however far removed from it he may have to be. Beckett takes that grey sunken cunt and gives it character, name, story.

Many times, Malone kisses his mother's 'old grey pear' (breast, I suppose) and may have pleased her a little. His lovers, usually heterosexual, and often said to be in love, are old, impotent, diseased, crippled, smelly and ugly. It is as if he took those images of dying and sickness and sparse-haired age, from Keats, and showed them in action, recognising, over and over again and without making too much fuss, that the old, the ugly and the sick may desire, be gratified, love, take and give sexual pleasure, and that the 'healthy' reader should admit his likeness. Sex ticks on, however minimally, in sickness and in health. In *More Pricks Than Kicks* the sexual kicks are indeed few, for though Belacqua is certainly not impotent he is a rather unwilling lover. Watt, too, finds coupling an exhausting business. Murphy's is probably the nearest we get to energetic love-making in Beckett, but although he enjoys the pleasures of the serenade, nocturne, and albada, he dislikes the part of himself that loves Celia. But even for Belacqua and Watt, love exists, and is a solace, however scotched or slighted.

Watt's relation with Mrs Gorman, the fish-woman, isn't really love, and he finally decides that he may have liked her just for the fishy smell, and she him for the stout. But their affair is played out with more affection and consolation than this rude explanation suggests (*Watt*, pp. 138–9):[3]

> Then he would have her in the kitchen, and open for her a
> bottle of stout, and set her on his knee, and wrap his right
> arm about her waist, and lean his head upon her right breast
> (the left having unhappily been removed in the heat of a
> surgical operation), and in this position remain, without
> stirring, or stirring the least possible, forgetful of his
> troubles, for as long as ten minutes, or a quarter of an hour.
> And Mrs. Gorman too, as with her left hand she stirred the
> grey-pink tufts and with her right at studied intervals raised
> the bottle to her lips, was in her own small way at peace
> too, for a time.

This affair bears a strong family resemblance to the later loves, also described comically, but with total acceptance, without repugnance for what might be found repugnant by the average insensitive reader. Murphy divides jokes into those that have once been good and those that have never been good, and most of Beckett's comic love-affairs are instances of life's bad jokes, though their badness is tender and heartening, and conveys the message that love like this is, at worst, better than nothing, and, at best, very like more salubrious, young, and elegant love-making. He stresses weakness, silliness, inefficiency, lack of good looks, pressure of time, fatigue and age, which are all problems that everyone must either have experienced or anticipated. As with the story of the gloved lover, the silliness and innocence of some of Beckett's people, Watt, Molloy and Malone, for instance, may remind us of the fool in many traditional dirty jokes, and the three subjects of innocence, ignorance and impotence are, as the groundsman in 'Draff' might say, classical. Beckett's sending-up of high-flown languages also makes its contribution to the amusing treatment of sexual half-heartedness (*Watt*, p. 140):

> Further than this, it will be learnt with regret, they never
> went, though more than half inclined to do so on more than
> one occasion. Why was this? Was it the echo murmuring in
> their hearts, in Watt's heart, in Mrs. Gorman's, of past

passion, ancient error, warning them not to sully not to trail,
in the cloaca of clonic gratification, a flower so fair, so rare,
so sweet, so frail?

In the trilogy there is more love and more sexual energy. Age
is the problem, but they do their best. Molloy possibly pleases his
mother by kissing 'that little grey wizened pear'. He admits her
terrible smell, and while he says 'Pah' realises that she may also
have said 'Pah', for, as he insists, he doesn't 'diffuse the perfumes
of Araby'. Molloy's willingness, pliancy, frankness and tolerance
remind us not too grimly of the rotting flesh and his matter-of-
factness is both funny and insistent (pp. 35–6):

And if they had removed a few testicles into the bargain I
wouldn't have objected. For from such testicles as mine,
dangling at mid-thigh at the end of a meagre cord, there was
nothing more to be squeezed, not a drop.

Molloy probably knew true love, though he isn't absolutely
sure (pp. 56–7):

It was she made me acquainted with love. She went by the
peaceful name of Ruth I think, but I can't say for certain.
Perhaps the name was Edith. She had a hole between her
legs, oh not the bunghole I had always imagined, but a slit,
and in this I put, or rather she put, my so-called virile
member, not without difficulty, and I toiled and moiled until
I discharged or gave up trying or was begged by her to stop.
A mug's game in my opinion and tiring on top of that, in
the long run. But I lent myself to it with a good enough
grace, knowing it was love, for she had told me so. She bent
over the couch, because of her rheumatism, and in I went
from behind. It was the only position she could bear, because
of her lumbago. It seemed all right to me, for I had seen dogs,
and I was astonished when she confided that you could go
about it differently. I wonder what she meant exactly.
Perhaps after all she put me in her rectum. A matter of
complete indifference to me, I needn't tell you. But is it
true love, in the rectum? That's what bothers me sometimes.
Have I never known true love, after all?

He isn't quite sure, but as usual, he reasons quite acceptably.
The discourse on the needs and nature of true love contains more
than irony. Molloy says it is characterised by the acceptance of
poor conditions (flying 'High above the tight fit and the loose'),
and by superfluous, supersexual attentiveness, like cutting the

beloved's toe-nails and massaging the beloved's rump. His explanation for refusing to repeat the experience is suspect but plausible, based, I suppose, on a sense of its uniqueness and perfection, which makes him want to keep the memory 'pure of all pastiche'. There is no one quite like Beckett for having it both ways, for doing what he says women do, giving the cake to the cat and eating it as well. It doesn't seem right to say that all the customary exalted definitions of love's value are here satirised or deflated, since Beckett insists that if they mean anything at all, they have to apply to all human conditions. Beckett certainly makes romantic definitions take a beating, from grotesque, brutally detached and ferocious humour. But he forces the extension of romantic value with powerful plausibility. Rank as love is, for Beckett's people, it behaves remarkably like love: suffers like love, consoles like love, and is not exempt from dirtiness, ugliness, smelliness, sickness and death. Love is thus particularised and related to traditions and human experience. On at least two occasions there is an uncertainty about the name of his true love, part of the total slipperiness of names in the trilogy, but part also of the admitted weakness of amorous memory.

The other member of the trilogy who knows true love is Malone's Macmann, whose idyll resembles Molloy's but has its own special features. Macmann has an affair with his keeper, Moll. They are not unsuccessful, in spite of impotence, 'summoning to their aid all the resources of the skin, the mucus and the imagination, in striking from their dry and feeble clips a kind of sombre gratification' (p. 261). The course of their intimacy is made to conform to traditions of love. Macmann learns the right language, 'the yesses, noes, mores, and enoughs that keep love alive' and he writes love poems while she writes love letters. They say the usual things, wish they had met while young, are grateful for finding each other, know what they have is a protection, company, and a solace when the wind blows at night. The conventions are of course changed by the age, impotence, and revolting aspect of the lovers. They are consoled for not having met sixty years ago by the elaborate argument that whereas they were very ugly in youth now they're scarcely worse than even their 'best favoured contemporaries'. Impotence gives new meaning to those 'mores and enoughs' as to the 'heart's labouring'. The account of the affair, with its shifting balance of feeling from one love to the other, and details of decline and death, is an off-hand and nasty way of describing something that has given shape and interest to thousands of romantic novels.

Beckett is insisting, as Moll insists, that sexual love can be nasty but still help. Love finds its warranty in the repulsive as in the sublime. Macmann's explanation of human need is remarkably sane, despite his insanity (p. 262):

> When you hold me in your arms, and I you in mine, it naturally does not amount to much, compared to the transports of youth, and even middle age. But all is relative, let us bear that in mind, stags and hinds have their needs and we have ours.

Or, as Malone puts it earlier (p. 243):

> For people are never content to suffer, but they must have heat and cold, rain and its contrary which is fine weather, and with that love, friendship, black skin and sexual and peptic deficiency for example, in short the furies and frenzies happily too numerous to be numbered of the body. . . .

Love is sometimes romantic, beautiful, even associated with nostalgia and dreams. This romantic image of love, however, gets discredited. The sense of beauty and youth, which it invokes or which is added to give it extra glamour or value, is permitted only in dreaming. Even memory sets it too firmly in the solid earth of experience. One of its purest appearances, set easily and obviously in dreaming, is in *From an Abandoned Work*, which is filled with odd but brilliant images of the past, the image of his mother, the image of blue, brightness, and the image of beloved objects (p. 142):

> Love too, often in my thoughts, when a boy, but not a great deal compared to other boys, it kept me awake I found.
> Never loved anyone, I think, I'd remember. Except in my dreams and there it was animals, dream animals, nothing like what you see walking about in the country. I couldn't describe them, lovely creatures they were, white mostly.

Insubstantial, but charming. Charming, too, is the off-hand and good-tempered lack of fuss and competitiveness. The narrator of this fragment is violent, given to sudden rages, but there is something very cool and calm about his account of his love-life, and the tacked on observations, 'I'd remember' and 'lovely creatures they were' have a nonchalance which combines with the inexplicable passions to create his character and his story. Even the dreams are given individuality.

But they have something in common. Where sexual love has charm, it is given a remoteness. In *Lessness* the remembered or imagined love has the calm melancholy of assured loss, 'Old love new love as in the blessed days unhappiness will reign again' and perhaps, 'Never but in dream the happy dream'. There is also the image of the lovers' shadows watched by Malone, who shares with several of the narrators a pure innocence about some sexual activities. He can't quite make out what is happening over the road, as he looks from his window, from his bed, at the shadows that move, come together, separate, join, stand up against the curtain, clasp, rub against each other. He describes the encounter with the precision and abstractedness of the eye that doesn't recognise what is happening, either because he is too old, or too remote, and then comes the sudden identification (pp. 238–9):

> . . . it is clear we have here two distinct and separate bodies, each enclosed within its own frontiers, and having no need of each other to come and go and sustain the flame of life. . . . Perhaps they are cold, that they rub against each other so, for friction maintains heat and brings it back when it is gone. It is all very pretty and strange, this big complicated shape made up of more than one, for perhaps there are three of them, and how it sways and totters, but rather poor in colour. But the night must be warm, for of a sudden the curtain lifts on a flare of tender colour, pale blush and white of flesh, then pink that must come from a garment and gold too that I haven't time to understand. So it is not cold they are, standing so lightly clad by the open window. Ah how stupid I am, I see what it is, they must be loving each other, that must be how it is done. Good, that has done me good.

This must be one of Beckett's most beautiful voyeuristic descriptions, and the forms, colours, and movement make the encounter as balletic as it is mysterious, for not only does Malone not know for a long time what they are doing, he doesn't even know if it is dawn, late night, or evening, only that they move together in the suddenly lit window which shows him that there really are people outside, that the terrifying Magritte-like image he has of the black night being painted on his pane, is not real. But after the delicate beauty, comes the reduction: 'they have loved each other standing, like dogs. . . . Or perhaps they are just having a breather, before they tackle the titbit. Back and forth, back and forth, that must be wonderful. They seem to be in pain.' It is the voice of experience now, added to that of innocence. And the knowing ends the beauty, rather as Alice and the fawn can only companion each other when they do not know they are girl and animal.

There is the other beautiful image in *Imagination Dead Imagine*, carefully drawn and measured, each white body lying in the white semicircle, vanishing and reappearing, freezing and heating. They do not move but the mirror shows breath and the eyes open and 'gaze in unblinking exposure', but only once overlapping, 'for about ten seconds'. Shudder is suppressed, but they are sweating and icy. And there is the shattering understatement, 'the bodies seem whole and in fairly good condition'. Perhaps there is no ground for including this as an image of sex, but it is an image of the human couple, locked in a position of non-embrace, and of non-sleep. They are all too successfully imagined, and their love-lessness seems imaginable when imagination has died.

Imagination creates the terrible embraces in *How It Is*, where the couples, unsexed, behave aggressively in order to make contact, invent and develop a code and a language, compel each other to sound and even song, use the same instrument, the tin-opener, to nourish, wound, speak to each other, and touch. *How It Is* presents a dimension of love in the light, associated with brightness, flowers, blissful nature, but the force of the embraces and aggressions in the mud, of those awful arse-wounds, is finally shown when they too are revealed as too good to exist, part of a terrible and terribly reduced dream of love that might be supposed to be awful enough to exist. Perhaps the most sickening displacements in all Beckett come in the hell-like life or life-like hell of this novel, where even the tormented contact is finally dispelled, and everything except mud and solitude said to be fictitious. To be made to regret such encounters and wounds is to have imagination stretched into a knowledge of isolation. No wonder such an imagination can create Malone's astonished gaze at copulation, Watt's embrace of Mrs Gorman's single breast, Macmann's tolerance of Mag's vomit, the compliance with every wish of the old man who didn't like to touch skin.

III

The *Texts for Nothing* are eloquent on the subject of the third solace, nature. The clerk or scribe of the fifth text wonders if he will ever see sky again and be free to move in sun and rain, but he then immediately discredits the nostalgic imagery as mere literary props (*No's Knife*, pp. 92–3):

> The sky, I've heard – the sky and earth, I've heard great accounts of them, now that's pure word for word, I invent nothing. I've noted, I must have noted many a story with

them as setting, they create the atmosphere. Between them where the hero stands a great gulf is fixed, while all about they flow together more and more, till they meet. . . .

And the sixth text has the narrator trying again to write a little story, 'with living creatures coming and going on a habitable earth crammed with the dead, a brief story, with night and day coming above . . .'. Beckett imagines solitude like no one else, he also transforms the sense of time and place, but he cannot usually dispense with some kind of natural habitat. He tries, to be sure, but the attempt to create a measurable and visible exterior in *Ping* only shows up the naturalness of the other invented places. And even the cube of *Ping* depends for its claustrophobia on a nature implied outside. The place and space of *How It Is* has a memory or dream or tradition or fiction of light, sun, air, but even its admitted actuality has mud, a mud in which no flowers grow. *Imagination Dead Imagine* has temperature and light, though tormentingly. But most of Beckett's people do relate to nature, if only across the gulf described in the fifth text, and do a certain amount to create setting and atmosphere. These solitaries, in pain and doubt, ignorant of meaning and identity, trying to make out the point of human existence through reports and stories, then trying to stop, trying to shut up, trying to die, do mostly live on an imaginable earth, with imaginable air, water, and fire. Beckett usually accepts an irreducible minimum of air, movement, and nourishment – the absence of such a minimum, its reduction through fantasy and abstraction, in *Imagination Dead Imagine* and *Ping*, is terrifying. But he generally needs the elements of earth, air, water and fire to provide the minimal living conditions, though living would not be his term. So his people tend to have a response to nature, often the acceptance of an elaborately described habitat. Like literature and like sexual love, nature, interrogated for meaning, sometimes offers one, sometimes doesn't. The effect of meanings and lack of meaning is not only helpful in creating people, it also helps the reader get some bearings, though getting them is not by any means a simple process of reassurance. Nature does not offer, as in the *Lyrical Ballads*, a familiar landscape transformed by the moonlight of imagination. Though Coleridge's use of suns and moons in 'The Rime of the Ancient Mariner' does sometimes come to mind when facing those dubious moons in *Molloy*. But our notions of familiarity and strange transformations have been moved on by surrealist art, and Beckett, like Henri Michaux, whom he occasionally resembles, is doubtless affected by the flora, fauna, and things of surrealist landscapes and seascapes. *Imagination Dead Imagine* and *Ping* owe something to cubism, too, and non- or semi-representational painting and sculpture. Beckett's landscapes are marvellously original and bizarre, but his nature is transformed by the people wandering through it (his travellers) or bogged down (his paralytics) more often than by visual inventiveness.

The first sentence of *Imagination Dead Imagine* says contemptuously that it is easy to imagine nothing, 'no trace anywhere of life', but hard though necessary to imagine a death or afterdeath of imagination. The first thing to go is landscape, 'Islands, waters, azure, verdure, one glimpse and vanished, endlessly, omit'. Beckett's natural landscape never had a very impressive presence even before imagination died. As early as *More Pricks Than Kicks* he was showing displeasing scenes, like the Hill of the Wolves in 'Fingal', with a 'ruin of a mill on the top, choked lairs of furze and brambles passim' or the view from the Hill of Fingal, 'its coast eaten away with creeks and marshes, tesserae of small fields, patches of wood springing up like a weed, the line of hills too low to close the view'. It lacks charm, though it certainly has visible life. In the story 'Walking Out' nature is more than unpleasant, and beauty is conferred only to reveal horror, as in the sheep-and-lamb-crammed landscape which Belacqua criticises for its lack of horses, where 'the grass was spangled with scarlet after-births, the larks were singing, the hedges were breaking, the sun was shining, the sky was Mary's cloak, the daisies were there, everything was in order'. E. M. Forster had to move to an Indian sun and landscape in order to destroy the pastoral sweetness of our fertile spring myth, Beckett successfully attacked an Irish pastoral while staying in Ireland. In 'A Wet Night' the rain which is falling in 'a uniform untroubled manner' evokes, in order to annihilate, Joyce's sympathetic snow at the end of 'The Dead': 'It fell upon the bay, the littoral, the mountains and the plains, and notably upon the Central Bog it fell with a rather desolate uniformity.'

No more could be expected of rain which is Beckettian, Irish, and purgatorial. The very last landscape in *More Pricks Than Kicks* presents a problem of classification to the groundsman ('Draff', *More Pricks Than Kicks*, p. 204):

What with the company of headstones sighing and gleaming like bones, the moon on the job, the sea tossing in her dreams and panting, and the hills observing their Attic vigil in the background, he was at a loss to determine off-hand whether the scene was of the kind that is termed romantic, or whether it should not with more justice be deemed classical. Both elements were present, that was indisputable. Perhaps classico-romantic would be the fairest estimate. A classico-romantic scene.

Nature is certainly there, but put in its place, with whatever attributes that muted admiration, irony, or satire require. (Beckett would probably exclaim at the presumptuousness of putting nature in its place.) It is possibly more accurate to say that Beckett does not allow natural landscape to have the part it generally has in previous literature. But he obviously has an eye for its dubious charms, as for those of literature and sex, even as he meditates its abolition. The existence of nature, diminished and subdued, is of some importance, both to Beckett's people and Beckett's readers. Where Nature is almost obliterated, in *Imagination Dead Imagine* or *Ping*, the reduction of the now unnatural landscape is painful, like the reduction of human vitality for which it provides a constricted space. None of the longer works can get along without nature. It seldom commands an enthusiastic or admiring response and it is extremely unstable, but it does provide welcome landmarks. (The plays can do without its richness, for it remains rich in most of Beckett's fiction, never as impoverished as Winnie's heap of sand in *Happy Days*, or the tree in *Waiting for Godot*. The nature of his fiction tends to be more sensuous and more elusive than the simpler symbolic settings and objects of the plays.) To like nature need not be a virtue. Moran likes nature, but he is one of Beckett's nastiest people, a pedantic Christian and a horrible father, and his romantic response to nature is part of his obnoxious certainty, and soon to be lost, since he has to come out of his domestic garden into Molloy's harsher and wilder territory. But his response to nature is plainly discreditable. First, he is misled by nature. About to leave, on the 'threshold of the Molloy affair' he sees in the sun's beams 'the sabbath of the motes' and wrongly concludes that the weather is fine. Earlier when Gaber is about to announce the Molloy quest, he enjoys nature, in spite of its internal discomfort, partially and selfishly inhaling 'the scent of my lemon-verbena' and listening to the blackbird and thrush, 'their song sadly dying, vanquished by the heat, and leaving dawn's high boughs for the bushes' gloom' as the contented spectator himself will soon do. On a later occasion he moves straight from an appreciation of sunset, 'in the west scarves of fine red sheen were mounting the sky' to his dinner, an unsatisfactory shepherd's pie. He has already remarked that the great joy which surged over him at the sight of the red sky ended in a sigh, 'for the joy inspired by beauty is often not unmixed', though what the reader observes as the mixture, the straight move from the shepherd's sky ('Red sky at night is the shepherd's delight') to the shepherd's pie is not in his mind. He has a foreboding about leaving his province for Molloy's, and his own is largely described in terms of his neat and possessively enjoyed garden, 'my house, my garden . . . my trees . . . my birds of which the least is known to me', where the Biblical echo manages to cast a slur both on Moran and the Almighty (like the Mary-blue sky in 'Walking Out'). Once he starts on the Molloy country that slight nastiness we find in 'Fingal' creeps in (pp. 134–5):

> But the principal beauty of this region was a kind of strangled creek which the slow grey tides emptied and filled, emptied and filled. And the people came flocking from the town, unromantic people, to admire this spectacle. Some said, There is nothing more beautiful than these wet sands. Others, High tide is the best time to see the creek of Ballyba. How lovely then that leaden water, you would swear it was stagnant, if you did not know it was not.

Much later, disintegrated and reduced in the Molloy country, he has a surge of the old romantic and heroic nature-feeling; he thinks gratefully of June's milk as he looks at the night sky, which promises an 'evening that brings out the lights, the stars in the sky and on earth the brave little lights of men'. This sounds a sublime consolation, but in a sentence or two the light goes out, he is alone and not liking it. At the end he returns to his garden, and it is unguentary, but dubious; something sinister about it makes his response shift and sway (p. 176):

> There was a bright side. They were lovely days. The winter had been exceptionally rigorous, everybody said so. We had therefore a right to this superb summer. I do not know if we had a right to it. My birds had not been killed. They were wild birds. And yet quite trusting. I recognised them and they seemed to recognise me. But one never knows. Some were missing and some were new. I tried to understand their language better. Without having recourse to mine. They were the longest, loveliest days of all the year. I lived in the garden.

The change in Moran's language is accompanied by a change in his feeling for nature. He is wary of cliché, of the language of fixity, expectation, and justice. He is less possessive of his territory. He has been in the Molloy country, and comes back more like Molloy and less like the Moran he was.

Molloy's attitude to nature is much closer to the usual one (I hesitate to call it a norm) in the stories. It wobbles from a sense of beauty to a sense of repulsion, from a romantic straining after a natural sublime to a rejection of such spuriousness. Molloy's word 'strains' is nicely ambiguous; early on he tells us his soul 'strains wildly' after certain things in nature,

> the fields, whitening under the dew, and the animals, ceasing from wandering and settling for the night, and the sea, of which nothing, and the sharpening line of crests, and the sky where without seeing them I felt the first stars tremble.

Apart from the warning refusal to speak of the sea, Molloy seems to strain after a pleasant calm and freshness, but it soon becomes clear that the natural description acts as a clumsy aid in Molloy's attempt to talk about things other than himself, for instance, cows and sky. It is also evident that nostalgia for nature can't be credited. The different bits of remembered landscape are at times dismantled, having been arbitrarily assembled by memory and fiction, for the putting together of cows, sky, sea, and mountains is all part of the admittedly tiring heaping up of things until there is no more room and no more light. At times the image is kept pleasantly before him but not for long, and not without being undermined, as in the description of him springing along rough sunlit quiet streets (on his crutches, of course), giving himself 'up to that golden moment, as if I had been someone else'. Warmth, light, calm, silence and languor are all appreciated, and have an emotional impact, 'I didn't feel unhappy', but it is evident that there is something wrong. Molloy is indeed acting like someone else, having an untypical response, and it may be one of those moments when his experience is contaminated by the experience of Moran who finds it easy to be warmed and consoled by nature. After a while Molloy reverts to the early image of straining and depreciates it, 'I was straining towards those spurious deeps, their lying promise of gravity and peace from all my old poisons, I struggled towards them, safely bound. Under the blue sky, under the watchful gaze.' This isn't simply a rejection of romantic nature, but the invocation of something menacing, as if the spuriousness were a real trap, the blue a hopeful gaze turned towards a victim. But the response to nature wobbles, as suits Molloy's self-styled 'long emotional confusion' and he can speak of the affection he feels for the surface of his 'way', 'bright or dark, smooth or rough, and always dear to me, in spite of all, and the dear sound of which goes and is gone, with a brief dust, when the weather is dry'. Molloy can list and reduce the items in a landscape, but he can also attend most closely to sights and sounds, as he does when he gets a little too close to his 'way', and lies with outstretched arms under a hawthorn (p. 27):

> The white hawthorn stooped towards me, unfortunately I don't like the smell of hawthorn. In the ditch the grass was thick and high, I took off my hat and pressed about my face the long leafy stalks. Then I could smell the earth, the smell of the earth was in the grass that my hands wove round my face till I was blinded. I ate a little too, a little grass.

Sometimes there is only a little wrong, as here, but sometimes there is a violent rejection, as with the sun and the moon, often suspect in Beckett. The Dantean moonspots are a problem for Belacqua, and Watt dislikes both moon and sun, though he has an unexplained lapse in favour of the sun. Molloy's moon casts a bright but far from lucid shine. One night he sees it suddenly, rather as Malone sees the lovers across the street, and describes it with a similar cool precision, in terms of the framing window-bars and the movement across the window, in three segments, the middle staying constant while the 'right gained what the left lost'. This at once gives rise to doubt and relativism, as he reasons that either outside or inside is moving. The reasoning is sound in the abstract but depends on a loss of common ground, so that the one seems as likely as the other, contrary to common sense, pragmatic experience, and scientific knowledge, all of which are occasionally reduced or ignored. The moon is therefore a dubious moon, not to be trusted, even though it seems 'a simple thing . . . that vast yellow light sailing slowly behind my bars . . . which little by little the dense wall devoured and finally eclipsed'. Nature is observed familiarly, but detached and transformed by Molloy's mind, so that it seems that the optical illusion that wall devours and eclipses is perhaps not illusory at all. Molloy's devotion to strict appearances continues with his account of the light and shadows on the wall, 'And now its tranquil course was written on the walls, a radiance scored with shadow, then a brief quivering of leaves, if they were leaves, then that too went out, leaving me in the dark.' The observation becomes lyrical, splendid, though always wary and provisional. And Beckett makes Molloy say so: 'How difficult it is to speak of the moon and not lose one's head, the witless moon. It must be her arse she shows us always'. The description is undermined first by interpretation and then by rough bathos about science, as it suits Molloy's book. (We are even told here that he has studied astronomy.) The course of the undermining is an intelligible if singular course of thought and feeling, moving from the moon at the window to the quivering light on the wall, from the sensuous response to that quivering to a rejection of . lunatic enchantment and power, backed by tradition. 'The witless moon', seems to carry a lingering feeling for the witlessness, but the wild and beautiful word is rudely and cleverly obliterated. If she has no wits, and makes us lose our head, then she is punished by the logic and science which sees only an arse. A couple of pages later on Molloy returns to 'this business of the moon', faces the fact that he will have to cope without having all his wits about him, but will 'none the less get done with it, as best I can, at least I think so' (p. 41):

> That moon then, all things considered, filled me suddenly with amaze, with surprise, perhaps better. Yes, I was considering it, after my fashion, with indifference, seeing it again, in a way, in my head, when a great fright came suddenly upon me. And deeming this deserved to be looked into I looked into it and quickly made the following discovery, among others, but I confined myself to the following, that this moon which had just sailed gallant and full past my window had appeared to me the night before, or the night before that, yes, more likely, all young and slender, on her back, a shaving. And then I had said, Now I see, he has waited for the new moon before launching forth on unknown ways, leading south.

Soon the feeling that he has unaccountably lost time is replaced by the calm recognition that he hadn't seen any moon at all, new or old, that his nights were moonless, but he has been seeing through someone else's eyes and seeing the sky 'different from what it is' and the earth 'in false colours'. Later on, on a moonless night, when there is no question of a moon or of any other light, the sounds of night are sweetly and gently rendered, in one of the lyrical passages in which Beckett excels (pp. 48–9):

> it was a night of listening, a night given to the faint soughing and sighing stirring at night in little pleasure gardens, the shy

sabbath of leaves and petals and the air that eddies there as it does not in other places. . . . And a good thing too.

Some of Molloy's lyrical images are strongly morbid, like the one of a great cloud (p. 65):

ravelling, discovering here and there a pale and dying sky, and the sun, already down . . . manifest in the livid tongues of fire darting towards the zenith, falling and darting again, ever more pale and languid, and doomed no sooner lit to be extinguished.

Even this description is undermined: he first identifies the 'phenomenon' as characteristic of 'his region', then admits that he isn't qualified to speak of its characteristics, having never left it and so knowing neither its limits nor the regions beyond. This confession is further qualified by the reminder that he is in bed, and remembering inadequately a time when he was on his bicycle, itself jolting and as a 'cycle', 'boundless'. This stroke of wit completes the undermining of the notions of 'region', of space, time, or person. Moon, sun, and also sea are all uncertain in this jolting and perhaps cyclical chronicle, though Molloy's set-piece description of the sea is not so much morbid and undecided as frankly arbitrary and time-consuming (p. 68):

But in order to blacken a few more pages may I say I spent some time at the seaside, without incident. There are people the sea doesn't suit, who prefer the mountains or the plain. Personally I feel no worse there than anywhere else. Much of my life has ebbed away before this shivering expanse, to the sound of the waves in storm and calm, and the claws of the surf. Before, no, more than before, one with, spread on the sand, or in a cave. In the sand I was in my element, letting it trickle between my fingers, scooping holes that I filled in a moment later or that filled themselves in, flinging it in the air by handfuls, rolling in it. And in the cave, lit by the beacons at night, I knew what to do in order to be no worse off than elsewhere. And that my land went no further, in one direction at least did not displease me. And to feel there was one direction at least in which I could go no further, without first getting wet, then drowned, was a blessing. For I have always said, First learn to walk, then you can take swimming lessons.

The instability of nature derives from the instability of the spectator, who is only remembered and therefore partly forgotten and partly made up, by an old, sick chronicler, urged on by others who commission and collect his work. What he remembers is of course even more unstable than what he saw, and that was 'naturally' confused and undermined by ignorance, optical and other illusions, tradition, distance and notions of significance. Space is affected by time, vision blurred by being turned into literature. (Beckett is nearly always carrying on a blatant or subliminal argument with Proust about the redemption of time through art.) The attempt to see what is characteristic is a discredited romantic notion, like that in the fifth text, of sympathetic climates and natural phenomena. In Molloy this is a peculiarly interesting question, since character and personality are undermined, Molloy's region being confused with Moran's. The whole tradition of sympathetic nature and pathetic fallacy is not only attacked as Coleridge attacked it in 'Dejection, An Ode', lamenting but insisting to his various imputed hearers that 'Ours is her wedding garment/Ours her shroud', but also attacked by the disrupted sense of personality which makes it impossible to say what 'ours' may be. But despite the various disruptions of nature's stability, she (if she may be so denominated) gives the novels a strongly sensuous dimension, sometimes pleasant, sometimes unpleasant. The aesthetic notion of nature is disrupted like the aesthetic aspect of sex. We are made to see the moon's arse as we are made to see Mag's gums and single tooth.

Nature in Beckett is always uncertain, then, but the uncertainties shift. In How It Is, some of the Texts for Nothing, and Lessness, it joins with sexual love and religion to define the glamour of what is sometimes memory, sometimes dream, sometimes dream masquerading as memory, sometimes fictitious narrative creating all the deceits of dreams and memories. In How It Is and Lessness, beautiful nature is part of the remembered, dreamed, imagined and never experienced good moments, but it also provides the unpleasant mud or grey sand of the present, which may also be ultimately discredited, as in How It Is, but have a firmness of impression and a continuity that the remembered figments or moments never possess. Beckett's sensuous powers create sounds and shapes of great power, like the remembered crocus in the light, the white horse, and the tone-poems of Ping and Lessness. Although Ping is an abstract and 'unnatural' construct, an enclosure shutting off the phenomenal world, it owes much to Beckett's brilliant sense of shape and colour, which in its turn can light and form the figments and moments of the unstable but sensitive language.

Such imagery is significantly promising but unreliable in *Lessness*. In the greys and whites and blacks of aridity, lessness and blankness, blue stands out. (It does so also in *Ping* where the eyes whose vision is so limited are light blue.) In the deprivations of the desert the blue is the only colour, belonging both to eye and sky, so suggesting the inseparability of the human sight and the natural scene. The eyes, 'little holes two pale blue', do not exactly see the sky, any more (*Lessness*, pp. 13, 19):

Face to calm eye touch close all calm all white all gone from mind. Never but imagined the blue in a wild imagining the blue celeste of poesy.

Never but imagined the blue in a wild imagining the blue celeste of poesy. Light white touch close head through calm eye light of reason all gone from mind.

Sight and scene share a colour, but that is all. What remains is the contrast of the sightless eye and reasonless mind, with the blueness. The word 'celeste' stands out as another word for the colour blue, possessing also musical meaning (a soft pedal of piano or stop on harmonium) and religious associations. But both 'celeste' and 'poesy' are dignified, exotic and technical words which insist semantically on the dimension of art and imagination. Their effect is rather like that of some of Wallace Stevens's more exotic flowers of language, and like Stevens too is the mingling of natural and aesthetic implications. The colour blue is also Stevens's image for the colour conferred on natural green by art, though he too makes the admission that it is impossible to unmake the blue, to imagine dead imagination. Though their sensibility, temperament and personality are strongly opposed, Beckett and Stevens join in many ways in the rejection of metaphysics, in the attempt to establish a provisional and cagey value for art in a world where imaginative powers have been discredited.

A cruel nature is drawn in *From an Abandoned Work*, where the violence of animals, humans, and plants joins monstrously at the end, to confirm the abandonment. Like Molloy, the narrator in *From an Abandoned Work* has his 'way', and it is appropriately and personally violent, like his rages, 'And in this way I have gone through great thickets, bleeding, and deep into bogs, water too, even the sea in some moods and been carried out of my course, or driven back.' I think he is the only one of Beckett's people to make his way through fire, the image of his bizarre and murderous irrationality, though this way is only (only!) imagined in a dream,

> And that is perhaps how I shall die at last if they don't
> catch me, I mean drowned, or in fire, yes, perhaps that is how
> I shall do it at last, walking furious headlong into fire and
> dying burnt to bits.

This extraordinary fragment also contains the stark beauty of the white horse, the Schimmel with the red band on its side, 'bright white, with the sun on it', which seems to provoke the blinding savage rage, in one of those entirely original fantasies which present a plausible causality. The strength of the visual stimulus seems a sufficient occasion for the rage, perhaps supported by the thought of the effects of light and patterns in epilepsy. This piece even presents a scene (almost but not quite sublime) of nature's vastness, in the striking sentence, 'One day I told him about Milton's cosmology, away up in the mountains we were, resting against a huge rock looking out to sea, that impressed him greatly' which is cooled by the preceding sentence, 'A very fair scholar I was too, no thought, but a great memory.' Beckett's natural images frequently approach the sublime, but the sublime has to be inhibited, he knows all about it, but we can't have it, it won't do here. The narrator of this story is even slightly comforted by the thought of the natural cycle, which doesn't often cheer up Beckett's people, and sentimentally or Moranically describes the tears he sheds for happiness, 'for love of this old earth that has carried me along so long and whose uncomplainings will soon be mine'. He imagines his recycling, first under the surface, then dispersed through earth and finally, 'a ton of worms in an acre, that is a wonderful thought, a ton of worms, I believe it'. It is such a wonderful thought, though horrid, that it too has to be discredited, 'Where did I get it, from a dream, or a book read in a nook when a boy, or a work overheard. . . .' Even this narrator, who shares nature's violence, in his love of trampling birds, butterflies and slugs (a hostility returned with interest by birds and stoats and ferns) and in his rages and murderousness, makes due acknowledgment to the literary tradition, though in its morbid moments. Both character and nature join here in imagery and action of frenzied savagery, and the few brilliantly lovely fragments are plainly figments and dreams which offer no opposition. Nature is abandoned in both senses, being savage and purposeless, as far as Beckett's people can make out.

Romantic nature is displaced along with romantic love, beautiful

nature along with graceful love. And it isn't surprising that nature-
lovers like Moran tend to be discredited also as Christians. The
men at the end of *Watt* are like Moran, sentimental about nature
and so about life, 'It's not a bad old bugger of an earth.' Isn't it
though – Watt thinks so. Of course, he is mad, but Beckett was
claiming the reliability (although not total) of madness before
Laing, though after Shakespeare. For Watt the leaves will soon rot,
but his dislike of sun, moon, earth and sky, the lot, isn't simply a
dislike of dying but a hostility to the whole bad business. Nature is
a fallacious source of benevolence and pleasure, providing less than
human love. She is bloody, rank, meaningless. If her earth provides
the two distinct hells of *How It Is* and *Lessness*, the unfantastic
nature of Watt is every bit as unpromising (p. 34):

> But by this time Watt was tired of the ditch, which he had
> been thinking of leaving, when the voices detained him. And
> one of the reasons why he was tired of the ditch was perhaps
> this, that the earth, whose contours and peculiar smell the
> vegetation at first had masked, now he felt it, and smelt it,
> the bare hard dark stinking earth.

Art, love and nature do for Beckett's people what they do for
everybody: they warm, they chill, they offer and they withhold
significance. The heat and cold, the approach and retreat of
meaning, may take unfamiliar shapes in these stories, but what
they do and do not do for people is utterly familiar. Passions and
appetites persist, however attenuated, however absurd.

NOTES

1 All references to *Molloy*, *Malone Dies* and *The Unnamable* are to the one-
   volume edition of 1959 (Calder).
2 For instance, the joke about a fool petting in his mittens. See G. Legman,
   Rationale of the Dirty Joke, New York, 1968, p. 119.
3 References to *Watt* are to the edition of 1963 (Calder).

Chapter 7

Bilingual playwright

Harry Cockerham

To examine seriously Samuel Beckett's bilingualism in his plays is to raise immediately the question of whether these are to be regarded as works of literature or not, a matter on which critical opinion, at least in France, has tended to fly to extremes. The practice of seeking to explain creative works in terms of trends and movements has already produced in some quarters a habit of seeing Beckett in line of descent from Artaud, as a creator of 'poems in space' or perhaps even of provocations for the stage in the surrealist manner – certainly as one in whose plays the written or spoken word counts for a good deal less than the staging. Artaud's theatrical aesthetic, with its apparent devaluation of the word, runs counter to the strongly literary French theatrical tradition, which was still being stoutly defended by Jean Giraudoux in the 1930s when Artaud was formulating his theory. Against those who have found 'for plays in which the French language is not insulted and weakened, an epithet which is apparently amongst the worst terms of abuse, that of literary plays', Giraudoux reaffirms conventional French sentiments by seeing theatre unapologetically as a branch of literature and by presenting the theatrical experience as essentially the experience of a particular style. For him, what our age expects of the writer is 'that he should reveal to it his own truth, impart to it, so that it may organise its thought and sensibility, that secret which the writer alone holds: style. This is also what it requires of the theatre.'[1] Moreover, this tradition has been maintained in France since Giraudoux's time, in different ways, in existentialist theatre, which is preponderantly literary, and in the poetic theatre of, for example, Jean Tardieu.

It is hardly surprising that, for those who share Giraudoux's thinking, the spread of Artaud's aesthetic should seem fraught with dire consequences for the theatre, but to seek to explain Beckett's theatre by reference to Artaud and to see it as evidence of a coming divorce between drama and literature and of the inevitability of a textless theatre is to blink the fact of its continuing dependence on the word, whatever might be Beckett's exploitation of the physical, a fact which has been underlined by his most recent play *Not I*. Winnie, in *Happy Days*, is well aware of this dependence:

141

There is, of course, the bag. . . . Yes, there is the bag. But
something tells me, Do not overdo the bag, Winnie, make use
of it of course, let it help you . . . along, when stuck, by all
means, but cast your mind forward, something tells me,
cast your mind forward, Winnie, to the time when words
must fail – and do not overdo the bag.

Beckett's very assiduousness in translating his plays shows that
verbal expression is still a value in his theatre and that, where he is
concerned at least, woe about the absorption of the theatre by the
dance or the mime is misplaced.[2] Indeed, there has been an
equally strong tendency amongst French critics, at the opposite
extreme, to see the plays primarily as written works, a tendency
summed up in Jean Vannier's view that in *Waiting for Godot*
Beckett defies that law of the theatre which would make of every
play the spectacle of an event, and sets before us nothing less than
the spectacle of the word or of language itself.[3]

No doubt the truth of the matter lies somewhere between these
extremes. Already in the *Préface de Cromwell* (1827), Victor Hugo
had seen the need for French theatre to place greater emphasis on
the visual and to make fuller use of it as a means of communication
between playwright and audience. In the French context it is an
essential part of Beckett's achievement to have integrated the
verbal and the visual in a theatrical 'language' in which the word is
neither more nor less important than gesture, movement, setting
and lighting but works in conjunction with these. It is not, therefore, in the hope of defining at all fully the theatrical experience
afforded by Beckett's plays that one can study their literary
qualities – and hence also Beckett's bilingualism – but only because
the text is an indispensable part, though only a part, of the
complex whole that is the play, one source, amongst others, of the
play's power and symbolic radiance.

The basic facts concerning Beckett's bilingualism are perhaps
well enough known for it to be unnecessary any longer, even in
Britain, to defend the view of him as at least as much a French as
an Irish writer. A resident in France for most of his adult life,
Beckett has written part of his output in French, part in English,
subsequently translating the greater part of his work, either alone
or in collaboration, into the other language. This bilingualism is a
feature especially of his work since the Second World War, but it
was an increasingly important factor even at a time when he was
writing mainly in English. Indeed the pattern of works composed

in both French and English was established in the later 1930s: some of his French poems of that period strongly resemble poems in English of similar date, whilst others exist in both languages. Arguments over whether he is properly a French or an Irish writer are therefore necessarily sterile and it may indeed be that his example and the fact of his existence as a bilingual writer will do much to break down barriers between national cultures and encourage a trend towards comparativism in literary studies. We are faced, not with a writer who abandoned one language for another (a not infrequent occurrence), but with the possibly unique phenomenon of one who, throughout his career, has divided his efforts and his interests between two languages.

Amongst the questions raised by Beckett's bilingualism, that of his French style has given rise to even more disagreement amongst critics, if that were possible, than has the problem of the meanings to be found in his works. At one extreme, the more detailed type of study has provided guarded and even astringent judgments, stressing the limitations of Beckett's French and point-ing to features which are directly attributable to his foreign origins.[4] Most commentators who broach the subject do so, however, only in the most general and frequently impressionistic fashion and tend to heap high praise on Beckett as a stylist. Thus for Jean-Louis Barrault, he is the modern writer who, by his concern for purity, simplicity, musicality, and careful selection in style, is most reminiscent of Racine. Jean-Jacques Mayoux's few reservations about Beckett's French are far outweighed by his enthusiasm for a style which he places above considerations of French or English. Beckett's voice and accents are seen as so characteristic as to rise above whichever language he writes in: they recall, not Racine, but Chateaubriand.[5] Similar disagreement is to be found amongst those who have compared the French and the English version of some of Beckett's plays. Again, most of these comparisons are brief and impressionistic and they often lead (for example on the question of whether Beckett is more amusing in French or in English) to conclusions radically opposed to one another but expressed all with equal passion. Even the one reasonably detailed study of the subject is at several points less than convincing, having perhaps suffered by appearing too early to be able to take into account the plays originally written in English.[6] Nevertheless, methodical comparison of the French and English versions of the five major stage plays at present available in both texts can shed much light on Beckett's bilingualism, some on his French style and a little even on the reasons for critical dissension on these subjects.

In translating his plays Beckett had a long experience to draw on. In 1952, Maurice Nadeau, one of the most aware of Paris critics, was able to say that until then Beckett had been known only to a small circle of friends and initiates, and then mainly as a translator. His career as a translator in fact stretched back at least to 1932, when he was rendering into English the poems of the French surrealists Breton and Éluard. Long practice does not, however, seem to have made him come to see translation as anything less than a highly demanding task. This much is borne out by one of his more recently reported remarks on the subject, made at a rehearsal of *Endgame* in London. On hearing his own translation of Clov's punning remark about his telescope (through which he has just scanned the audience and seen 'a multitude in transports of joy'): 'Ça alors, pour une longue-vue c'est une longue-vue' ('That's what I call a magnifier'), Beckett is said to have exclaimed: 'It's a rotten line. Bad translation. . . . The more I go on the more I think things are untranslatable.'[7] There are a number of lessons in that remark. It shows the seriousness with which Beckett approaches the task of translation, his meticulousness over details, the importance he attaches to humour and wordplay in his plays and his irritated awareness of how a translation can fall short of the original. It also raises the fundamental question of why Beckett chooses to write each of his works in two languages, a question which has attracted surprisingly little critical attention and which is not satisfactorily answered by the fact of the wider audience this practice enables him to reach. It says much for Beckett's artistic zeal that he is concerned not to leave the translation of his works, into either language, to others but persists so earnestly in a task from which a lesser artist might have felt his success as a creative writer should have liberated him. More than that, it gives to the English and French translations of his works an authenticity not enjoyed by translations of other authors and raises the question how far his translations are such and how far, since they come from the author himself, they become distinct works of art, fresh treatments of the original subject with their own qualities and characteristics. Such considerations make his translations worthy of the same attention as the original versions and justify, indeed make necessary, detailed comparisons between the two.

Between the French and the English versions of the plays[8] there exist, in the first place, certain types of difference which do not, however, provide a basis for making distinctions as to quality or character. Thus the English *Waiting for Godot* can occasionally be more wryly poetic than the French, as in the remarks of Estragon (not in the French) at the end of Act I about the moon: 'Pale for weariness . . . of climbing heaven and gazing on the likes of us.' Or indeed in Act II, where the haunting exchange between Estragon and Vladimir about their surroundings, an exchange already poetic in the French, is if anything more so in the English:

ESTRAGON:	C'est pour ne pas penser.	It's so we won't think.
VLADIMIR:	Nous avons nos excuses.	We have that excuse.
ESTRAGON:	C'est pour ne pas entendre.	It's so we won't hear.
VLADIMIR:	Nous avons nos raisons.	We have our reasons.
ESTRAGON:	Toutes les voix mortes.	All the dead voices.
VLADIMIR:	Ça fait un bruit d'ailes.	They make a noise like wings.
ESTRAGON:	De feuilles.	Like leaves.
VLADIMIR:	De sable.	Like sand.
ESTRAGON:	De feuilles.	Like leaves.

On the other hand, Beckett is not always so successful in rendering the poetry of the French. The alternating four and five syllable lines of the starkly poetic exchange about the tree, in Act I, lose much of their rhythm, and thus power, in translation:

ESTRAGON:	Qu'est-ce que c'est?	What is it?
VLADIMIR:	On dirait un saule.	I don't know. A willow.
ESTRAGON:	Où sont les feuilles?	Where are the leaves?
VLADIMIR:	Il doit être mort.	It must be dead.
ESTRAGON:	Finis les pleurs.	No more weeping.

– whilst the yearning of Estragon's vision of the benefits Godot will bring is lost in the English, where the passage is omitted: 'Ce soir on couchera peut-être chez lui, au chaud, au sec, le ventre plein, sur la paille. Ça vaut la peine qu'on attende, non?' [1][9]

The same cancelling out of differences is to be found in the matter of passages in the one or the other language which throw light on meaning or appear to affect the interpretation of parts of the plays. In a question and answer omitted from the English *Waiting for Godot*, the French text explains what Pozzo means by the word 'knook' applied to Lucky [2]:

VLADIMIR:	Qu'est-ce que c'est, un knouk?
POZZO:	Vous n'êtes pas d'ici. Etes-vous seulement du siècle? Autrefois on avait des bouffons. Maintenant on a des knouks. Ceux qui peuvent se le permettre.

145

More importantly, the title of the French *Happy Days* figures in the body of the play in a way which suggests that it should be taken as a reference to Winnie's past, and not only, as might be thought, as an ironic comment on her present: 'Charlot Chassepot! Je ferme les yeux – et suis de nouveau assise sur ses genoux, dans le clos à Fougax-et-Barrineuf, derrière la maison, sous le robinier. Oh les beaux jours de bonheur!' [3] The English original of the relevant sentence had read simply: 'Oh the happy memories.' On the other hand, Estragon's sarcastic response, 'Catulle' [4] (he has already seen himself as an impoverished poet), when asked his name in Act I of *En attendant Godot*, is replaced in the English by the infinitely more suggestive 'Adam', which has been seen as a reference to the theme of expulsion from Paradise and thus indicative of Estragon's view of his condition as one of exile. The possibility remains open, however, that it is no more than a characteristically bitter joke from Estragon, who regards Pozzo as being a little too inquisitive anyway.

It is a much less straightforward matter to establish that the same balance exists, between the French and English versions, in regard to their comic quality, although this could be deduced from the fact that Beckett is pronounced funnier in each of the two languages by roughly equal numbers of commentators. Despite the fact that the French *Waiting for Godot* is described on the title-page as simply a 'pièce en deux actes' [5], whilst the English is 'a tragicomedy in two acts', Ruby Cohn finds the French play more comic, because more colloquial, than the English one. But this is to ignore the impression created by an accumulation of increased comic emphases in relatively small details in the English translation. Many of these are in Estragon's responses to Vladimir, for example his formula for explaining why Vladimir should be the first to hang himself on the tree (French text: 'Qui peut le plus peut le moins' [6]): 'If it hangs you it'll hang anything.' Or his extravagant reaction to Vladimir's mild reproach when he appears to lose interest in his comrade's musings on the crucifixion story ('J'écoute' [7]): 'I find this really most extraordinarily interesting' – or again his reply to Vladimir's routine inquiry about the state of his foot ('Il enfle' [8]): 'Swelling visibly.' Similarly, when Pozzo, having made grotesquely long-winded preparations to answer Estragon's question why Lucky doesn't put down his bags, at last arrives at his point, Vladimir's reaction in the French ('Attention') becomes much more openly sarcastic in the English (to Estragon): 'Make a note of this.' A comparable failure on the part of the French text to match the humour of the English is to be found at a notable point in *Happy Days*: rather flatly the French replaces by Winnie's hesitations over the correctness of the expression 'Le temps est à Dieu et à moi' [9] the highly amusing passage in the original English where she puzzles over whether her hair should be referred to as 'them' or 'it', and finally puts the question to Willie (who is bald!): 'What would you say, Willie, speaking of your hair, them or it? The hair on your head, I mean . . .'. WILLIE: 'It.'

Nevertheless, if Beckett might thus be thought to be funnier in English, there are other passages which would tend to bear out the opposite view. *Happy Days* in French reinforces at a number of points the humour of the original English. For example, Winnie received her first kiss in the English simply from 'a Mr Johnson, or Johnston, or perhaps I should say John*stone*'. In the French, with quiet sexual humour, Beckett makes this first lover a physiotherapist: 'Un kinési ou mécanothérapeute Demoulin . . . ou Dumoulin . . . voire Desmoulins, c'est encore possible' [10]. Finally, what Willie reads aloud from the paper in the English ('Wanted bright boy') becomes in the French a joke no longer just on his inactivity but on the situation of both characters exposed to the silence and to the merciless heat of the sun: 'Coquet deux-pièces calme soleil' [11].

Moreover, whole categories of humour which are present in the French versions are either absent or much less noticeable in the English ones. A noteworthy example is that of the joke based on the foreigner's image of the Englishman, which Beckett, as an Irishman, was able to share with a French audience, but which he seems to have thought unlikely to amuse an English one. To Estragon's 'Calm . . . Calm . . . The English say cawm' the French text had added a joke about English phlegm: 'Ce sont des gens câââms' [12]. When Nagg tells his tale, in *Endgame*, about the Jewish tailor and his English client, a stage-direction in the French (but missing from the English) tells us that 'il prend un visage d'Anglais' [13]. On the other hand, one joke about the English is preserved in the translation of *En attendant Godot*: Estragon's mimicking of their pronunciation of 'très bon'.

Although on occasion Beckett can produce a brilliant translation of French word-play, as when Clov's amusing mispronunciation of *coïte* as *coïte* [14] is rendered by a play on the English *lying* and *laying*, in general this is another kind of humour which, whether because of the sheer difficulty of translation or because punning is much more of a national sport in France than in English-speaking countries, is lost to the reader of the English versions. Here Beckett's dissatisfaction over his English rendering in *Endgame* of 'Ça alors, pour une longue-vue c'est une longue-vue', a play on the noun for a telescope and the adjective-and-noun meaning 'a distant view', has already been instanced, but there are many other examples. Sometimes Beckett solves the problem by substituting humour of another kind. When Pozzo, suddenly noticing the absence of Vladimir, who has gone to the lavatory, reproaches Estragon for letting him go off ('Vous auriez dû le retenir' [15]), Estragon, in a punning reply, jokes about his friend's kidney ailment: 'Il s'est retenu tout seul' [16] (English text: POZZO: 'He might have waited!' ESTRAGON: 'He would have burst'). Generally, however, play on words is either less successful in the English (in *Play* the second woman's 'What do you take me for, a something machine?' is vastly improved in the French: 'Tu me prends pour quoi, une machine à machin?' [17]) or is omitted altogether. This is the case with the humorous passage in Act I of *En attendant Godot* where Estragon is unable to remember whether he read the Bible at the secular school he went to as a boy or at a French Borstal (la Roquette) [18]:

ESTRAGON: La Bible . . . J'ai dû y jeter un coup d'œil.
VLADIMIR: (*étonné*). A l'école sans Dieu?
ESTRAGON: Sais pas si elle était sans ou avec.
VLADIMIR: Tu dois confondre avec la Roquette.

In *Fin de Partie*, when Clov says he can't feel Nell's pulse, Hamm's amusing confusion of *le pouls* (pulse) with *les poux* (lice) is, again, entirely omitted from the English: 'Oh pour ça elle est formidable, cette poudre' [19]. No doubt the most striking loss of this kind to the English reader is the humour Beckett derives from a mixture of real and invented proper names in Lucky's speech in the French *Waiting for Godot*, where the punning is dazzlingly rich. It is true that the crudeness of the names of two of the spurious authorities Lucky refers to – Fartov and Belcher – would be lost on a French audience, although they appear in the French text, but the infinitely more complicated humour of the other proper names used has been replaced by mere pale imitations in the English. Thus the English 'Acacacacademy of Anthropopopometry of Essy-in-Possy' had been that of Berne-en-Bresse in the French, an amusingly obscure or provincial-sounding town which in fact doesn't exist. It recalls Bourg-en-Bresse, a centre not of learning but of gastronomy, and Beckett's replacement of Bourg by the Swiss Berne is probably to be explained by the association with the verb *berner*, to hoodwink or hoax. Similar resonances are present in the names of most of the 'scholars' Lucky mentions. Puncher and Wattmann in the English text are a rather lacklustre Anglicisation of the French Poinçon et Wattmann – a *wattman* in French being a tramdriver, so that Poinçon (*poinçon* = ticket-punch) is his conductor. This helps to explain the 'public works' they are involved in, whilst both names are vaguely reminiscent of those of actual authorities such as James Watt or the French mathematician Louis Poinsot. The range of suggestion of the English Testew and Cunard is limited when compared to the vistas opened up, for the amateur of puns, by the Rabelaisian French names they are derived from: Testu et Conard. The most obvious association here is with *têtu et conard*: mulish and (in coarse slang) stupid. There are also the echoes, given the context, of French words for testicle (*testicule*) and vagina (again in slang: *con*). Finally the names are also those of real people in the world of learning: Testu, author of an *Histoire universelle des théâtres de toutes les nations* (1779–81) or Jean-Léo Testut,[10] author of a standard medical textbook, *Précis d'anatomie descriptive*, which has appeared in many editions since 1926 – and Conard, the eminently respectable Paris publishing house responsible for standard editions of numerous French authors. Finally Steinweg et Petermann (Steinweg and Peterman in the English text) are slightly more recondite because of the German element. For an English audience familiar with underworld slang (peterman = cracksman) the second of these two names could seem absurdly humorous. For a French audience it would be amusing in a different way (*péter* = to fart). It seems likely, however, that the joke is even more intricate and characteristically Beckettian in that it brings in a knowledge of German and of elementary etymology: these two German authorities are as dry (or as dense?) as stone, since *stein* = stone and *Peter* = Greek petros = stone. This would also account for the fact that in the remainder of Lucky's speech stones are mentioned seven times.

One last type of humour present in French but less noticeable in English is that of Beckett's jokes about his French style, which reveal him as somewhat self-conscious in his use of French. Lucky's false start to his speech: 'D'autre part, pour ce qui est . . .' (in the English: 'On the other hand, with regard to – ') is a parody of learned prose and also a piece of self-parody by Beckett, since John Fletcher points out[11] that the use of this expression is one of his mannerisms, for example in *Molloy*. More striking still is the humour inspired by the intricacies of French grammar when, in Act II, Estragon and Vladimir argue over whether the tree was there the previous day. In asserting that it was, Vladimir uses a very complicated French construction and pauses in the middle of his argument to check that he has got the mood and tense of the verb right [20]:

ESTRAGON: Il n'était pas là hier?
VLADIMIR: Mais si. Tu ne te rappelles pas. Il s'en est fallu
d'un cheveu qu'on ne s'y soit pendu. (*Il réfléchit.*)
Oui, c'est juste (*en détachant les mots*) qu'on-ne-s'y-
soit-pendu. Mais tu n'as pas voulu. Tu ne te rappelles
pas?

No translation of this has been attempted in the English version, but a rather unsuccessful one is offered for a similar joke a few moments later when Vladimir, agreeing with Estragon that it is difficult not to look at the skeletons around them, uses a very idiomatic French expression which Estragon, perhaps finding it amusing, perhaps not understanding it, makes him repeat:

ESTRAGON: Il n'y a qu'à ne pas regarder. / You don't have to look.
VLADIMIR: Ça tire l'œil. / You can't help looking.
ESTRAGON: C'est vrai. / True.
VLADIMIR: Malgré qu'on en ait. / Try as one may.
ESTRAGON: Comment? / I beg your pardon?
VLADIMIR: Malgré qu'on en ait. / Try as one may.

Was Beckett aware of the inadequacy of this translation? An amusing exchange nine lines later in the English version, but not present in the French, sounds very much like an attempt at compensation, especially since it involves the use of a French expression:

ESTRAGON: Que voulez-vous?
VLADIMIR: I beg your pardon?
ESTRAGON: Que voulez-vous?
VLADIMIR: Ah! que voulez-vous. Exactly.

In view of all this there seems to be little justification for regarding either the French or the English versions of the plays as funnier. Scrutiny of the points at which the versions differ from each other significantly reveals the fact that, in translating his plays either way, Beckett takes great care to maintain the humour of the original whilst at the same time often varying its character.

On the evidence of the first two plays it has also been claimed that Beckett is more vigorously crude in French than in English. No doubt some of his word-play has helped to create this impression, but in *Waiting for Godot* alone there are many places where the English reinforces the vulgarity of the French. Estragon cuts short the discussion about the Gospels in Act I with an obscenity if anything stronger in English than in French ('Les gens sont des cons' [21]): 'People are bloody ignorant apes.' When Estragon says of his carrot that the more he eats the worse it gets, Vladimir responds in rather refined French ('Je me fais au goût au fur et à mesure' [22]) which becomes in English: 'I get used to the muck as I go along.' Vladimir's suggested name for Lucky's dance ('le cancer des vieillards' [23]) is infinitely cruder in the English, which Beckett has confirmed as scatological: 'The hard stool.' When Estragon and Vladimir are annoyed by Pozzo's pleas for help in Act II, their French (ESTRAGON: 'Casse-lui la gueule.' VLADIMIR: 'Vermine' [24]) is milder and less violent than their English: 'Kick him in the crotch'/'Crablouse'. 'Finally, when the two decide to while away a few moments with an exchange of insults, these are specified in the English but not in the French: 'Moron! Vermin! Abortion! Morpion! Sewer-rat! Curate! Cretin! . . . Crritic!'

Nevertheless, when the later plays are taken into account, there is on balance little to choose between Beckett in French and Beckett in English in the matter of coarseness. Krapp's description of his younger self as 'that stupid bastard' becomes merely 'ce pauvre petit crétin' [25] in French, but in the same speech, by way of compensation, 'hard to believe I was ever as bad as that' becomes 'difficile de croire que j'aie jamais été con à ce point-là' [26], and 'the sour cud and the iron stool' even more bluntly repugnant: 'Merde remâchée et bouchon au cul' [27]. The truth of the matter is not that Beckett makes more use of coarseness in either the French or the English versions, but that in translating into whichever language, he is careful at least to maintain if not to increase the note of vulgarity. Similarly, neither the English nor the French Beckett is more economical. *En attendant Godot* lost about three pages and *Fin de Partie* a good two pages of text when translated into English, but what is less generally recognised is that *Happy Days* is abbreviated in the French translation at well over a dozen points, whilst *Comédie* omits the one and a half pages of notes headed 'Light', 'Chorus' and 'Urns' which precede 'Repeat' at the end of *Play*. This is in keeping with the general progression in Beckett's theatre towards an ever greater concision and density.

Systematic comparison between the French and the English versions of the plays thus casts doubt on the notion that Beckett is more poetic, or comic, or crude, or economical, or less enigmatic in the one language than in the other. Instead it reveals in Beckett what might have been expected of one who from very early in his career was a professional translator as well as a creative writer: a high level of consciousness and conscientiousness in reproducing his works in a second language. If he gives in to the temptation to improve at certain points by additions or, more often, by abbreviation, he does so without altering the essential quality of the original.

More interesting still, the comparison makes it possible to isolate the few genuine characteristics of the French versions not found, on the whole, in the English. In one way or another, usually by his resort to a technique of compensation, Beckett reveals his awareness of most of these points of difference between the versions – punning, linguistic humour, jokes about the English – and attempts to overcome the problem they pose, but there remains one such feature which, with apparent perverseness, he seems intent on preserving for the French versions: their colloquial quality. It is surprising how often, in *Waiting for Godot*, the familiar or picturesque character of the French goes by the board as Beckett translates straight and prosaically. Vladimir's 'Ah non, là tu te goures' [28] becomes 'Ah no, there you're mistaken'. His colourful reproach to Estragon, 'Pour jeter le doute, à toi le pompon' [29], becomes the rather flat 'Nothing is certain when you're about'. His remark about their rights, 'Nous les avons bazardés' [30], is translated 'we got rid of them' and his inquiry to Estragon 'Qui t'a esquinté?' [31] merely 'Who beat you?' Estragon's speech is similarly altered at more than one point. His remark to the effect that Godot had said he would come 'après le turbin' [32] is not translated but replaced by 'You think', and in Act II, when Pozzo asks why the two friends don't answer his question as to whether it's evening, Estragon's reply, 'C'est parce qu'on ne voudrait pas vous dire une connerie' [33], is replaced by the much less vigorous, 'Give us a chance.'

In the later plays the same process is seen in reverse when the French translations at a number of points reinforce the familiarity of the original English. Only at one point – in *Comédie*, when the second Woman's 'Go away and start poking and pecking at someone else' becomes merely 't'en iras harceler quelqu'un d'autre' [34] – does the English appear noticeably more colloquial. On the other hand the same play adds 'tu pues la pute' [35] to the translation of the Man's 'I smell her off you, she kept saying'. The translation of the Man's 'She put a bloodhound on me, but I had a little chat with him. He was glad of the extra money' makes greater use of popular parlance: 'Elle me colla un privé aux fesses, mais je lui dis deux mots. It fut ravi du rabiot' [36]. Similarly his remark, 'We had fun trying to work this out', is more vivid in the French, 'Tordante salade. Nous avons bien ri' [37], whilst the second Woman's 'He went on about why he had to tell her' produces 'Il me fit un exposé. Pourquoi il avait dû vider notre sac' [38]. Finally *Krapp's Last Tape* provides at least one similar example when the already mildly colloquial exclamation 'Ah finish your booze now and get to your bed. Go on with this drivel in the morning' is rendered even more colourful in translation: 'Vide ta bouteille et fous-toi au pieu. Reprends ces conneries demain' [39].

One last remarkable quality of the French texts of which, not unnaturally, few traces are to be found in the English, is the extent to which they reflect Beckett's absorption of French background and culture. This is more than just a matter of substituting French for English names, as happens for example in *Oh les beaux jours* and *Comédie*, or of replacing in the former play the English version of 'I love you so' from *The Merry Widow*, with the French. It is true that Beckett is content to translate literally into French such items from Winnie's cultural baggage as 'Woe, woe is me – to see what I see' or 'Oh fleeting joys – oh something lasting woe', but this is not his invariable practice in such circumstances. Snatches of French songs replace English ones in both *La Dernière bande* and *Oh les beaux jours* and on occasion Beckett culls from his memory lines from the French classics to suit particular purposes. When Willie crawls into his hole in *Happy Days*, Winnie, no doubt ironically, quotes to him Guiderius's song over the body of Imogen, supposed dead (*Cymbeline*, IV, 2), 'Fear no more the heat o' the sun'. In the French version this is replaced by 'Qu'ils pleurent, oh mon Dieu, qu'ils frémissent de honte', a slight misquotation from Racine's *Athalie*, Act II, where the Chorus chants [40]:

> Qu'ils pleurent, ô mon Dieu, qu'ils frémissent de crainte
> Ces malheureux, qui de ta cité sainte
> Ne verront point l'éternelle splendeur!
> C'est à nous de chanter, nous à qui tu révèles
> Tes clartés immortelles,
> C'est à nous de chanter tes dons et ta grandeur.

Plainly the line from Racine is just as ironic in this context, though in a different way, as the one from Shakespeare. It is one with those numerous pious ejaculations in which, with startling illogicality in her situation exposed to the merciless and unending light and heat of being, Winnie hymns the Creator's 'clartés immortelles': 'sainte lumière', 'oh le beau jour encore que ça va être', 'de grandes bontés' [41], etc. It emphasises, as do all these exclamations of wonder, perhaps the fatuousness of Winnie, perhaps her resilience. Both reactions have been voiced, but neither can be entirely avoided, and in such ambiguity lies much of the play's power to move.

Endgame, too, affords an example of literary quotation used to ironic ends in the closing monologue of Hamm, where 'You cried for night; it falls: now cry in darkness' translates the second line of Baudelaire's famous sonnet *Recueillement*, addressed to his grief [42]:

> Sois sage, ô ma Douleur, et tiens-toi plus tranquille.
> Tu réclamais le Soir; il descend; le voici. . . .

The irony lies in the so slight effect created on Hamm, for whom it is just 'a little poetry' to while away the play's closing moments ('Joli ça . . . Et puis? . . . Instants nuls, toujours nuls . . . [43]) by this sublime attempt of Baudelaire to conjure and conquer grief through its perfect expression in poetry. Hamm is himself a failed writer, for whom no such consolation through literature is possible.

Beckett derives equal irony, in the same play, from Clov's song, sung towards the end in response to Hamm's maudlin plea for 'quelques mots . . . que je puisse repasser . . . dans mon cœur . . . quelques mots . . . de ton cœur' [44]. The song, which is omitted from the English version, expresses Clov's disgust and cynicism [45]:

> Joli oiseau, quitte ta cage,
> Vole vers ma bien-aimée,
> Niche-toi dans son corsage,
> Dis-lui combien je suis emmerdé.

By its bathetically coarse final word Clov's song rejects through mockery a certain idea of love: 'on m'a dit, mais c'est ça, l'amour, mais si, mais si, crois-moi, tu vois bien que – que c'est facile' [46]. This time it is not Baudelaire whom the lines recall but rather the Romantic and sentimental love lyric typified in some of the poems of Gautier, for example 'Plaintive tourterelle' in *Émaux et Camées* [47]:

154

Plaintive tourterelle,
Qui roucoules toujours,
Veux-tu prêter ton aile
Pour servir mes amours . . .

Vole et que ton pied rose
Sur l'arbre ou sur la tour
Jamais ne se repose,
Car je languis d'amour . . .

Va droit sur sa fenêtre,
Près du palais du roi,
Donne-lui cette lettre
Et deux baisers pour moi . . .

– or perhaps even more the end of 'Absence' (*Poésies diverses*) [48]:

Descends dans sa gorge divine,
Blonde et fauve comme de l'or,
Douce comme un duvet d'hermine,
Sa gorge, mon royal trésor;

Et dis, mon âme, à cette belle:
'Tu sais bien qu'il compte les jours,
O ma colombe! à tire d'aile,
Retourne au nid de nos amours.'

Although Beckett is often said to be fully bilingual it is important to remember that he is not bilingual in the sense of having possessed two languages since childhood. His French was learnt at a comparatively late stage and as a foreign language, so that in the acquiring of it the order of events was for him the opposite of what it would have been for a native speaker: first the formal study, then, to the extent that this happens when a language is thus acquired, the unconscious imbibing of everyday patterns of speech, vocabulary and idiom. This is what chiefly distinguishes Beckett from the native French writer and also helps to explain certain features of his writing.

Verbal expression in Beckett's plays in French reflects the man in his diverse roles in France, and in the different phases of his acquisition of the language: as student, teacher and academic, as writer and frequenter of literary circles and, especially during the Occupation, as in many ways an ordinary Frenchman in a variety of temporary jobs. From all these sources came Beckett's extraordinarily wide stylistic register, ranging from the sublimely poetic through various shades of humour and seriousness to a bitter and blunt realism. This variety is one of the strengths of his plays and is relevant to the much debated question of why he chose to write in French.

Different explanations have been offered of Beckett's characteristically enigmatic answer to this question: 'Parce qu'en français il est plus facile d'écrire sans style' [49]. It suggests perhaps no more than that Beckett was concerned not to impose a recognisable personal style on his material or on his audiences. We are very far here from the kind of literary theatre characterised by uniformity of style and it is much less easy to say of Beckett than of, say, Giraudoux, that he has his own style which in all his plays overlays character. Eloquence and stylistic elegance are repeatedly parodied in his theatre – in Pozzo, in Hamm and even in Winnie. The key to the special quality which Beckett brings to writing for the French theatre seems to lie in what comparison between the French and the English versions of his plays enables one to isolate as the distinguishing mark of the former: that conscious, even self-conscious playfulness to be seen in the delight in word-play, linguistic jokes and that language-within-a-language that is French slang. What seems to attract him about French is the very fact that it is less second nature to him than is English, that his relationship to it is different and makes him more able to manipulate it consciously. Any writer is a student of language, but one operating in a foreign language is so in a very special sense. One is constantly aware of Beckett in his plays, not as a littérateur striving after fine writing as the final justification for the work, but rather as a student of the French language, and thence of language itself, listening patiently to his characters and consciously registering all.

It is in this way that Beckett is able to create the impression of a naturalism of spoken language which is new at least to the French theatre, so new indeed that it was at first rejected out of hand by audiences accustomed to what Alain Robbe-Grillet has termed the comfort of fine theatrical speech. It is thus significant that what Roger Blin most admired in *En attendant Godot* on his first acquaintance with it was the naturalness of its dialogue, and that he found this so revolutionary as to make much other writing for the stage difficult to listen to. Language itself may or may not be, as some have maintained, the subject of Beckett's theatre, but what in a theatrical sense is of more immediate interest is that Beckett has made language a source of dramatic excitement of a new kind. At their best, his plays have a pace and tempo which are maintained by the sheer brevity of many if not most of the exchanges. This brevity (it is one of the ironies of Beckett's theatre that he creates authentic, living dialogue for the theatre between characters who have very little of consequence to say to one another) is a fundamental source of the energy and excitement of the plays, a kind of tension which Beckett creates out of situations the opposite of tense. Moreover, the excitement has to do not just with the brevity of the exchanges but with the uncertain direction of the conversation (or indeed of the monologues), its rich tonal variety. Comic, parodic, sarcastic, vulgar, bitter, anguished or philosophical by turns, it makes a kind of mosaic of human moods. It is not the least of Beckett's achievements as a writer for the stage that he so renews the art of dialogue and of monologue as to convince us that the language he uses, so far from amounting to a personal style overlaying character, is on the contrary generated and governed by the haphazard and everchanging moods, whims and subjects of conversation of his characters.

NOTES

1 'Discours sur le théâtre', in *Littérature*, Idées NRF, Gallimard, Paris, p. 186.
2 See for example J. Robichez, 'Le Théâtre depuis 1950', in *Histoire de la littérature française*, Armand Colin, Paris, 1970, vol. 2, p. 988 (collection U).
3 Quoted in *Les Critiques de notre temps et Beckett*, Garnier, Paris, 1971, p. 139.
4 See J. Fletcher, *Samuel Beckett's Art*, Chatto & Windus, London, 1967, ch. 6.
5 See 'Samuel Beckett and the universal parody', in *Samuel Beckett: A Collection of Critical Essays*, ed. Martin Esslin, Prentice-Hall, New Jersey, 1965, pp. 90–1.
6 Ruby Cohn, *Samuel Beckett: The Comic Gamut*, Rutgers University Press, New Jersey, 1962, ch. 12: 'Beckett self-translator'.
7 *Fin de partie*, ed. J. and B. S. Fletcher, Methuen, London, 1970, p. 86.
8 Editions referred to are as follows: *Waiting for Godot*, Faber & Faber, London, 1965; *En attendant Godot*, ed. C. Duckworth, Harrap, London, 1966; *Endgame*, Faber & Faber, London, 1964; *Fin de partie*, Editions de Minuit, Paris, 1957; *Krapp's Last Tape*, Faber & Faber, London, 1965; *La Dernière bande*, Editions de Minuit, Paris, 1959; *Happy Days*, Faber & Faber, London, 1966; *Oh les beaux jours*, Editions de Minuit, Paris, 1963; *Play*, Faber & Faber, London, 1968; *Comédie*, Editions de Minuit, Paris, 1966.
9 Approximate translations of most of the passages of quoted French will be found at the end of this chapter. In the text, they are indicated by a number within square brackets.
10 I owe this observation to M. Jean-René Démoris.
11 Fletcher, op. cit., p. 99.

TRANSLATIONS

[1] Perhaps tonight we'll be sleeping at his place, warm and dry on the straw and with full bellies. It's worth waiting, isn't it?

[2] VLADIMIR: What's a knook? POZZO: I know you don't belong to these parts. Do you even belong to these times? People used to have jesters. Now they have knooks. Those who can afford it.

[3] Charlot Chassepot! I close my eyes – and am in the back garden again at Fougax-et-Barrineuf, sitting on his knee under the robinia. Happy days!

[4] Catullus.

[5] Two-act play.

[6] He who can do more can do less.

[7] I'm listening.

[8] It's swelling.

[9] Time is God's and mine.

[10] A kinesi or mechanotherapist Demoulin . . . Dumoulin . . . or perhaps even Desmoulins, that too is possible.

[11] Neat two-roomed flat, quiet, sunlit.

[12] They are ca-a-a-alm people.

[13] He puts on an English face.

[14] [*Coite* = quiet; *le coït* = coition.]

[15] You should have restrained him.

[16] He restrained himself.

[17] [Here the French adds an element of word-play to the English: *machin* resembles *machine* but means 'what-d'you-call-it'.]

[18] ESTRAGON: The Bible. . . . I must have glanced at it.
VLADIMIR: (*surprised*). At the school without God? [i.e. non-religious school.]
ESTRAGON: Don't know whether it was without or with.
VLADIMIR: You must be mixing it up with Borstal.

[19] Oh, that powder's marvellous for that.

[20] ESTRAGON: It wasn't there yesterday.
VLADIMIR: Of course it was. You just don't remember. We came within a hair's breadth of hanging ourselves from it. (*He thinks.*) Yes, that's right (*separating the words*) of hanging ourselves from it. But you didn't want to. Don't you remember?

[21] People are silly buggers.

[22] I get used to the taste as I go along.

[23] Old men's cancer.

[24] ESTRAGON: Sock him in the face. VLADIMIR: Vermin.

[25] That pathetic little idiot.

[26] Hard to believe I was ever as bloody stupid as that.

[27] Crap long-chewed and a corked-up arse.

[28] You're kidding yourself.

[29] At casting doubt you really take the cake.

[30] We flogged them.

[31] Who did you over?

[32] After the daily grind.

[33] Because we don't want to say something bloody silly.

[34] You'll go away and torment somebody else.

[35] You stink of whore.

[36] She stuck a tail at my backside, but I had a word with him. He was delighted to make a bit extra on the side.

[37] A hilarious mix-up. It gave us a good laugh.

[38] He told me a long tale. Why he had had to spill the beans about us.

[39] Empty your bottle and hit the hay. Go on with this bloody nonsense tomorrow.

[40] Let them weep, oh God, let them shake with fear, those unfortunates who will never see the everlasting glory of your holy city! It is for us to sing, we to whom you reveal your immortal light, it is for us to sing of your bounty and your majesty.

[41] Immortal light: holy light; oh this is going to be another happy day! great mercies.

[42] Be good, my Grief and calm yourself down.
You begged for Evening; it's falling; here it is.

[43] Nicely put, that. . . . And now? . . . Moments for nothing.

[44] A few words . . . to ponder . . . in my heart . . . a few words . . . from your heart.

[45] Pretty bird, leave your cage,
    Fly away to my true love,
    Nestle in her bodice and
    Tell her how bloody fed up I am.

[46] They said to me, That's love, yes yes, not a doubt, now you see how . . . how easy it is.

[47] Plaintive dove,
    Always cooing,
    Will you lend me your wing
    To serve my love. . . .

    Fly off and let your pink feet
    On tree or tower
    Never settle
    For I am lovesick. . . .

    Go straight to her window
    Near the king's palace,
    Give her this letter
    And two kisses for me.

[48] Alight in her exquisite bosom,
    Fair and fawn as gold,
    Soft as ermine fur,
    Her breast, my royal treasure;

    And say, my soul, to the fair one:
    'You know he is counting the days,
    Oh my dove! fly swiftly back
    To our love-nest.'

[49] Because in French it is easier to write without style.

Chapter 8

Film and the religion of art

Martin Dodsworth

I

Beckett's *Film* will not be thought a success by many people: the interesting question is 'what makes it fail; and beyond that lurks another: how it was that this failure was allowed to come into existence. Why was it not stifled at birth?' (Since birth, of course, it *has* been stifled as far as English audiences are concerned, since copies have proved almost totally inaccessible to them.)

Admirers of Beckett show a natural tendency to explain the film's unsatisfactory quality in terms of the techniques used in its making. *Film* is a doppelgänger story: in it, we see the protagonist literally pursued by the eye of the camera. He attempts to protect himself from all possibility of being looked at through any kind of eye, particularly from being looked at in the face; but he is defeated. As he dozes in his rocking-chair, the camera sneaks round from its position at his back and there is a confrontation between the protagonist (O, the observed, in Beckett's script) and the pursuer (E, the eye), who is now seen as it were through O's own eyes, and is seen to be O's double. This confrontation makes it necessary that we should be able to distinguish clearly between O's point of view and E's, but the necessity is more deeply rooted in *Film* than this would suggest. Even before the confront-ation proper (which Beckett terms an *investment*) Beckett asks that the audience should be able to distinguish E's perception of O from O's own perceptions of his surroundings. Beckett toys with the notion that these two different points of view might be conveyed to the audience simultaneously, but rejects it, not on the grounds of practicability, but because it might leave the spectator confused. Instead he opts for 'a succession of images of different *quality*, corresponding on the one hand to E's perception of O and on the other to O's perception' of his surroundings. This is the solution to the problem adopted by Alan Schneider, the director of *Film*, who also takes up Beckett's suggestion that 'brief sequences' should establish the O quality of vision right from the start of the film.[1]

Predictably enough, since Beckett himself points to the difficulty, it has been suggested that a failure to distinguish adequately between the points of view of O and E can account for much of what is wrong with *Film*. The suggestion does not seem to me acceptable, for various reasons: it exaggerates the possibility of confusion between E shots and O shots (to my mind the difference is clearly established from the moment of the first O shot), it exaggerates the importance of this differentiation which cannot but be explicit in the 'investment' section proper anyway, and it contrives to overlook radical and, as I shall try to show, essentially Beckettian defects in the film. We can learn something about Beckett's characteristic qualities, good and bad, by a consideration of the failure of *Film*.

It cannot be denied, however, that there is a good deal wrong with its execution. Buster Keaton was not first choice for the part of O – understandably. Chaplin was the right person to want because Chaplin's body and in particular his walk are expressive as Keaton's walk and body are not: and this consideration is an important one when the actor is to be seen most of the time from behind. Zero Mostel and Jack MacGowran had both worked in Beckett productions before, and both had a sympathy for his work which was lacking in Keaton. The part is in any case a taxing one since much depends on the expressiveness of O's face when he is at last confronted by E. Alan Schneider judged that 'Buster, finally given his chance not only to let us see his face but to see him act, let loose from deep inside somewhere. When we finally saw it, that face paid off. . . .' But this is surely wishful thinking. Keaton's look when faced by E has to recall the look on the face of the elderly couple in the street and of the old lady on the stairs when they too are confronted by the camera. And though in this respect his performance may be better than that of the others, it shares with them an exaggerated, theatrical, altogether unfilmic quality. The notion that a look can be repeated ('same expression as couple in the street': 'that look') is not ridiculous, but similarity or identity of one look with another takes on meaning only as far as its context is a whole facial repertoire, conspicuously absent from *Film*. It is the fact that the couple in the street, the old lady, and O are drawn together by a single facial expression that is important; but in the absence of a sense of their different-ness this drawing-together strikes one as an idea, a thought on the part of the author, rather than as a surprising identity in the experience of the characters concerned. It is possible that someone like Jack MacGowran could have made of the look a less self-consciously shocking moment of recognition for the audience. But Keaton is not notably successful, and it is reasonable to suppose that this was because Beckett demanded too much of his actor at this point. 'An agony of perceivedness' is what Keaton has to express, though we are barely to perceive his face before the agony appears;

to ask this of the actor is much. Alan Schneider in any case allowed this 'agony' to find expression as a rather commonplace horrified gape, perhaps making 'that look' easier for the minor actor to produce, but diminishing the power of Keaton's own performance.

Schneider comments on the other actors in the film in his essay 'On directing *Film*'. The couple in the street are described (more or less accurately) as 'bad but bearable'; a glimpse of the characters not used in the opening street sequence quickly explains why they were thought to be bearable. As for the old lady on the stairs: 'The flower lady, Sam thought, was beautiful. So did I.' Indeed, she performs her little piece of melodrama well: 'Gradually same expression as that of couple in street. She closes her eyes, then sinks to the ground and lies with her face in scattered flowers.' Her performance, however, is not such as to make us forget the melodramatic nature of the act. Again, how could it be? What she has to do is no more rooted in a lived continuum of acts than Keaton's 'look' in the confrontation.

Film, then, shows actors battling against the odds with an intrinsically disobliging scenario. Both author and director could have done more for their cast.

The defects in realisation are not, however, solely connected with the actors' performances. In two respects at least the film deviates from its scenario to its own disadvantage, and in one further respect Beckett's wishes are observed when they should have been disregarded.

Schneider fails to respect the scenario in the sequence where Keaton has to eject dog and cat from the room, and also in the street setting. As far as the dog-and-cat sequence is concerned, Schneider was to some extent a victim of bad luck, since what happened was that in an early take Keaton dropped the dog a bit too hard on the other side of the door and the dog wouldn't trust him any more; the result was that the sequence does not conform to Beckett's 'foolish suggestion' for it in his notes to the scenario, which could have brought out more clearly the film's ambiguous relation to the comedies of the silent cinema and also have lightened the tone of that part of *Film* to good effect. One can't help feeling, however, that this bad luck stemmed from Keaton's not being at ease on or off set during the making of *Film*: even Schneider's laudatory references to him come out sounding wrong and they plainly didn't get on in any real sense of the term.

Beckett's scenario describes the street setting as follows: 'Dead straight. No sidestreets or intersections. Period: about 1929.

Early summer morning. Small factory district.' The setting used
in the film itself is unsatisfactory in several respects. Although
architecturally it may belong to the 1920s, or even earlier, it does
not belong to a small factory district of 1929, though it possibly
belongs to a run-down small factory district of New York in the
mid-1960s. What is small now is not necessarily what was small in
1929, what is small in New York is not necessarily small elsewhere.
What Beckett's scenario required was for the opening shots to
suggest a place and a time. Schneider's opening does neither. His
street could be anywhere in a large city (not evoked by Beckett)
and the time of day could be anywhere between six in the morning
and six at night. The scenario further suggested 'moderate anima-
tion of workers going unhurriedly to work. . . . One cab, cantering
nag, driver standing brandishing his whip.' We are in the world of
Mercier et Camier and the *Nouvelles*. All this is missing from the
completed *Film*. Schneider's inexperience of direction led to a good
many useless, and so unused, shots, and the rest that would have
been usable had to be rejected because, in Schneider's words, 'the
performances, except for Buster's, were terrible'. (One trouble
looks, from the stills, to have been that Schneider was thinking in
terms of theatre rather than cinema when he cast his extras.)

Did it matter that Beckett's opening was in this way reduced?
Beckett himself sanctioned Schneider's omissions. 'He had never
been sure all those people belonged in that opening anyway. They
gave it and the film a different texture, opened up another world.'
The scenario suggests that Beckett had populated his opening for
thematic reasons only: 'All persons in opening scene to be shown in
some way perceiving . . . i.e. all contentedly in *percipere* and
percipi.' Such thematic reinforcement might seem superfluous:
hence Beckett's consent to the enforced abridgment. Yet what is
lost is more than a reminder of the pervasiveness of looking and
being looked at in the world, which is contented enough with all
its habitual seeing. Beckett's original scene also made the point
that the protagonist was *not* like anyone else: he moves against the
grain of all the others who are 'going unhurriedly to work'. They
are in pairs: he is solitary. He is different, not representative of the
mass. This would not be suggested in Schneider's *Film*. It might
further be argued that 'opening up another world' to that of the
protagonist was essential to the way Beckett conceived of *Film*
and that for this reason he should not so readily have abandoned
his opening. Finally, the original opening would not simply have
made the protagonist's untypical quality plain, it would also have
rooted the events of *Film* in a dimension of experience necessarily

shared with the audience, and the lack of such a dimension is one of the defects of the completed *Film* just as its slighting is of the scenario.

The suggestion from Beckett which Schneider ought not to have taken up was one we have noted already, that the audience should be prepared for the differentiation of O's point of view and E's once O is inside the room by putting brief sequences in the O style into the preceding parts of the film. This was a mistake. An audience unprejudiced by a reading of the scenario is in any case not likely to understand the difference between O shots and E shots until E confronts O, if then. Simply to have more of these different-quality shots is not to make them more acceptable or comprehensible for the audience. Furthermore – and this is the more important objection – the introduction of these shots cuts up the film at a point where continuity is desirable. There must be a sense that O is pursued by E, and this sense of pursuit can only be had if the audience feels not that it is watching a film composed of individual shots which have subsequently been put together but that it is pursuing O itself with the camera. Comparisons with conventional pursuit sequences, which are often made up of a variety of shots, are not in order here since they are working for different aims and with different material: speed or care, for example, are qualities often to be suggested as well as the simple quality of pursuit, and the pursuer himself is visible and needs to be seen. In *Film* only the camera movement can give adequately the sene sof pursuit and Beckett's suggestion prevented his idea from realisation on film with maximum intensity.

II

So far we have been looking at qualities in the realisation of Beckett's scenario that make *Film* a failure. These have to be cleared out of the way before we can think clearly about what Beckett himself set out to do, what went wrong before the scenario fell into the hands of Schneider, Keaton and the rest, and what all this can tell us about the quality of Beckett's *œuvre* in general. And first: what *kind* of work is *Film*?

A useful analogy can be made between *Film* and John Cage's 'Lecture on Nothing' (first printed August 1959), for this brings out the essentially modern quality of what Beckett has done. Cage's lecture is set out on the page in a fashion reminiscent of poetry, and its musical structure is described by the author as follows:[2]

There are four measures in each line and twelve lines in each
unit of the rhythmic structure. There are forty-eight such
units, each having forty-eight measures. The whole is divided
into five large parts in the proportion 7, 6, 14, 14. 7. The
forty-eight measures of each unit are likewise so divided.
The text is printed in four columns to facilitate a rhythmic
reading.

Much of the lecture is given up to commentary on its own progress:[3]

Now begins the third unit of the second part.
Now the second part of that third unit.
Now its third part.
Now its fourth part (which, by the way, is just the same
length [in number of words – M.D.] as the third part).
Now the fifth and last part.

But the 'Lecture on Nothing' does not altogether exclude ideas.
As Cage himself puts it: 'Most speeches are full of ideas. This one
doesn't have to have any. But at any moment an idea may come
along. Then we may enjoy it.'[4]

In fact, there is quite a large and self-assured idea behind Cage's
demonstration: 'I have nothing to say and I am saying it and that
is poetry as I need it.' And again:[5]

Our poetry now is the realisation that we possess nothing.
Anything therefore is a delight (since we do not possess it
and thus need not fear its loss). We need not destroy the
past: it is gone; at any moment, it might reappear and seem to
be and be the present.
Would it be a repetition? Only if we thought we owned it,
but since we don't, it is free and so are we.

The analogy between *Film* and the 'Lecture on Nothing' is
partly a matter of their formal qualities. In both the content is
minimal in relation to the time taken up in performance – the
structure, that is, is apparently elaborated well beyond the needs
of the 'subject': 'The film is divided into three parts. 1. The street
(about eight minutes). 2. The stairs (about five minutes). 3. The
room (about seventeen minutes).' Keaton told Schneider con-
fidentially that 'he had made a lot of movies in his time and didn't
see how this one could possibly play for more than four minutes.
He had timed it.' In fact, even with its abbreviated Part 1, *Film*
runs for twenty-two minutes.

Cage's lecture pretends to be about nothing, yet this cannot be and is not really the case: it is inclusive of an idea which determines its structure and, whether the author likes it or not, gives such a barren sequence of phrases as that already quoted ('Now begins the third unit . . .' and so on) a meaning which it would not possess in any other context, that is, that 'our poetry now is the realisation that we possess nothing'.

Beckett's *Film* is not free from an interest in nothingness. O's exclusion of the world from his room, of all eyes that might be thought to be watching him, is an attempt, imaginatively at least, to annihilate other people. His falling back into the rocking-chair when, as he thinks, all eyes have been turned from him recalls Murphy's use of it: 'it gave his body pleasure, it appeased his mind. Then it set him free in his mind.' Although Murphy's mind 'excluded nothing that it did not itself contain' Murphy uses the mental freedom afforded him by his rocking to bring himself as near as he possibly can to nothing, 'a mote in the dark of absolute freedom'. He seeks, and obtains, 'the sensation of being a missile without provenance or target, caught up in a tumult of non-Newtonian motion'.[6] We may hazard that something of the same sort is what O is after.

Nevertheless, *Film* does not present itself so clearly as a structure inclusive of an idea as Cage's lecture. O's quest for nothingness, if it is that, picks up a good deal more in its abortive progress to fulfilment than does the lecture. It is, for example, possible to attach a 'story' to the events of *Film*. Indeed, Beckett does so in his notes to the scenario:

> This obviously cannot be O's room. It may be supposed it is
> his mother's room, which he has not visited for many years
> and is now to occupy momentarily, to look after the pets,
> until she comes out of hospital. This has no bearing on the
> film and need not be elucidated.

This exercise in narrative reconstruction is not required by the film, and it contravenes the filmic rule equivalent to the literary principle that we should concern ourselves only with the words on the page. Discussing whose room it is that O is in is like arguing about the distance between the castles of Goneril and Regan in *King Lear*. Yet Beckett appears to want us to flirt interestedly with aspects of *Film* that aren't even properly speaking available to us. The suggestion about the room is made and then briskly withdrawn.

Beckett's note performs an ambiguous function, rather like that of the photographs which O examines and then destroys as he sits in his rocking-chair in the room which may or may not be his mother's. (As far as the room is concerned, compare the opening of *Molloy*: 'I am in my mother's room. It is I who live there now. I don't know how I got there.' In *Film* we know how O gets to the room but not whose room it is, nor whether O lives there.) The photographs record a man's life, from infancy to graduation day, marriage and fatherhood, and finally to his condition at the age of thirty: 'Looking over 40. Wearing hat and overcoat. Patch over left eye. Clean-shaven. Grim expression.' The fact that there are seven photographs suggests an ironic foreshortening of the seven ages of man. Beckett's notes imply, but do not state, that these are photographs of O himself. In the film the last photograph makes this explicit. And yet the photographs explain nothing about O or about themselves. They tell us neither why he is what he is now nor truly what he was in the past. Of course they invite us to tell a story to ourselves about him: O enlisted, went to fight, leaving his wife and child behind and returned from the wars to find them dead, or that they had abandoned him. But it might be that he took to drink and ran away from them, or that he was himself in some way responsible for their deaths. And so on. The minimal content of *Film* is far more open to speculative extension of this kind than Cage's 'Lecture on Nothing'.

In this respect it is similar to Beckett's television play *Eh Joe*; and since the scenario for *Film* has been published in the same volume as *Eh Joe*, and the two works are complementary to each other, it may be worth commenting on the relation between them.

Film depends on a mobile camera in pursuit of a protagonist who seeks to avoid its gaze. In the interests of this visual pursuit, sound is deliberately restricted – reduced to one soft 'sssh!' heard (if heard at all) in the street sequence, a sound which appears to be permitted only in order to emphasise the silence which otherwise pervades.

Eh Joe depends on sounds, on a monologue which Joe seeks to avoid hearing. In the past he has boasted of his ability to quell the voices within his head, which belong to specific people, by a process he has termed 'mental thuggee'. Just as O's destruction or evasion of the eyes of witness proves useless, however, so Joe is assured that his efforts are without point: when he has strangled the voices of all the dead that may speak to him, there will still be his own voice to hear, and beyond that, his God's. In the interests of this pursuit of Joe by the voice in his head, what we see in *Eh Joe* is deliberately restricted. The camera moves to follow Joe round the room as he locks himself into it but then confines itself

to an ever more intense scrutiny of Joe's face, in ten basic movements viewing it in larger and larger close-up. Just as sound is used
to emphasise the silence of *Film*, so in *Eh Joe* the mobility of the
camera is used to draw attention to the way in which it is held by
the sight of Joe.

Beyond this complementarity of the two plays there lies an
essential similarity. In both we sense a formal elaboration well
beyond the needs of 'subject'. In *Eh Joe*, that is little more than an
anecdote: the voice of a woman tells Joe how a girl committed
suicide for him, painfully, and still declaring her love for the man
who had driven her to death: 'There's love for you. . . . Isn't it
Joe? . . . Wasn't it Joe? . . . Eh, Joe? . . . Wouldn't you say? . . .
Compared to us. . . . Compared to Him. . . . Eh Joe?' Despite the
telling of this story with numerous repetitions, however, the
circumstances, motivation and quality of Joe's perfidy (if it was
that) in regard to the girl remain obscure and available for speculation much as the past history of O. *Eh Joe* encourages a natural
tendency in us to construct a story about the persons and events
referred to in the course of the monologue, yet there is not simply
one story that will fit the facts in our possession. For example, it
may be that Joe acted as he did because of the way in which his
parents, or one of them, acted to him. Not all his acts of mental
thuggee are necessarily culpable, or equally so. The fringe of
uncertainty about the action is like that about the sequence of
photographs in *Film*. Into both works there enters a principle of
indeterminacy, to which Beckett's note on O's room draws
attention. The aspect of indeterminacy is a further connection
between *Eh Joe* and *Film* and the aesthetic of John Cage. (Of
course, no work of art can determine how it is to be interpreted
precisely: on the other hand, the area of what is determined can
vary significantly in relation to that which is not. In the case of
these two Beckett works, the argument is that what is determined,
what *must* be deduced from them, is small relative to what is not.)

The second of John Cage's three lectures 'Composition as
Process' deals with indeterminacy, and particularly with 'composition that is indeterminate with respect to its performance'. Morton
Feldman's *Intersection 3* is taken as an example of such a composition, which, in so far as he can advocate anything, is advocated by
Cage. He describes Feldman's work as permitting an infinite
number of performances which may or may not be based on a
systematic notion of interpretation. If the performer decides to do
without consciously organised principles of interpretation he may,
for example, decide to go[7]

inwards with reference to the structure of his mind . . . to a point in the collective unconsciousness of Jungian psychoanalysis, following the inclinations of the species and doing something of more or less universal interest to human beings; or to the 'deep sleep' of Indian mental practice – the Ground of Meister Eckhart – identifying there with no matter what eventuality.

(The latter possibility suggests an entry into that area of mind where Murphy feels himself 'a missile without provenance or target'.)

According to Cage, 'composition which is indeterminate with respect to its performances . . .' is 'necessarily experimental. An experimental action is one the outcome of which is not foreseen'.[8] What he says about composition applies to any art which is given over to indeterminacy. It cannot respect any of the principles or conventions usually associated with art, for in determining the artist's manner of proceeding and the audience's responses, they fetter his art. The kind of art which Cage advocates is necessarily an anti-art, and, as his references to Meister Eckhart indicate (they are many, and fundamental to an understanding of his aesthetic) it is religious in spirit. 'Our poetry now is the realisation that we possess nothing'; it is at once a substitute for the religion of the past, which is no longer ours, and it is religion itself – for what can be more religious, in an old-fashioned sense, than this avowal that 'we possess nothing'?

Indeed, this religious basis for indeterminacy in art leads one to the discovery that the 'freedom' of Cage's work is illusory. What underlies it is a theory, about which he will talk endlessly, and which rigidly determines the kind of music he can write, does so, in fact, as rigidly as the rules which he has rejected. Something of the same kind applies to Beckett in the works under discussion. Although he leaves room for speculation on individual elements in either composition, there is little room for doubt as to the central proposition which makes such speculation possible and, one suspects, of doubtful relevance in the author's view. Far from being undetermined, these works are *over*-determined, subduing art to the necessities of a particular kind of religious belief – one which many will find unacceptable and which Beckett lacks the means in his art here to enforce.

Susan Sontag sees the progress from art to anti-art as something inevitable if the artist regards himself, or allows himself to be regarded, as possessed of a religious insight:[9]

172

As the activity of the mystic must end in a *via negativa*, a theology of God's absence, a craving for the cloud of unknowing beyond knowledge and for the silence beyond speech, so art must tend toward anti-art, the elimination of 'subject' (the 'object', the 'image'), the substitution of chance for intuition, and the pursuit of silence.

The argument does not have universal validity, but it does fit the case of Beckett quite well. Both *Film* and *Eh Joe* flout decorum in the manner of anti-art, and both ask to be viewed in a religious spirit, as the embodiment, however imperfect, of the desire for some kind of experience that is free, in particular, from what Sontag calls 'the distracting individuality of "ordinary" life'.[10] *Film*, we may say, fails because it lays too proud a claim on religious qualities: *Eh Joe* is more successful because its commerce with religious aspiration is of a more doubtful kind. Before any justification of this can be attempted, however, we need to describe the kind of spiritual adventure with which *Film* concerns itself.

III

As Richard Coe, among others, has shown, Beckett's work has affinities with both oriental religion (particularly in *Murphy*: we have already drawn attention to the similarity between Cage's reference to the 'deep sleep' of Indian mysticism and the darkest area of *Murphy*'s mind) and Sartre's philosophy. Beckett's attitude towards Sartre remains obscure. Coe believes that *The Unnamable* makes use of 'two specific concepts out of *L'Être et le néant*'. It is arguable that the mud in *How It Is* derives not only from Dante, but also from Sartre's concept of *le visqueux*, which stands for the ambiguity of the relation between ourselves and the external world, also in *L'Être et le néant*. The same book offers in its discussion of *le regard* the most apt commentary on *Film*. Beckett's interest in Sartre hardly needs explanation – as Coe remarks, he was, in *Murphy*, 'an *existentialiste avant la lettre*' – but it is worth recalling that Beckett was *lecteur d'anglais* at the Ecole Normale Supérieure at the time when Sartre was studying there (and also Maurice Merleau-Ponty).[11]

Sartre at any rate helps us answer the question: 'Why does O avoid, as far as he possibly can, being looked at by E or anyone else?' The condition of being looked at is one of crucial significance for human beings in Sartre's view, since he believes that it is only because others look at us from outside ourselves that we are able to internalise that look and so become conscious of ourselves as distinct from the world in which we move. For Sartre, that is never a pleasant business, for several reasons. First, it involves us in acknowledging the existence of another person, who is beyond our control, ultimately unknowable, and so a threat to the world which had previously been completely identified with our own self. Second, the other person sees us as an object. He assesses us in terms of this or that possible form of behaviour: he typecasts us. In doing so he limits our freedom of action by complicating the motives for action. We do not now simply act: we act in the context of his expectations and these must be taken into account by us. Third, this results in a radical and irreparable split within our self. We can no longer exist entirely as the *en-soi*; we develop the *pour-soi*, being-for-itself. The level of being-in-itself is that at which we existed entirely prior to being caught in the look of the other person. At this level we are aware of our self as having plans and thoughts, but our self is indistinguishable from the plans and thoughts it has. As soon as we have been looked at, and are conscious of the fact, however, we become aware of our self as an object perceptible to others, as a body separate from other bodies, having plans and thoughts which are now registered as distinct from our self, since they are inevitably subject to the compromise and impurity of existence in a world of others. Whilst part of us remains at the level of the *en-soi*, being-in-itself, part of us now exists at this new level of manipulation and finitude, the level of the *pour-soi*, of being-for-itself.

Beckett's scenario originally proposed showing people in the street other than O and the couples whom he jostles 'in his blind haste'. These were to be all going in the same direction and all in couples; further, they were all to be 'contentedly in *percipere* and *percipi*'. The last detail makes it explicit that, in Sartre's terms, they have accepted the split between *en-soi* and *pour-soi* and are happily living the life of the latter. Such happiness must be fundamentally a form of lying to oneself, since it involves a denial of the pain arising from the split in consciousness into the two levels or forms of existence. All those who are looked at by E suffer the full 'agony of perceivedness' however; held by that gaze they are no longer able to lie to themselves about the suffering which underlies their lives.

O's flight from E and his removal of all possible sources of being looked at cannot be explained as an attempt to preserve the bad faith of the life of the *pour-soi*. He is as much in flight from that life as he is from E who penetrates its falsity. O's destruction of the photographs is not only a way of removing eyes that might possibly be imagined looking at him in the room: it is also a denial of himself as a being in time, as possessed of a past. According to Sartre, time is an aspect of the *pour-soi*:[12]

> L'en-soi ne dispose pas de temporalité précisément parce qu'il est en-soi et que la temporalité est la mode d'être unitaire d'un être qui est perpetuellement à distance de soi pour soi. Le Pour-soi, au contraire, est temporalité. . . . (The *en-soi* has no claims on the temporal precisely because it is *en soi*, being-*in-itself*, and because the temporal is the mode of existence inseparable from a being which is in its own regard [*pour soi*] perpetually at a distance from itself. The *pour-soi*, on the contrary, is the temporal. . . .)

In the destruction of his past and in his avoidance of the consciousness of being looked at, O is seeking not to protect himself in the life of the *pour-soi* but to regain the bliss of the *en-soi*. Such an endeavour must fail, because once the look of the other person has been internalised it cannot be removed. Even locked in the room with all physical eyes removed, destroyed, or covered, O is still looking at himself. He cannot shake off his own consciousness of self. (Were we permitted to look through the eyes of the flower-lady or the couple in the street at their moments of agony we should see an image not of O, but of the person concerned.) E is a generalised self-consciousness, an eye of God bringing each person face to face with himself. E's face bears an expression 'impossible to describe, neither severity nor benignity, but rather acute *intentness*': he *is* this intentness turned inward upon the individual. *Film* is an illustration of the impossibility of ever regaining the serenity of the *en-soi* once a consciousness of other persons has entered the mind; indeed it could be described as a revelation of this impossibility, and the word should be given its full religious force.

It is proper to invoke religion here for two reasons. First, Sartre's philosophy is a metaphysic and it is one which is felt to be of as vital personal concern to his reader as to him. A metaphysic upon which depends personal salvation (and an understanding of the impossibility of some kinds of personal salvation) deserves to be called religious, and such a metaphysic underlies *Film*. Second, a reading of Beckett's early study of *Proust* shows his willingness to term such an adventure as O's a religious one. Since the point is an important one and since, also, it may be as well to emphasise authentically Beckettian as well as Sartrean sources for *Film*, some consideration of the Proust book seems necessary here.

Beckett reads Proust primarily as a thinker, and his book is an exposition of the thought of *A la recherche du temps perdu* in which little distinction is made between what Proust thinks and what Beckett. For example, he appears to accept Proust's account of the instability of created things and the justification of habit as a protection of ourselves from knowledge of the incessant change which is the true condition of human life (a change emphatically enough present in the life of Belacqua Shuah, we might recall, who marries three times in the course of the ten chapters of *More Pricks Than Kicks*):[13]

> Habit is a compromise effected between the individual and his environment or between the individual and his own eccentricities, the guarantee of a dull inviolability, the lightning conductor of his existence. . . . Breathing is habit. Life is habit. . . . Habit then is the generic term for the countless treaties concluded between the countless subjects that constitute the individual and their countless correlative objects. The periods of transition that separate consecutive adaptations (because by no expedient of macabre transubstantiation can the grave-sheets serve as swaddling-clothes) represent the perilous zones in the life of the individual, dangerous, precarious, painful, mysterious and fertile, when for a moment the boredom of living is replaced by the suffering of being.

The opposition of 'the boredom of living' to 'the suffering of being' anticipates by thirty years that of the '*percipere* and *percipi*' in the street at the beginning of *Film* to the 'agony of perceivedness' with which it concludes. Sartre is an intervention merely in Beckett's internal monologue.

Proust's reality is one that is painful to observe because habit will not willingly give up its claim to 'a dull inviolability' and because the perpetual changes of the real world frustrate the spirit in its natural longing for 'the free play of every faculty'.[14] It involves an acknowledgment of the inevitable defeat of all desire:[15]

> No object prolonged in this temporal dimension tolerates possession, meaning by possession total possession, only to be achieved by the complete identification of object and subject. The impenetrability of the most vulgar and insignificant

176

human creature is not merely an illusion of the subject's jealousy. .... All that is active, all that is enveloped in time and space, is endowed with what might be described as an abstract, ideal and absolute impermeability. So that we can understand the position of Proust: 'We imagine that the object of our desire is a being that can be laid down before us, enclosed within a body. Alas! it is the extension of that being to all the points of space and time that it has occupied and will occupy. If we do not possess contact with such a place and with such an hour we do not possess that being. But we cannot touch all these points.'

To apprehend reality as the object of our desire is to apprehend our own limitations with regard to it. We can never encompass it, and yet only habit protects us from a constant yearning for it, a love which can only be possessed outside space and time.

Proust claims by involuntary memory to overcome the limitations of time, space, and mortality:[16]

The identification of immediate with past experience, the recurrence of past action or reaction in the present, amounts to a participation between the ideal and the real, imagination and direct apprehension, symbol and substance. Such participation forces the essential reality that is denied to the contemplative as to the active life.

When, at the conclusion of *A la recherche du temps perdu*, in the Guermantes courtyard and library, Marcel experiences a succession of such moments as involuntary memory makes possible and is able to identify them, to perceive their essence, Beckett describes him as suffering 'a religious experience in the only intelligible sense of that epithet, at once an assumption and an annunciation' and later the intervention of involuntary memory alone is 'a mystical experience'.[17]

It is such an experience that is attempted by O; we cannot say whether he achieves it since the figure of E may or may not be the unchanging reality which Beckett, as opposed to Proust, believes to underlie 'the boredom of living'. O's room and his destruction of the photographs both possibly derive from Proust – his cork-lined room and his opposition to realism, 'the penny-a-line vulgarity of notations'.[18]

It may be significant in this connection that when *Proust* came to be reprinted in this country it was together with the *Three Dialogues – Beckett and Georges Duthuit* which make clear that

Beckett does not share Proust's belief in an intuitive art based on moments of intuition into reality afforded by the involuntary memory. The dialogues begin by Beckett's sketching an impossibly pure kind of experience as the goal, it would seem, of art – experience of an objective reality freed from all entanglement with subjective interpretation: 'Total object, complete with missing parts, instead of partial object.' They conclude by admitting that such an aim is impossible: Beckett praises the artist Bram van Velde as 'the first to admit that to be an artist is to fail, as no other dare fail, that failure is his world, and the shrink from it desertion, art and craft, good housekeeping, living'.[19] No Proust he.

Film illustrates the extent of Beckett's debt to the Proustian religion as well as his quarrel with it. Much can be learned if we compare O's actions with the commentary on solitude in *Proust*:[20]

> For the artist who does not deal in surfaces, the rejection
> of friendship is not only reasonable, but a necessity. Because
> the only possible spiritual development is in the sense of
> depth, the artistic tendency is not expansive, but a
> contraction. And art is the apotheosis of solitude.

O's solitude is productive of nothing but an 'agony of perceivedness' and we are to understand that this is the ultimate reality we can ourselves perceive.

Again, *Film* makes no statements. It is about an intuition, and it asks for an intuitive response which would make this exposition redundant. It approximates, consequently, to music, 'an art that is perfectly intelligible and perfectly inexplicable', to music which for Proust can hold 'the ideal and immortal statement of the essence of a unique beauty, a unique world' but which for Beckett, though it also affirms 'the "invisible reality" that damns the life of the body on earth as a pensum',[21] has nothing to redeem either body or spirit.

IV

Film is not merely about the failure of religious experience, that is, experience of a metaphysical reality, even such as Murphy achieves, to console; it is religion itself, for it requires to be believed in by an intuitive act of assent. It is useless to work out what it is about in the way in which we have done because all that happens is that what it is about usurps what it is. It is a parable from Beckett's not very private religion. One can, of course, discuss the parables of the New Testament without reference to their specifically religious context, as representations of a reality which is the product of common human endeavour, or as demonstrations of an ethic rooted in nature rather than a metaphysic. It is also possible to speak of *Film* in this way. But whereas the New Testament parables root themselves in a human reality in order to speak of what is beyond it, *Film* disdains such rooting. The schematic representation of the shared world of habit, of the *pour-soi*, does nothing to draw us into the central experience of *Film*, which imperiously demands our assent to its premises, whilst doing virtually nothing to express them cogently. *Film* is written for a world in which Merleau-Ponty's rival account of the nature of seeing called 'L'Œil et l'esprit'[22] does not exist. The schematism of *Film* belongs to a schoolmaster whose mind is closed because he knows himself right, and Beckett's religion as it manifests itself here has all the meanness of a Calvinism where salvation is utterly impossible.

The point is not that *Film* fails as 'art', but that it fails to interest us in its own right. In the context of Beckett's own work, it takes on a significance which hardly belongs to it in itself. Just as Beckett in *Proust* puts Proust's thought before all consideration of the force with which it is conveyed, so in *Film* the artist as thinker has taken precedence over the artist as uniquely endowed with a capacity for imagining and expressing human acts. 'The artistic tendency' here is certainly a 'contraction' both in the bounds of O's experience and in our experience of O. The threat of such a contraction is familiar enough in Beckett's work, but it is not often realised: 'you must go on, I can't go on, I will go on.' Malone works out a scheme by which the last months or days of his life can be regulated, but his life exceeds any rules he can make for it; *Malone Dies* thrives on the tension between rules and what exceeds them. Only in a few minor works, of which *Film* is the chief but among which are also found the two 'acts without words' and *Breath,* is this ambiguous tension missing. The need for certainty to which Beckett succumbs when he produces dogmatic work of the order of *Film* is the need which he fruitfully resists in his best work.

Perhaps it is significant that in none of these works is the medium words, for the rootedness of language in the irremediably human seems of itself to act as a curb on Beckett's absolutist aspirations. Bearing this in mind, we can see *Eh Joe* as an attempted amends for the simplistic endeavour of *Film.* (Their *formal* resemblance has already been considered.)

Joe, like his counterpart in *Film*, shuts out the world from his room; but he is tormented by more than the fact of self-conscious-

ness. He hears the voice of an internalised other remorselessly
accusing and paining him. The fact that he is looked at does not
appear to enter his mind, despite the intensity of our look; indeed
what we see is of less consequence for us than what we hear, even
though what we see is unusually distressing and painful to us. The
experience depicted in *Eh Joe* and our own experience of it seem
to involve a retraction of the significance attached to seeing in
Film.

Let us suppose that the voice which Joe hears is an embodiment
of the Proustian 'involuntary memory'. It is certainly a horrifying
parody of it. Its relation to reality is of a far more complex kind
than the figure of E presented to O. In *Eh Joe*, for example, it is
open to us to believe that the protagonist is unhappily subject to
hallucination. The behaviour of the flower-lady and the couple in
the street make this impossible to believe as far as O is concerned.
We are free to believe that the voice in *Eh Joe* is the internalisation
of Joe's guilt, or that he refuses to acknowledge guilt, or that the
voice is a phenomenon from beyond the grave. Its accusations may
be true or false. If true, then it may be right or wrong to torment
Joe as it does. It is possible to see *Eh Joe* and to feel exclusively
pity for Joe and anger that he should have to submit to hearing
the voice. This is because the reality with which it presents us
is genuinely overwhelming. It does not make complete sense
because there is too much of it for us or for Joe to come to terms
with, even notionally as we do so easily where *Film* is concerned.
The language of *Eh Joe* is inherently ambiguous. When the voice
speaks of her last time with Joe as 'Last I was favoured with by
you', she is rejecting the idea that it was a favour but also suggesting that it might have been a favour even if she failed to recognise
it as such. Rival versions of reality are implicit here, and *Eh Joe*
as a whole reminds us of the difficulty of opting for a view of
reality that takes into account adequately other people's
experiences. *Film*, without language, can only offer a view of
reality which we are free to accept or reject but which does not
draw us into the perplexities out of which it is supposed to arise.

The defect of *Eh Joe* is not the schematism of *Film*, a fatal
giving-in to the diagram which, for example, in the game of chess
in *Murphy* is seen for what it is, but is rather an overreaching
gesture towards humanity. *Eh Joe* actually invokes 'love': 'There's
love for you. . . . Eh Joe?' But in doing so it sullies the word with
its own ambiguous irony: for was it love the girl showed in her
suicide? Would it have been love even if she did, as the voice
affirms, die 'taking Joe with her'? These are a different kind of

question from the one about 'favoured' implied in the previous paragraph. What the voice says about her own relations with Joe has an authority, even an authoritative ambiguity, that she cannot have when talking about someone else's relations with him. If she really knows about the reality of what the other girl did and felt in her last solitary hours, then her own metaphysical status is clarified and we have a mawkish and repulsive story of moral retribution from beyond the grave. If on the other hand the 'love' she attributes to the other girl is her own fantasy then she takes on a psychological credibility at odds with the ambiguous nature of her existence in Joe's mind. Beckett's attempt to produce a more deeply human version of his parable on the impossibility of human self-subsistence ends up flirting with sentimentality and muddle.

Looked at together, *Film* and *Eh Joe* remind us of the continual temptation for Beckett of falling back on the schematic and dogmatic and of the difficulty he has in resisting it. His work of the last ten years surely reflects an increase in this difficulty as it tends to define itself more and more narrowly in terms of diagram and sentimentality. The Beckett I value is the comic artist of *Endgame* and *Happy Days*, the profoundly ambiguous and humorous creator of *Malone Dies* and, his neglected masterpiece, *From an Abandoned Work*. In *Film* and to a less extent in *Eh Joe* there is a regrettable return to the cockiness of youth (of *Proust* and *More Pricks Than Kicks*), an elevation above morality and human value which is objectionable also in Cage and is a blight on all anti-art that does not ironise its own aspirations into comedy. A religion which maintains now, as it did forty years ago, a belief in original sin as 'the sin of having been born'[23] must surely in the human interest be rejected. An art which depends so completely on that religion and which imagines it in such poverty as *Film* can hardly succeed to hold our interest. Beckett's bringing of it into being is a powerful reminder of the limitations placed on his creative genius.

NOTES

1   Samuel Beckett, *Film: Complete Scenario/Illustrations/Production Shots*, Faber & Faber, London, 1972, pp. 58–9. Beckett's scenario and notes, but not Alan Schneider's essay 'On Directing *Film*', are also printed in *Eh Joe and Other Writings*, Faber & Faber, London, 1967. Since the texts are brief, I have considered it unnecessary to give detailed references for quotations from *Film, Eh Joe* or Schneider's essay, which is of course to be found in the separate *Film* volume.

2 John Cage, *Silence*, MIT Press, Cambridge, Mass., 1966, p. 109.
3 Ibid., p. 112.
4 Ibid., p. 113.
5 Ibid., pp. 109, 110.
6 Samuel Beckett, *Murphy*, Ch. 6.
7 Cage, op. cit., pp. 36–7.
8 Ibid., p. 39.
9 Susan Sontag, 'The Aesthetics of Silence', in *Styles of Radical Will* Secker & Warburg, London, 1969, pp. 4–5.
10 Ibid., p. 5.
11 See Richard Coe, *Beckett*, Oliver & Boyd, Edinburgh, 1964, pp. 73–4.
12 J.-P. Sartre, *L'Être et le néant*, Gallimard, Paris, 1957 (1943), p. 255.
13 Samuel Beckett, *Proust* and *Three Dialogues–Beckett and Georges Duthuit* Calder & Boyars, London, 1965 (paperback, 1970), pp. 18–19.
14 Ibid., p. 20.
15 Ibid., pp. 57–8.
16 Ibid., p. 74.
17 Ibid., pp. 69, 75.
18 Ibid., p. 76.
19 Ibid., pp. 101, 125.
20 Ibid., p. 64.
21 Ibid., pp. 92–3.
22 Gallimard, Paris, 1964; translated in Maurice Merleau-Ponty, *The Primacy of Perception*, ed. James M. Edie, Northwestern University Press, Evanston, Ill., 1964, as 'Eye and mind'.
23 *Proust . . .* , p. 67.

Chapter 9

The space and the sound in Beckett's theatre

Katharine Worth

I

A drama of the interior, oblique, dream-like and ethereal, that is also intensely physical, concrete, insistently aware of itself as theatrical process. This paradox is my subject. I want to consider the physicality of Beckett's dramatic technique, his way of handling space and light in the stage plays, sound in the radio plays, so as to draw his audience into a disturbing and releasing experience of inwardness and heightened perception.

The stage plays keep us visually alert, partly by reminding us that we are an audience and should be sharing in the actors' flaunted consciousness that the whole thing is a performance. Reminders vary from cheeky, music-hall comments as they take a look over the auditorium – 'Inspiring prospects', 'I see . . . a multitude . . . in transports . . . of joy' – to a more doubtful and fitful apprehension which can have an odd effect on one's own sense of identity; Hamm brooding 'All kinds of fantasies! That I'm being watched!', Winnie feeling herself 'clear, then dim, then gone, then dim again, then clear again, and so on, back and forth, in and out of someone's eye'. Or the man in *Play* wondering 'Am I as much as . . . being seen?'

Our role, then, is to watch, to keep our eyes on a stage space that is made to work on us with extraordinary precision and force as space. No stage directions can ever have been more spell-bindingly explicit than Beckett's on such matters as the placing of windows or the plotting of lights. He uses stage directions as a sculptor uses tools, to create dynamic relationships between the seen and the unseen areas of the stage, making the unseen a vital element in the dramatic experience. In the later plays, light is his chief tool for creating this sense of double space. In the first two, the off-stage area supplies a strange extension of the visible stage. *Waiting for Godot* and *Endgame* are complementary in this as in so many other ways. We are excited in the one by an entrance, in the other by an exit, that never happens: the ways in and out of the stage assume extraordinary importance. Both had their first performance in proscenium theatres – 'wings' figure in the stage directions of *Waiting for Godot* and *Endgame* still needs a frame to provide the indispensable door and windows. But *Godot* can be played anywhere and retain its special scenic power.

The 'in the round' production it often gets probably best expresses its distinctive quality of frightening openness and emptiness; the stage seems from the start a place people will pass through, not settle down in; featureless except for the moon that rises in the second act and the tree that is such a dubious landmark:

ESTRAGON: . . . You're sure it was here?
VLADIMIR: What?
ESTRAGON: That we were to wait.
VLADIMIR: He said by the tree. (*They look at the tree.*) Do you see any others?

. . . .

ESTRAGON: . . . We came here yesterday.
VLADIMIR: Ah no, there you're mistaken.

. . . .

ESTRAGON: In my opinion we were here.
VLADIMIR: (*looking round.*) You recognise the place?
ESTRAGON: I didn't say that.

The visible bareness already makes a powerful impact, but Beckett increases it by building up the impression of an off-stage area that infinitely extends the bareness and emptiness and multiplies the opportunities for wandering freely that Estragon and Vladimir so terrifyingly have. The off-stage world is kept before our attention by a continuous stream of exits and entrances, from small ones like Vladimir's necessary trips to the spectacular, noisy appearances of Pozzo and Lucky and the quieter, but almost equally troubling, entrance of the Boy, bearing his equivocal message from Godot, towards the close of each act. The characters lead a complete and separate life, it seems, in this off-stage scene; like the actors they are (and are not) they go there to sleep, apart from each other, and Estragon has nightmare experiences, always the same, of being assaulted and beaten in a ditch.

It is a world that seems to change effortlessly according to who goes out into it. Sometimes it has real geographical features – the Mâcon country is out there, and the Pyrenees: 'I've always wanted to wander in the Pyrenees', says Estragon; 'You'll wander in them', Vladimir promises. But it is a fairy-tale place too, where Pozzo might sell Lucky at a fair and afflictions descend with a magical suddenness that makes Estragon's comment on Pozzo's blindness – 'Perhaps he can see into the future' – seem entirely appropriate. It is the fabulous country where Godot can actually be spoken to, and also the humdrum bit of lane that Vladimir has to rush to in order to relieve himself. And through it all, it remains the

186

real off-stage, as we are comically reminded when Estragon directs Vladimir, 'End of the corridor, on the left' and he shouts back, 'Keep my seat.' It's the Void, and there is plenty of it, as Estragon remarks drily. The joke about the off-stage Gents reminds us, in a peculiarly direct way, that the auditorium is part of the Void too; that we, as an audience waiting for entrances on the stage, are exposed to the same threat as the actors, the possibility of a real entrance that will push everything into a new dimension of salvation or damnation, the entrance of Godot. Beckett reveals to us our own feelings about this formidable possibility in a slapstick sequence that beautifully relies on our being sharply aware of the actors as actors, agitated about the someone who is actually there, off-stage, coming closer all the time. Estragon runs on in a panic, shouting 'They're coming!' Vladimir translates this into 'Godot is coming', tries to drag Estragon off-stage to meet him more quickly, shouting 'We're saved!' Estragon resists and runs in terror about the stage trying to get out, while Vladimir comments sardonically. First he tries the other stage exit, comes back still panicking 'We're surrounded!', then the backstage – 'Imbecile! There's no way out there' – then recoils from the prospect of going out over the auditorium – 'Well, I can understand that' – finally takes Vladimir's advice to hide behind the only piece of stage furniture, the tree, and crouches there ridiculously, still very much in view. 'Decidedly this tree will not have been of the slightest use to us', says Vladimir.

It is a good joke, but there is a queer actuality in all this that keeps us wondering. Did Estragon see someone or something coming? When they take up their look-out positions on either side of the stage and peer into the off-stage, there is apparently nothing there and Vladimir suggests that he might have had a vision. But after all, a little later 'someone' does appear, the grotesque combination of blind Pozzo attached to dumb Lucky by the short rope. And the prospect of Godot comes up again in a confused, threatening form. 'Is it Godot?', Estragon keeps asking and Vladimir seems to be saying that it is with his 'At last!', though in fact he is only saying 'Reinforcements at last!', as Estragon finally realises. 'I knew it was him', he says, with child-like triumph when Vladimir identifies 'poor Pozzo'. But we know he didn't, and we are not quite sure about Vladimir either: didn't he think for a moment that Pozzo might be Godot, and aren't we a bit unsure ourselves? Doesn't some of the dark, cruel atmosphere that hangs about Pozzo transfer itself to our idea of Godot and make the prospect of his entrance a more and more alarming one? So it is a relief when the play ends without the entrance being made, a relief with irony in it – we did so nearly expect someone called Godot to erupt from the wings. There is also the quite opposite feeling of disappointment – it is a severe anti-climax, after all. Now it seems he won't come, and Estragon and Vladimir have no more reason to be on this bit of stage than on any other spot in the Void. They are returned to their awful freedom to be anywhere, with no place marked out as home.

The bare, open stage is a powerful image of that sad homelessness. And yet it is because it is so bare, featureless, lacking in homeliness, that we can feel to the full their achievement in making a relationship which is in itself a kind of homely place. They quarrel, get irritable, wonder about separating; as Vladimir says, 'One isn't master of one's moods.' But they have tolerance, understanding, continuing care for each other. They create a domestic ambience, discussing the day's menu – carrots or turnips – pondering a change of boots, Vladimir singing Estragon to sleep, soothing him in his nightmare. Out of the complex of emotions roused by the continuing bareness of the stage without Godot, this sense of their touching achievement prevails. Where they stand together talking on a stage with no chairs, no aids to comfort except a tree and a moon, *that* is home, an oasis of human warmth and closeness in the terrible open spaces of the Void.

There is a bare stage again in *Endgame* and again it has to serve for home, but a grim one this time, the kind that is also a last stop. From this space the off-stage scene has been only too successfully excluded, it might seem. No danger of alarming entrances by person or persons unknown, no chance of entrances at all, nor views of the outside for any of the characters except Clov and he has to climb laboriously on a ladder – oh, the oppressing fatigue of that business in the theatre – and use his telescope to see the scene he reports so dourly and discouragingly to blind Hamm. Hamm and Clov know as well as Estragon and Vladimir did that they are actors in a theatre – 'What is there to keep me here? The dialogue' – but even the auditorium is remote for them: Clov has to look through his telescope to see the 'multitude . . . in transports . . . of joy'. 'That's what I call a magnifier', he says, a wry joke against the audience that effectively brings us into the play and makes us know our distance from it too: this is a world we can't easily get access to.

The visual constriction of the box stage, under the unvarying grey light – a physically depressing condition in itself – is overpoweringly oppressive, the sense of no exit terrifying. The two tiny windows are so high, so almost useless: the one door so narrow. Jack MacGowran playing Clov thought of himself squeezing through it like a rat going into its hole, an idea clearly suggested by the text; there *is* a rat in the kitchen. Beckett calls this door an 'aperture'.

For all but one of the four characters the door does not exist; everything has to happen on the stage and everything does happen there, from Hamm's pee to Nell's dying. No going off-stage to sleep or find another space: they can't even change position unaided in the space they have. But Clov is free. He can go out of the door and this is something he does continually, in and out, sometimes so unnecessarily, forgetting what he went out for in the first place, that he almost seems to be practising going out, as his stiff, staggering walk suggests someone who is just learning to co-ordinate the movements needed for walking. Don't we follow him with our eyes, longing for release from the grey room, follow with the mind's eye as he actually goes through the door that would let us out? And when Hamm has himself wheeled to the windows to feel the sunlight on his blind face, don't we want to wrest it open for him and let in the sun and the great open view of land and sea we know from Clov is out there? It becomes almost intolerable that we can't see through the windows, go out of the door: they have become desperate focal points.

So the off-stage scene has not been excluded after all. Unseeable, except as it is reported by Clov, ungettable at, yet it powerfully exists, a strong magnet, irresistibly drawing one of the characters towards itself.

Irresistibly, one might say, only in the obvious sense that Clov has to keep going through the door, but this doesn't seem to take him very far. The door leads into the kitchen and the kitchen is just another box, ten feet by ten feet; as he smugly remarks: 'Nice dimensions, nice proportions.' And he hardly moves in it: when Hamm asks him how he spends his time there he says that he watches the wall; and sees his light dying.

Constriction, dying light; the off-stage doesn't seem a very lively extension of the visible stage. And yet it is livelier in a way, as we get comical reminders: there's a flea hopping about, for instance, and a rat that seems to hang on to the raw, natural life it has: that seems the implication in Clov's funny, cryptic line: 'If I don't kill that rat he'll die.'

But what of the world outside the windows, what would Clov be committed to if he were able to make that bigger exit that he finally appears dressed for, so jauntily and incongruously, in his panama hat, tweed coat and umbrella, ready for all weathers?

Critics have on the whole stressed the deathliness of the imagined scene, favoured Clov's word for it – Corpsed. It is the universe after some cataclysm, a Hiroshima, a Deluge, which has left the appropriately named Hamm lord of the ark of survivors, with his human family and a selection of animals, though only one of each, to indicate that this Deluge myth is a dark variation on the biblical one, with the possibility of replenishing the earth cut out. And of course it is the astonishing achievement of *Endgame* to give us while in the flesh so full an experience of what it might be to die. We do go into a world of last things, where life and vigour are being slowly and painfully extinguished: we suffer the end of action, the end of sight and the power to move one's limbs, of hearing, of sexual love: there is a real death in the play and mourning; Nagg crying in his dustbin while Nell quietly dies in hers; one of the most touching death scenes on any stage. Perhaps if the off-stage scene could be exposed, we would indeed see, as John Fletcher says, that 'One window looks out on a dead plain, the other on a becalmed sea.'[1]

But in that ritualistic separation of the windows, the earth window and the sea, a more potent suggestion comes through. The sense of genesis gets strongly into the play: the echo of that voice we all know from childhood, sounding out of the Book of Genesis, calling the dry land earth and the gathering together of the waters, seas, and finding creation good. The echo merges with the echoes of Noah and reinforces them: not just from the part of the myth that deals with Deluge as destruction but the other part, the climax, the ending which is also a beginning, everything starting again, all freshly washed by the waters that poured out, as the Authorised Version has it, from the windows of heaven. Perhaps the stillness outside that Clov describes hasn't after all to be seen in his terms – of leaden waves and nothingness – but as the hushed expectancy of a universe waiting for creation, for the breaking of the waters.

This seems to be what Hamm and Clov in their strange way are waiting for. Hamm is irked by the dryness: he keeps Clov on the move, looking out for change:

HAMM: Have you looked?
CLOV: Yes.
HAMM: Well?
CLOV: Zero.
HAMM: It'd need to rain.
CLOV: It won't rain.

Clov is relieved: it is his relief at finding no change that the play opens with: the long-drawn-out business with the ladders; his laugh as he studies the prospect. Later he gets a comical shock – 'Christ, she's under water!' – when he looks out of the wrong window and sees a flooded earth. But – 'It'd need to rain.' The sense of the need for water is strongly there, along with Hamm's craving for a green world and tides. 'If I could drag myself down to the sea!', he meditates, 'I'd make a pillow of sand for my head and the tide would come'; he wonders whether there is still green beyond the hills, invokes Flora, Pomona, Ceres. Of course his literary flights are always suspect, but these are backed up by the journeys he makes so laboriously to the windows, Clov pushing, to feel the sun and sea. Again we have a joke about the wrong window – there's no light on earth – and of course he wouldn't hear the sea, Clov tells him, even if he were to open the window; nothing happens at the sea window either. But in this context, the very notion of the window being opened is exciting: a breath of far-off air seems to draw nearer. The comic business with the windows, the talk of earth and sea, Hamm's dreams of Flora and Ceres, have the effect of bringing the idea of sun, rain, sea into the room and making them seem infinitely desirable. This is an effect to do with life, not death. Clov may resist the idea, pour cold water on Hamm's fantasies, but by the end of the play we've come to recognise that Clov's pessimism is his instinctive reaction to Hamm's masterful and often cruel ebullience. He enjoys saying 'No more': no more pain-killer, no more sugar plums, no more tide, though he goes too far when he says 'No more nature'. As Hamm observes dryly, 'You exaggerate.' 'In the vicinity', Clov adds, and we laugh, but the laugh is against him this time. Even in the vicinity nature is irrepressible: the flea is caught but the rat gets away: Nell dies but outside the 'muck-heap' window at the very end a small boy appears. Clov rather horribly picks up the gaff and offers to go after him, but even if Hamm didn't dissuade him, wouldn't he miss the boy as he did the rat? He may dread life but he has to play Hamm's game, climb ladders to look out of windows, study the earth to see if the waters have broken.

The 'something' that is taking its course in *Endgame* begins to look like a movement towards birth as well as a kind of death; a difficult act of generation. The generations are very much there in the room: old Nag, the 'accursed progenitor', Hamm, who says. 'I'll have called my father and I'll have called my . . . (*he hesitates*) . . . son,' Clov, who may be the son. And outside a small boy. coming late into the play to suggest young life continuing.

In an earlier draft of *Endgame* Beckett pointed up this theme of generation by the grotesquely farcical device of having Clov appear in the disguise first of a woman and then of a boy. He has also recorded[2] – remarkably – his imaginings of life in the womb:

Even before the fetus can draw breath it is in a state of barrenness and of pain. I have a clear memory of my own fetal existence. It was an existence where no voice, no possible movement could free me from the agony and darkness I was subjected to.

These are hints towards the kind of interpretation I have been suggesting, but we don't need to have that kind of evidence to feel in *Endgame*, very largely through the great impact of the setting, a struggle into life that is somehow bound up with dying, with the presence of the old parents inside and the boy outside, with all the business of looking out of the windows for signs of water and the dread of it, with the slow compulsion towards the narrow door.

The peculiar grey light of *Endgame* is one important means for giving the stage space its distinctive, between-worlds quality. In the plays that follow, light takes on a more active and dominant, not to say domineering role.

A consistent pattern of symbols can be sensed behind these physical patterns of light and dark. Just how fully thought out it is, James Knowlson has indicated in his interesting short study of Beckett's light symbolism.[3] He reproduces some jottings from Beckett's notebook for the German production of *Krapp's Last Tape*, including lists of light and darkness emblems which give the impression of a whole system in the background, though the style of the emblems doesn't suggest a rigid notation but rather a free and fluid play of images which keep a flavour of variegated nature about them. Light emblems include agreeables like mild zephyr and clear water and also quickening fire, which could be more equivocal, as it is in *Happy Days*: darkness emblems disconcertingly include sirocco as well as the more to be expected mist and vapour. There is a reassuring particularity in this, a sense of both overlap and contrast, which softens the schematic effect and suggests that light symbolism might function in the plays, as indeed I think it does, in a natural, undogmatic way that allows for lifelike inconsistency and variety both within individual plays and from one play to another.

There are also some more knotty and crabbed comments, when Beckett starts to talk like one of his own theologically minded critics. Krapp giving the black ball to the white dog might represent the sacrifice of sense to spirit, he notes, and this somehow connects with the abstruse relationship the character is said to have with the light over his table: '. . . Krapp decrees physical (ethical) incompatibility of light (spiritual) and dark (sensual) only when he intuits possibility of their reconciliation intellectually as rational-irrational.'

For those who really do feel something like this going on in the play, it has no doubt gained an extra dimension but it seems safe to assume that there will not be many to do so. It would certainly be hard to guess from the tone of the exegesis that the play would be such a comic and touching piece, that the dry bones of the symbolism could be so triumphantly converted to living flesh. Traces of the bones do show in it, as in other plays, especially *Endgame*, which has its own dog, also heavily loaded with colour symbolism. Dogs seem to bring out the pedant in Beckett, though certainly the black dog in *Endgame* just about earns its passage by prompting some nice jokes between Hamm and Clov, as when Hamm's obsession about whiteness – 'He's white, isn't he?' – is neatly dissolved by Clov's dead-pan 'Nearly'.

But the times when we feel in uneasy need of a key to understand what is going on are very few. As for a key capable of opening up all doors, that would be a hard idea to entertain, when the plays in performance make such a stunning effect of individuality and newness. The same sparse elements recur – space and light, heads and voices – and each time something totally unexpected springs from them; a changed mood, a harsher or softer tone, a new slant. In *Krapp's Last Tape* the light does, I think, come in the end to suggest a kind of spirituality, but we don't need to travel by the thorny route suggested in the note to arrive at that view.

The play offers an instant image of double space, a stage startlingly divided; most of it in darkness, only round Krapp's writing table a powerful light. Perhaps the first impression is one of loneliness. A whole stage blacked out, its possibilities unused, the action shrunk to the table with the strong white light over it that pleased the Krapp of thirty years before so greatly:

> The new light above my table is a great improvement. With all this darkness round me I feel less alone. (*Pause.*) In a way. (*Pause.*) I love to get up and move about in it, then back here to . . . (*hesitates*) . . . me. (*Pause.*) Krapp.

Ironic and sad lines heard now, with the old man still alone; making no more use of all that stage than to shuffle across to restock himself with drinks and tape and so back to the table.

193

There is also something ludicrous and repellent about his total self-absorption, as Beckett suggests by making him a bit of a clown, with white face and purple nose, given to antics like slipping on a banana skin and looking up words in a huge, pantomime-style dictionary. At such moments the ring of light is a minuscule circus, with the performer who is also a writer going through his tricks and making wry jokes against himself. His last book sold seventeen copies, eleven at trade price; 'Getting known' he says comically. We laugh, but he doesn't show any signs of hearing: the joke falls into the darkness that cuts him off so effectively from all kinds of company except his own voice, so pompously and meticulously recorded on the tapes.

So he is lonely, aging, pathetic and absurd. But the patterning of light and dark allows for other effects which subtly modify these first strong impressions. There are those repeated journeys across the unlit stage into the darker shadows at the back; they build up a sense of weary effort, slow and laborious, as in the business of peering at the spools with his short-sighted eyes, to get the right tape on, make the 'sifting' process work. In the German production which Beckett himself directed, Martin Held most movingly suggested a kind of virtue, even heroism, in this patient toil. Something was being retrieved for us from the dark, obscure area of the stage where Krapp's life goes on beyond the range of our sight (we can only hear the plop of cork in bottle) and brought into the lighted circle of his consciousness to be registered fully.

He brings himself into the light too in this other sense. As he sits there obsessively playing back his younger voice we can see that in some ways he hasn't changed; that it isn't meaningless to speak of 'me . . . Krapp'. Old and middle-aged Krapp laugh at the same jokes, especially the bitter joke of hearing still earlier Krapp record his youthful aspirations: old Krapp can go one better here and laugh where his middle-aged self doesn't at all those good resolutions to drink less. He still loves words – 'Spooool! Happiest moment of the past half million' – though it appears that his memory for them has slipped when he has to look in the dictionary for 'viduity', a word used so confidently by his earlier self; one of the sadder changes time has brought about in him, it seems, along with the general deterioration of his sensuous life; the minimal sex, the 'sour cud and the iron stool'.

But there have been changes that are not so depressing, that do seem like a move into the light. And after all we can't be so sure about the failing memory for words: maybe the younger Krapp looked up 'viduity' especially to make a good impression on tape:

it's the kind of thing he might do, to judge from the pompous, pedantic style that old Krapp has come to detest, switching off whenever the tape begins to declaim in a lofty, generalising way about beliefs, spiritual realities and so forth. We're really bound to agree, to be glad for him that he has been able to shed that windbag; the sequence he has come to prefer must surely strike us too as infinitely preferable; an afternoon with a girl in a punt, a sensuous consummation that broke the bonds of self; an ecstasy: 'We lay there without moving. But under us all moved, and moved us, gently, up and down, and from side to side.'

And smaller, trivial things flood back with that memory and are also seen anew, seen with such intensity that life begins to appear infinitely worth living, whatever its hazards and miseries, even the miseries of old age:

> Be again in the dingle on a Christmas Eve, gathering holly, the
> red berried. . . . Be again on Croghan on a Sunday
> morning, in the haze, with the bitch, stop and listen to the
> bells. (*Pause.*) And so on. (*Pause.*) Be again, be again.
> (*Pause.*) All that old misery. (*Pause*). Once wasn't enough
> for you. (*Pause.*) Lie down across her. (*Long pause.*)

The play ends with the tape recorder running on past the idyll in the punt into the sequence where the Krapp who rejected that love argues against the doubt he felt even then: 'Perhaps my best years are gone. When there was a chance of happiness. But I wouldn't want them back. Not with the fire in me now. No, I wouldn't want them back.' And old Krapp lets it run, staring in front of him, thinking thoughts we can guess from that last tape, a pathetic figure in the lighted ring of memory, 'eaten up by dreams', as Beckett says. But the pathos is only part of the effect; the sentimentality that might have threatened, especially when the defensive burlesque elements have faded out, is never really a danger. The light has by the end acquired positive values that take us well beyond nostalgia: the table has become the place where a great reorganisation of memory has been achieved and understanding enlarged, ours of Krapp and Krapp's of himself. The precious moments of his life float up from the darkness that hid them when they were happening and they can be experienced not as a tired memory but as if for the first time; fresh, new, living with an intenser life.

The sense of an undifferentiated, unsifted darkness all around is obviously very important for this complex final effect. When the play was televised a vital element went out of it (even though Patrick Magee, the original Krapp, was playing with his usual fine sensitivity). There was no off-stage, could hardly be: inevitably when the camera followed Krapp on his journeys it created a significant area, a dark meaningful tunnel; it was no longer the half-unused and unseen, unappreciated stage, out of which Krapp has laboriously wrested light and meaning.

The staginess of Beckett's technique is uncannily absolute, defying translation to another medium. So it is again in *Happy Days* and *Play*; space and light are fearfully present in these plays; pressurising the characters, refusing to be ignored, as we do normally ignore them once we have taken in the scene of the play.

It might be easier to miss the full force of the light in *Happy Days*: unless it is accentuated in production, as Beckett requires, it could seem no more than an ordinary, if very bright, full stage lighting. Of course we couldn't miss the heat effects in the scene, the scorched grass in front of Winnie's mound, the parasol that catches fire, nor the continual allusions to light and heat; Winnie wondering if she will end up charred to a cinder, advising Willie to slip his drawers on before he gets singed, starting her day with an invocation that is like a parody – 'Hail, holy light'.

But that isn't quite the same as being exposed ourselves to uncomfortable physical pressure from the light and the whole scene, as we so firmly are, for instance, in *Play*.

A visually bold production is needed to realise Beckett's directions and hints and make us feel the 'blazing light' as the 'hellish blaze' it is for Winnie. We need also to have our attention drawn (productions I have seen seldom do this) to the strange backcloth he calls for – 'Very pompier trompe-l'œil backcloth to represent unbroken plain and sky receding to meet in far distance'. This backcloth does what none of the earlier plays had done, rules out the idea of change and chance, obliterates the off-stage: no unseen unpredictable vast here, no unrecorded vital darkness as in *Krapp's Last Tape*. No possibility of darkness at all: Winnie's times of sleep – rationed by the inexorable bell – have all to be taken under the scorching glare. There are no breaks in the dry plain, the red desert where everything seems to be drying up especially the sexual life that has been so central in her imaginings.

For some critics, her insistence on making the best of all this is a sign of stupidity, a wilful refusal to face facts and recognise the horror of her situation. But the horror surely lies in her being prevented from doing anything but look at the scene around her, the harsh facts about her own physical deterioration and Willie's comic, appalling inadequacies as her one faithful follower and listener.

She sees Willie with awful accuracy, directing his smallest movement, helping him into his hole like a bossy nanny: 'Not head first, I tell you! (*Pause.*) More to the right. (*Pause.*) The *right*, I said. (*Pause. Irritated.*) Keep your tail down, can't you.' And she applies the same merciless scrutiny to herself. Characteristically the play opens with her dispassionately studying her teeth in the mirror:

> (*Testing upper front teeth with thumb, indistinctly*) Good Lord!
> (*pulling back upper lip to inspect gums, do.*) good God! –
> (*pulling back corner of mouth, mouth open, do.*) – ah well –
> (*other corner, do.*) – no worse (*abandons inspection, normal speech*) – no better, no worse – (*lays down mirror*) – no change – (*wipes fingers on grass*) – no pain – (*looks for toothbrush*) – hardly any. . . .

That 'hardly any' is a measure of her accuracy as a self-scrutiniser. And she can also see herself as others might see her. In each act she conjures up for us observers to whom she is no more than a curious object; Mr and Mrs Shower or Cooker – sinister names in this fiery context – who gape and wonder and size up her physical qualities – 'Can't have been a bad bosom, he says, in its day. (*Pause.*) Seen worse shoulders, he says, in my time. (*Pause.*) Does she feel her legs? he says.'

So she does see it how it is. And yet she is determined to see it how it never was and perhaps never could be: in the teeth of her handicaps, she continues to create her other world around her, her musical comedy world of perpetual romance where she is the merry widow and Willie a phlegmatic Count Danilo, hardly likely to be converted by the end of the play, as his prototype was, to the Merry Widow vision of sex as a thing of passion, faithful love, undying flames. A ridiculous vision, it looks, in a way: the middle-aged woman in low bodice and pearl necklace immured to the waist and then the neck, with only poor old Willie, squinting at his pornographic postcards, for partner. And yet still she demands romance, holding a musical box to her bodice-clad bosom and swaying – as best she can – to the music of the Merry Widow waltz.

We must laugh at the absurdity, though surely without contempt; it would mean contempt for a rather large percentage of the human race, after all; Beckett's choice of *The Merry Widow*, one of the most popular of all musical comedies, as the model for

Winnie's dream, suggests rather that he is hinting at the universa-
lity of this kind of dreaming. A similar suggestion is made, it seems
to me, in the stage direction, 'very pompier trompe-l'œil', where
'pompier' indicates just that kind of mixture of highly coloured
and highly conventional that could appeal to large numbers of
people besides women like Winnie.

Still, the dream is full of absurdity, and it has disagreeable, even
repellent aspects too. It is so very self-centred; hard luck for
Willie, one feels, to have to play audience to all those little scenes
where the spotlight falls on Winnie being courted and adored by
other men. He can hardly read a snippet from the newspaper he so
understandably buries himself in without having it snatched up and
converted to fodder for romance. 'His Grace and Most Reverend
Father in God Dr Carolus Hunter dead in tub', he quotes, and
instantly Winnie is back in the past, sitting on Charlie Hunter's
knees 'under the horse-beech . . . the happy memories!'

The dream can make her tart, even cruel, to Willie who falls so
very far short of it. When he makes his enormous effort at the end
and comes crawling on all fours towards her, resplendent in top
hat and tails, he is received with mockery:

> Well this is an unexpected pleasure! (*Pause.*) Reminds me of
> the day you came whining for my hand. (*Pause.*) I worship
> you, Winnie, be mine. . . . What a get up, you do look a sight.

There seems to be a touch of fear in this response. 'Don't look
at me like that', she says, when he lifts his face to hers: at the very
end her smile goes out as he gazes at her. She wanted him to look
at her once, but now there is so little for him to feast his eyes on;
and then, there is something rather alarming, primitive and
earthy as well as comically matter-of-fact, about Willie; he crawls
out of his hole for the last time, as the ambiguous stage direction
tells us, 'dressed to kill'. But there is elation too in this extraordinarily complex ending: it's now that she sings the words of the
Merry Widow waltz, ending with 'You love me so!'

In fact, Winnie's dream has been made to show many facets by
the time we reach the enigmatic climax, with the two looking
silently at each other, Willie on all fours, she a head in the ground.
It has been turned round and round, 'shown', as Winnie has been
shown, under that hard light that refuses concealment and makes
the accessories of the dream, the lipstick, the mirror, the Merry
Widow hat and parasol look such puny and pathetic objects. 'No
damask', she says, squinting down at her cheek when she has

lost the use of her hands, and leaving us, as her habit is, to finish the quotation: 'She never told her love, But let concealment like a worm i' the bud, Feed on her damask cheek.'

The unfinished quotation is full of irony; part comical – 'she never told her love' must be a joke against someone who never does anything else – and part bitter. Concealment, romantic privacy, are no longer possible for Winnie: it is only Willie who can still creep into the shade, as she warns him to: 'Go back into your hole now, Willie, you've exposed yourself enough.'

The sexual pun is a reminder that Winnie has one foot in Willie's world: she enjoys being shocked by his smutty postcards and she can be tolerant of his nastier habits, like eating his own snot. But she isn't satisfied with that reality. Against all the odds, she insists on asserting the superior reality of her inner world. Is the harsh light revealing only how meretricious that world is and forcing her to see it? Perhaps, but that isn't quite how it comes over. Her imaginative vitality, for all its absurd, self-regarding side, is impressive, heroic in the circumstances; one has the impression that Willie would have petered out long before if she hadn't been there to stimulate and goad him. Her mind may be a ragbag, her taste questionable and her grasp on her favourite poets not very firm – 'What is that unforgettable line?' – but still, poetry exists for her; Shakespeare, Keats, Milton reverberate in her mind: she has air and fire in her despite the heavy earth that is closing round her and getting tighter all the time.

Finally, I think, it seems more impressive than absurd that she continues to defy the light and hold on to her strange ragbag of dreams, re-creating her parasol after it has been set on fire, bringing Willie out of his hole in his wedding clothes by the force of her longing for that imagined delight. In the final scene, the light has in a way triumphed: she is utterly helpless and exposed – no lipstick, no concealing hat, pretensions stripped away, and we feel the terror of this as she does – 'Don't look at me like that'. But there is all that power in her too, the power that has preserved an image of Willie and herself as golden lovers, in a world of beechen green and shadow numberless. She has Charlie not Willie in mind, as it happens, when she slips into her quotation from *Ode to a Nightin-gale*: 'Ah yes . . . then . . . now . . . beechen green . . . this . . . Charlie . . . kisses . . . this . . . all that . . . deep trouble for the mind.' But the associations evoked by 'beechen green' go far beyond the specific memory of Charlie's kisses: it is a richer context for herself and Willie that she creates with her laconic allusion to the Keatsian vision of delight and transience:

> That thou, light-wingèd Dryad of the trees,
> In some melodious plot
> Of beechen green, and shadows numberless,
> Singest of summer in full-throated ease.

Their summer has shrivelled up, lost its romantic shadow, and yet the full-throated song persists. When the play ends with Winnie singing and Willie crawling to her, another Keatsian ode swims into mind: like those figures on the Grecian urn they are fixed, it seems, in their feeling for each other. 'For ever wilt thou love, and she be fair!' Grotesque realisation of that dream, and yet how touching that it should survive at all under the pitiless light: that Willie should get into his top hat and try, so ludicrously and poignantly, to be again for her what he was; and that she should want him to.

In *Happy Days* the horror of the light is its sameness. In *Play* it is, rather, the inexorable movement as the spotlight travels round the heads in their urns, plucking them out of darkness and returning them to it in a cycle that threatens to recur indefinitely. What might be the purpose of these alternations of light and darkness is the burning question for both the audience and the victims.

The two separate phases of the action are strongly marked off from each other by a change in the characters' relationship with the light. In the first they seem unconscious of it: they go through their 'play', the tale of their adultery, unaware that the spotlight is actually arranging the pattern of the narrative, cutting them off in mid-phrase to allow someone else in, juxtaposing lines to get suggestive effects that highlight their contractions and evasions.

'So I told her I did not know what she was talking about', says M, and the spot switches wickedly to W2 face to face with W1 and brazenly echoing his denial of their liaison: 'What are you talking about? I said, stitching away.'

The spot is making the play, in fact, out of the individual narratives; it has to, because the characters themselves are almost totally incapable of seeing beyond their own parts. They are narrow parts, aptly represented by the abbreviations which are their only names in the text: M, W1, W2; as in a French's catalogue which codes plays for amateurs according to the number of their male and female roles. 1M. 2F – that is their plot in a nutshell: it is also the way they have chosen to think and feel about themselves. 'What a male!', W1 says, complacent even when she is tormenting herself with thoughts of M's infidelity. 'And of course with him no danger of the . . . spiritual thing', W2 reflects. Both women accept and admire the sexual voracity which so comically turns out, in the second phase, to have given him permanent hiccups.

The three characters are all rather brilliant narrators. They make us see their play as vividly as if they were going through it in the flesh, reclining in morning-rooms and drawing-rooms and doing their nails by open windows instead of being as they are stuck in their urns. It's not one play we see, however, but three; the different versions of a common plot that the spotlight/director gets them to perform: each in turn is drawn into the light to present the story of their adultery; they half report, half act it out, mimicking, quoting, giving us bits of dialogue with appropriate changes of voice and style. Through this strange mishmash of narrative and dialogue, the 'play' comes over as an event that has trapped them in a mesh of lies and deceit, the deceit they have practised on each other and the self-deceit that allows each one to place him or herself so hard and square on the centre of the stage as the charac-ter deserving all the sympathy. The spot has great fun pointing up the phoniness of their 'memories'. Its quick switches from one to another make the style veer hilariously from the super-genteel pseudo-literary they like to think of as their own to something much slangier, tarter and very funny which they are all at home in though they tend not to acknowledge it: 'Judge then of my astoundment when one fine morning, as I was sitting stricken in the morning room, he slunk in, fell on his knees before me, buried his face in my lap and . . . confessed.'

So W1 as she hears herself. She comes over very differently through the medium of W2: 'I smell you off him, she screamed, he stinks of bitch.' Not just a rival's invention, this: it's the tone she falls into when she stops presenting herself and instead lets her feelings rip: 'Pudding face, puffy, spots, blubber mouth, jowls, no neck, dugs you could. . . .'

Comical shifts of tone and style but disturbing too: so much dishonesty in the affected tones, the false pity of W2's 'Poor thing', for instance, and such venom and hatred in the coarse vigour of the natural speech.

There are some faint movements towards honesty and natural-ness of a less savagely egotistical kind, especially in the man. He does stop occasionally to question how much truth there is in his non-stop performance: 'So I took her in my arms and said I could not go on living without her. I don't believe I could have.' But his emotional confusion is so deep, the woman's egotism so unyielding, that it's hard to imagine them ever breaking out of their impasse, clearing their minds and coming to a state of better feeling.

And then comes the 'change'. 'Finally it was all too much.' As they all in their different ways reach this point of breakdown, the light snaps out and after a five-second blackout, three half-strength spots come on simultaneously. These changes of light have been much reworked by Beckett: the French text offers an alternative method of handling the spot based on experience from the English performance, and as R. L. Admussen points out in an article on the early drafts[4] it was quite late in the evolution of the text before the notion of the single spotlight, the 'unique inquisitor' was conceived.

In a situation as concentrated as this, even the finest change in the lighting is crucial, so responses must inevitably vary according to the productions one has seen. In my own experience it seemed that a totally new situation was created when the single inquisitory light went out, and after a moment of darkness the characters all became visible at the same time under the equal light of separate spots, were heard speaking all at once and in lower tones; it was as though we were getting down to a deeper level where the possibility of true communication might begin to exist. Momentarily the fearful isolation and separation was relieved. Relief is certainly an element in the characters' responses to this new situation, though at the start of it they are a long way from knowing what they have to be relieved about. 'When first this change I actually thanked God. I thought, It is done, it is said, now all is going out –' The man says this with the terrible single spot back on him, so we know how far he is from 'going out' in the sense of being spared the light. The kind of relief he is being offered is harder to come by: it seems to depend on the characters' *not* sinking into darkness.

To know, as they now do, that the light is on them is an intensely painful experience and yet we can see for ourselves that it has already been a salutary one. They have been prised out of those self-centred narratives, where they fancied themselves in complete control – even over other people's lines – into something much closer to being real dialogue. The being at the other end doesn't seem to reply but the sense of someone listening gets strongly into the play through the break with narrative and the move to a powerfully direct mode; spasmodic, agitated questions, appeals, confessional gasps. The impression builds up of a living, personal relationship which they try hopelessly to refuse – 'Get off me', 'Go away and start poking and pecking at someone else' – but their brilliant ruthless director has moved on from plot to work on character: he sees what the actors need to do to get it right but won't supply answers: they have to be needled into doing that for themselves.

The method works. They begin to worry about the false notes in the parts as they have been playing them so far, struggle to imagine what is required of them:

Is it something I should do with my face other than utter? Weep?

Is it that I do not tell the truth, is that it, that some-day somehow I may tell the truth at last and then no more light at last, for the truth?

Looking for some-thing. In my face. Some truth. In my eyes. Not even.

This 'not even' points to a nightmare possibility which the man especially is bothered by. The director is not really directing: the light is: 'Mere eye. No mind. Opening and shutting on me.'

That would be a nightmare for the audience as well as the actors. But our experience of the play tells us that this isn't how it is. The actors, after all, know less than we do about the light. While they were still oblivious, we were aware of it, arranging, cutting, piecing together their plot; it is easier for us to see it still at work making a new pattern, highlighting phrases, returning insistently to key motifs.

What is the nature of the pattern that forms out of the fragments of the discarded plot? The characters are inclined to see it as a pattern of judgment and punishment: 'Bite off my tongue and swallow it? Spit it out? Would that placate you? How the mind works still to be sure!'

They think of the spotlight as a judge weighing them in the balance and finding them wanting: 'What do you do when you go out? Sift?' 'You might get angry and blaze me clean out of my wits. Mightn't you?' And this is often how the play is taken in by its critics.

But is it all pain and punishment? The ordeal is intense but I think we must feel too that there is something good in it. New, softer notes have crept into the style. The man muses, for instance, wondering if the women ever meet 'and sit, over a cup of that green tea they both so loved, without milk or sugar, not even a squeeze of lemon'. A gentle image this, that would have seemed absurdly ill at ease in the hard, deceptive flow of the first narrative. 'We were not civilised', he reflects and suddenly we realise how far they have travelled already from the coarse, unkind passions of their sexual bondage. For the very first time we hear love spoken of as pleasure: the possibility of sympathetic human relationships opens up as the sexual cacophony dims and we get snatches of purer, tenderer sound. The man dreams of taking out a little dinghy on a May morning, 'the first to wake to wake the other two' and we may feel with shock that perhaps this was always the vision behind the insatiable sexual appetite that has landed him with his comic hiccups and made the women so confident that with him there was 'no danger of the . . . spiritual thing'.

When lines from the old plot drift in now, as they still do, they are incongruous: 'She had means, I fancy, though she lived like a pig.' The light isn't interested: it dowses itself when the characters seem to be getting stuck in those tired old phrases. When it recalls them from darkness they have moved further away from the first script. The dream of the May morning emerges, the movements of sympathy get a little stronger, the phrases once used so virulently begin to hang in the air like a dirge for them all; 'Pity them', 'Poor creature. Poor creatures'. In those simple shifts from singular to plural – something it takes a Beckettian structure to realise with dramatic force – the great process of change that has already taken place is movingly suggested.

But is this promise of hopeful change undermined or even entirely negated by the play's structure, that awesome repetition, line for line, of the whole action, and the suggestion made by the closing sequence, that if it were to be played through again it would be exactly the same and so on for ever and ever? Human beings turned into tape recorders – a vision of hell more ghastly than Sartre's *Huis-clos* with which *Play* is sometimes compared. The comparison with *Huis-clos*, however, points up just those aspects of *Play* which make it seem less like hell than purgatory. To my mind, the hope of change or salvation survives the threat of damnation made by that repetitive structure. The dizzying sensation of a process gathering momentum for a third time round is sombre and terrible but powerfully stimulating too; the repetition could seem an element in a process of regeneration, a process that is infinitely slow and painful but is already well advanced: in the next cycle, if we could see it, there might be a tiny modification, another shift from singular to plural, perhaps, or a delicate change of vocabulary, which would be the beginning of yet another phase in the difficult development of the three damaged beings.

Change is, after all, what we experience in an extraordinarily physical way through the impact of the setting: those spectacular changes from darkness to light and back again which we learn to associate with the subtle changes of tone, mood and style that tell of the great moral development the characters undergo. In the short space of time that *Play* takes to perform, they have moved from falsity, discord and hatred to honesty, sad reflectiveness, fuller sympathy; a change of the same order as the reconciliations of Shakespearian tragedy.

In a way the fear is not so much that they will have to go on but that they will not be able to, may break in the process. 'And what of the terrified spirit/Compelled to be reborn?' *Play* might almost have been written out of those lines of Eliot's. Can these characters survive their painful reshaping? The play ends not in the light but with their being returned to darkness. This is what they have been longing for, the old dark state, when they were untormented by the light of consciousness; the sensual dark, the dark of sleep and rest; even the dark of mindlessness is contemplated as preferable to the light. And yet at the same time they know the light is better. 'Dying for dark—and the darker the worse. Strange.'

Finally, it seems to me, one may even begin to hope that the light hasn't given them up, to wish for their ordeal to be renewed, as it will be, the next evening when the spotlight wakes them up again. Even though we have been left grimly fixed at this stage of the ordeal, between the threat of extinction and the threat of hell, the changes the light has already brought about are an intimation that heaven might exist too. In such a context that is a moving revelation.

There seems no end to the variations Beckett can play on the themes of space and light. Even a slight work like *Come and Go* offers a totally new arrangement. There are affinities with *Krapp's Last Tape*, but here the ring of light is a soft and kindly thing: it holds the three women together and somehow upholds them. When each in turn goes out into the dark, the other two discuss with pity and horror the fate that threatens the absent one, but neither she nor we are allowed to know it: within the circle of light none of them is concerned with her own troubles, only with thoughts and memories of each other, sitting with clasped hands 'as in the old days', feeling invisible rings, seeming indissolubly joined in the gentle radiance of memory.

The leap from this fragile piece in minor key to the powerful *Not I* is a measure of Beckett's staggering variety and resourcefulness. One might have thought after *Play* that no shock of equal power could be generated from those same limited materials: dark, light and speaking, heads. But it happens in *Not I*. Perhaps, even, the visual shock is more drastic: that fluorescent mouth, writhing high up in the darkness of the stage and emitting its stream of disordered sound, the faintly lit figure opposite, also raised above ground level, in its loose black djellaba that conceals sex, age, all marks of personal distinction.

The loss of gravity, the asymmetry are deeply disturbing. Where are those beings, what kind of connection is there between them? In wrestling with these questions, as we are forced to by an arrangement that keeps us looking across the stage at an awkward angle from the mouth without a body to the body apparently without a mouth, we are drawn pretty far into the terrible experience of dissociation Mouth tells of: how at seventy, strangely wandering in a field picking cowslips, she suddenly found herself

> in the . . . what? . . . who? . . . no! . . . she! . . . (*pause and movement*) . . . found herself in the dark. . . .
> she did not know . . . what position she was in . . . imagine!
> . . . what position she was in! . . . whether standing . . . or sitting . . . but the brain . . .what? . . . kneeling? . . . yes . . . whether standing . . . or sitting . . . or kneeling. . . .

The stream of sound pours on and as we start to pick out recurring phrases – 'no love,' 'no love of any kind' – a deeper dissociation reveals itself, till when she gives the last of her terrible shrieks ' – who? . . . no! . . . she! . . .' – that odd, cryptic spatial relationship between babbling Mouth and silent Auditor has become a meaningful thing, a mute expression of a divided state of being, a fragmentation that Mouth is struggling to understand and the Auditor to help her understand, or so it might seem from the absolute attention he is giving her. She can only gasp out the scattered elements of her experience, so, like her, we have to grope our way to a full view. She remains divided to the end, fixed in her 'vehement refusal to relinquish third person', and we are left with a great range of choices for our own interpretation. We may take it as an experience of dying, of death, of schizophrenia or some other mental purgatory; see the Auditor as priest, psychiatrist, friendly mentor; probably we hardly feel able to distinguish among these or like views.

However we read it, it is a story to rouse pity and terror; an account of massive deprivation; premature baby and abandoned child growing up in a world that gives her no affection, only judgment – 'no love of any kind'; 'stand up woman, speak up woman'. An experience of seemingly total alienation, which the Auditor is apparently unable to relieve: when he reacts to her shrieks of 'who? . . . no! . . . she!' by raising and dropping his arms to his sides, the gesture expresses 'helpless compassion'.

Is this, then uniquely for Beckett, a vision of absolute despair? Certainly it is an especially harrowing play, and perhaps it is harder to identify the sources of solace. Yet it seems to me they exist and that in the spatial arrangement alone, there are delicate intimations that some benevolent force might be guiding and controlling the seemingly uncontrollable event, giving Mouth those glimpses of a paradisal state which she begins and ends with: 'God is love . . . tender mercies . . . new every morning . . . back in the field . . . April morning . . . face in the grass . . . nothing but the larks . . . pick it up.'

If she could pick this up and keep it, shut out all the rest, including the mockery that her experience seems to have made of 'God is love', that would be heaven. The struggle to do it is agonising, but it is being made, and the presence of that attentive listener suggests, perhaps, that she is nearer it now than she has ever been in her poor starved life. Someone is listening, that is a start, and although she is so fixed in her defensive third person, there is also a sense of enormous potential freedom in the play: both beings are free-floating, released from matter: they have terrifying freedom to create their own dimension. Seen from this viewpoint, the Auditor standing so high and still has something angelic, Dantesque about him; a Virgilian guide, he seems, waiting for the moment when the struggling spirit is free to follow him. If *Waiting for Godot* and *Endgame* are plays of earth and water and *Happy Days* is fire, then *Not I* is the play of air. It is the furthest Beckett has yet gone – but who knows how far he could go? – in drawing power and meaning from the empty spaces of the stage.

II

In the plays written for the air, this airy dimension might be thought harder to come by: no chance for total silence here; no hidden areas of darkness in a medium where all is dark; no off-stage to suggest mysterious continuance. But as always Beckett turns restrictions to advantage. The impossibility of silence becomes a dynamic condition of the action: Henry in *Embers* desperately tries to suppress the sound of the sea that rushes in to fill all the pauses in his monologue; the Opener in *Cascando* is caught in a troubling relationship with a voice that is always there, gabbling its tale of Woburn, whenever he goes through the inescapable ritual of 'opening'. The sound-effects studio is made to function as the nearest thing to an off-stage the medium is capable of: it gets into the plays as the alarming region, somewhere in the space around them, which bombards the characters with sound and which they can mysteriously draw on for their great efforts at self-expression, Croak or the Opener calling for music; Henry choosing among sounds of shingle and horse hooves; the Rooneys, waiting for appropriate rural noises to come in on cue; they are all aware of themselves as producers engaged in a continual struggle to get their sounds right.

That struggle must have had particular personal meaning for Beckett at the time he turned to radio. Coming back to English as first language with *All That Fall* in 1957 after so many years of writing in French clearly had its awkwardness: English was 'abstracted to death', he had said, and now he was back with this recalcitrant tongue, fighting off abstractness. The sense of the awkwardness gets very strongly into the plays, gives them a rather special, private intensity as well as a quirky, self-mocking irony. Artist characters are central; conductors, wrestling with the slippery sounds that will go their own way, even to the extent of acquiring capital letters and emerging as full-blown characters.

It is arguable that the privacy is exclusive, makes for a certain remoteness. Certainly these are cryptic pieces, but it seems to me that Beckett succeeds in opening his problems of communication to us and in making us aware how much in fact they resemble our own. Take Henry in *Embers* for instance. His habit of talking aloud to people who aren't there comes over partly as the special compulsion of a writer grappling with difficult materials: his hopeless attempts to get the story of Bolton and Holloway right takes us deep into the obscure area of the mind where the artist makes his choices among the jostling elements of his private life. But he is also and all the time a distressed old man such as we might meet anywhere, talking to himself in a railway-station waiting-room late at night, perhaps, or on some street corner; reminding us that we come very close to this ourselves sometimes, when we inwardly rehearse or recapitulate some desperate conversation, maybe under stress even voice our share in an imaginary dialogue as he does. The Henry who might be any of us comes forcefully through the medium of his wife's voice, worrying about the effect his perpetual talking is having on their young daughter and pressing him to see a doctor. Or there is Mrs Rooney, so bothered about those patches of dead language in her dialogue. We're encouraged to see the professional aspect of this; as a radio character she would indeed fade out, become a 'big pale blur' if her language ceased to convince, but although Beckett wittily allows her knowledge of her situation, that doesn't prevent her anxiety from coming over in quite ordinary terms too, as the expression of a simple human need for self-expression: she has a hard time trying to communicate her feelings through a style that makes them seem terribly over-emphasised: a not unfamiliar experience for most people, one would guess.

Perhaps it is remoteness of another kind that has prevented the radio plays from receiving much critical attention. Recordings are sadly inaccessible; *All That Fall* has been heard more often (which means presumably that more unofficial copies exist), but the other plays have had few airings. The BBC may arrange replays on request, but in the present unsatisfactory copyright situation, no public performances are allowed, even in an educational context, as we discovered when we made our attempt to borrow *Words and Music* for our original lecture series. In that case, the need to hear material sounds (especially of the music) was so compelling that I was led into an attempt to make a new production, though even before I had seen John Beckett's score, which makes taxing instrumental demands, it was apparent that the intricacies of the sound relationships in the play would be far beyond the skill and resources of amateurs: it had to be a professional produc-tion, and this is what we are now engaged on.

Beckett's concreteness in this sphere makes difficulties for his critics: one can only hope that the effect will be to stimulate more productions, as well as efforts to change the copyright situation so as to make the recordings that do exist more accessible.

In *All That Fall* there are some teasing variations of tone. The play was written to come out of the dark, Beckett says; our delicate task is to separate the true dark from the false one the rhetoric offers. It is delicate because there is so much pressure from the naturalistic elements (robuster in this than in any other of the radio plays) to take that rhetoric at its face value, give it the wrong kind of weight.

Of course it is sometimes obvious that we are meant to laugh at Mrs Rooney's comically florid style, with its exaggerations and sentimentalisings. She often invites us to herself with her caustic comments and deliberate-seeming bathos; when she outlines her idea of happiness, for instance: 'Would I were lying stretched out in my comfortable bed, Mr Barrell, just wasting slowly, painlessly away, keeping up my strength with arrowroot and calves-foot jelly . . .' or demands of Mr Tyler, 'What kind of a country is this where a woman can't weep her heart out on the highways and byways without being tormented by retired bill-brokers!'

But there are those other times when she seems to be unaware of her own exaggerations, and we are not so sure how we should be responding. How seriously do we have to take her, for instance, when she laments over her lost Minnie, or the hinny with the great moist cleg-tormented eyes, or the hen Mr Slocum runs over? And is there a real difference of feeling between those fulsome outbursts and her simple expression of pity for the old woman alone in the ruinous old house playing over and over to herself the recording of Schubert's *Death and the Maiden*.

One tone slides so almost imperceptibly into the other that we need all the help we can get from material sounds to distinguish between the posturings and the genuine article. Beckett's witty stage directions show how much he depends on our having this evidence. The tone colour of the non-verbal sounds is constantly fluctuating; at one extreme the persuasive melancholy of Schubert, at another the irony of those comically histrionic 'rural' noises that so regularly undercut melancholy and sentiment:

The cows – (*brief moo*) – and sheep – (*brief baa*) – ruminate in silence. The dogs – (*brief bark*) – are hushed and the hens – (*brief cackle*) – sprawl torpid in the dust. We are alone. There is no one to ask.

It is more difficult for the reader than the listener to stay continuously aware of this disrespectful, tongue-in-the-cheek undercutting; easier to fall into the error of taking Mrs Rooney's vale of tears philosophy for general comment, a reflection (albeit in comically grotesque form) of Beckett's own dark view of human life. The play often has been taken as that, rather than as what the nuances suggest it is, a part amused, part wry and sombre probing of a state of mind that sees everything in dark terms. Mrs Rooney does so consistently draw out tales of illness (especially female illness) and disaster in everyone she meets on her road; she is so lugubrious, so complacent about her superior capacity for feeling the pain of others: a real Mrs Gummidge, she seems, liable at any moment to come out with, 'I'm a lone lorn creetur', and 'I feel it more than other people'. She makes Mr Slocum retract his daring suggestion that it is a blessed thing to be alive in such weather and out of hospital; rebukes Mr Tyler – 'Have you no respect for misery?' – for interrupting her tears over little Minnie. Yet in the next breath she tells us that little Minnie would be in her forties now, or fifty maybe; a piece of bathos it's not at all easy to place. Is she codding in such moments, inviting the listeners to join in the joke against herself, or is she seriously playing for sympathy but overdoing it so wildly that she alienates and repels it instead?

She knows herself that this happens. 'I estrange them all', she says, 'They come towards me, uninvited, bygones bygones, full of kindness, anxious to help. . . . A few simple words . . . from my heart . . . and I am all alone . . . once more.' A 'few simple words' is a joke, but like the joke about 'little' Minnie, it is registered in a complex tone. We can't dismiss these sayings as jokes or grotesquerie any more than we can simply take them straight. The modulations of tone build up a more subtle impression; behind the theatrical exaggerations there seems to be a genuine, intensely private grief, to do with childlessness, that is being projected on to the scene at large, turning the whole world into a sad hospital for hysterectomies and in the process estranging the much longed-for sympathy.

On the homeward journey with Dan, we are given a glimpse into that privacy. The tone changes; Mrs Rooney still has her sentimental lapses (called forth by lambs especially), but now they are held in check by his bracing and astringent humour. Impossible to offer the facile pity she spends on hens to a man who ruminates on his blindness, 'The loss of my sight was a great fillip. If I could go deaf and dumb I think I might pant on to be a hundred', or makes his grim jokes against children, 'Did you ever wish to kill a child? . . . Nip some young doom in the bud.'

Obscure connections open up between her distracted volubility and his formidable reserve. By the time she hears the news he has so deliberately kept from her about the child's death on the line, the complex pattern of their feelings is becoming clearer: his revulsion from children seems part of a deep will to non-involvement that is somehow related to her grief over her childlessness: little Minnie is more than ever a fantasy, but in the context of their strange, but touchingly close relationship, the grief has become more real. When she breaks down in telling the story of the child who wasn't properly born and he says, 'Poor Maddy'; when the strains of *Death and the Maiden* are heard again and she says, 'Poor woman', the pity seems unforced and genuine. We know now we are in the Rooney mood, have always been there really; the affectations were a distortion created by the private shadows. It is a sombre ending; the child's death, the sound of wind and rain and dragging footsteps; but something has come out of the dark; the Rooneys have been understood, the true voice of feeling has made itself heard, though wavering through all the excess; perspective has been restored.

To arrive at that clearer perspective we have to be alert to some fine nuances of sound. So too in *Embers* (BBC, 1959), although here we are straining from the start to know what kind of solidity events and characters have, who and what is real.

The play opens with an ambiguous suggestion that all is fiction. Henry is heard, (disconcertingly like a real producer) calling for sound effects. 'On', he says, and there is the sound of boots on shingle; 'Down', and it dies away. He controls the sounds, it seems, as he controls the story of Bolton and Holloway, the two 'grand old men' and the mysterious 'great trouble' he keeps returning to in his narrative; that traumatic interior, the still room, fire burning low on the hearth, one old man pleading desperately with the other for help: 'Please! Please!'

This first impression of a man in control is never quite lost: rather, it is kept in tension with exactly the opposite impression of a man who has totally lost control. Sometimes the same sound produces this peculiar double effect. Horse hooves, for instance come in as a conventional sound flashback at one point: Ada mentions Addie's riding lessons and there to order is the noise of walking hooves. But everything to do with Addie rouses an obscure, wild irritation in Henry. The trot turns to a gallop, Addie wails, the wail is amplified to a 'paroxysm' and suddenly cut off; the sound has got out of control, gone back to being what it was when he first called for it in the opening 'conversation' with his dead father: 'A ten ton mammoth back from the dead. Shoe it with steel and have it tramp the world down.' And one sound he has no control over at all; the 'sucking' noise of the sea that is heard in every pause: it is the last sound we hear, wordlessly undoing his closing words: 'Nothing, all day nothing. (*Pause.*) All day all night nothing. (*Pause.*) Not a sound.'

These sounds, so painful and uncontrollable, give a solid lifelike quality to Henry's own story, make the sea-shore, though so strange a place, seem at first much more real than the made-up place in the story he is so patiently inventing and manipulating; that 'white world' where he is free to choose what shall be seen and heard, whether the room should have shutters or hangings, the old men stand or sit, what names they should have. We are invited to hear him in the act of composition, feeling for a name he hasn't yet invented.

Ring then at the door and over he goes to the window and looks out between the hangings, fine old chap, very big and strong, bright winter's night, snow everywhere, bitter cold, white world, cedar boughs bending under load, and then as the arm goes up to ring again recognises . . . Holloway . . . (*long pause*) . . . yes, Holloway, recognises Holloway, goes down and opens.

Then Ada is called for and again there is this extraordinary sense of doubleness. She seems in a way more real than anyone else Henry conjures up: he doesn't have to imitate her voice, as he does his father's, or keep her at a distance, inset like Addie (that unloved dream child): she has her own voice, sounds close, actually there, warning him about sitting on the cold stones, sharing his memories; their first experience of sex on that same beach, the disappearance of his father, who perhaps was drowned there.

And yet she is troublingly unreal and unsubstantial. She was there before he called her, she says enigmatically, her voice is low and remote, she gets increasingly vague, won't even venture a guess as to how old their daughter might be: it is impossible to visualise her; she is much less there in that way, in fact, than Bolton in the story, with his 'old blue eye, very glassy, lids worn thin, lashes gone, whole thing swimming', holding his candle and pleading with Holloway, for an injection, it seems. That interior, with the 'dreadful' sound of the embers shifting on the hearth is the scene that stands out most sharp and clear, in spite of the mockingly literary style of the narrative.

These are disturbing oscillations of reality: most disturbing of all, perhaps the moment when shadowy and yet so real Ada sows doubt about the reality of the sound we and Henry are hearing so clearly:

I don't think you are hearing it. And if you are, what's wrong with it, it's a lovely, peaceful gentle soothing sound, why do you hate it? (*Pause.*) And if you hate it why don't you keep away from it? Why are you always coming down here? (*Pause.*) There's something wrong with your brain, you ought to see Holloway, he's alive still, isn't he?

The mention of Holloway is a shock that must set us thinking differently about the story. Was that hesitation over the doctor's name not a faltering of invention but a mental block set up against some traumatic memory? Is the story an attempt to express

213

something about his obsessive, uneasy relationship with his father; is Ada called up as a listener because she really was there in the old days – these are the only listeners who are any use to him now, he says – or is she as much a fiction as one suspects Addie to be?

Finally, when Ada is snuffed out and Henry is left trying to finish his double narrative, the dividing line between the stories has been dissolved: the real-life story has come to seem more like fiction and the fiction more like a mirror of real life. Both have acquired a new, ghostly reality, such as Ada has, and the father who is so very nearly there – in the old men, in Henry's one-sided conversation with him, in the suggestive sound of the sea.

Just what that closing sound suggests is the question we are left with. It's a hard one to answer without a sound recording fresh in mind (and I haven't that advantage), but it does seem as if the doubleness that is such a striking feature of this play must somehow enter into our interpretation. No doubt about its being an awesome sound, dreadful, even, as something so unwanted and unstoppable must be. Yet in affecting Henry as it does, keeping him talking and telling stories, it is also keeping life going. He may abandon the Bolton story as a failure: 'not a sound, white world, bitter cold, ghastly scene, old men, great trouble, no good. (*Pause.*) No good.' But the vitality in the Jingle-like staccato suggests that the stories will go on: perhaps the sea is our assurance that they will: there is a promise of continuation in it, in contrast to that other 'dreadful' sound that Henry hears and we don't; the embers fading on the hearth, with their threat of chilly decline, uncreative winter. The sea stirs up anguish but it is a wakeful anguish, the kind that makes things live: the old father has not completely drowned after all; the sea comes in with a rush at the end to contradict Henry's exhausted reflections on waste and nothingness.

If the full effects of the sounds in *Embers* are hard to gauge unheard, how much harder (except for the Beethovens among us) to measure the role of the music in *Cascando* (BBC, 1964). We don't even get help from stage directions as in *Words and Music* (BBC, 1962), where Music will offer Words 'an improvement on foregoing' or become 'warmly sentimental'. Music in *Cascando* is only a dotted line. And yet the counterpointing and harmonising of Voice and Music is crucial to the play's meaning. As though they had linked their arms, the Opener says: the mystery preoccupies him. Where does Music come from? 'Is that mine too?', he broods, thinking resentfully of the people who rationalise his strange vocation: 'It's his, it's his voice, it's in his head.'

He seems to be resisting that suggestion by cultivating an

214

impersonal, automaton-like style – 'It is the month of May . . . for me. (*Pause.*) Correct' – and ushering in and cutting off Voice and Music as if he had no more to do with them than that.

As the play goes on the impersonality breaks down. He can be heard getting more like Voice as both he and Voice increasingly show affinities with the Voice's 'character' Woburn. 'A long life . . . already . . . say what you like . . . a few misfortunes . . . that's enough', Voice will say, and the notion of a long life and its vicissitudes drift into the Opener's remarks – 'I have lived on it . . . till I'm old. Old enough' – and into the Woburn tale. Woburn is said to be journeying across the hills, down to the sea, in a boat, out to the island in search of a place to sleep 'elsewhere'. The Opener speaks of Voice and Music giving him 'outings'; Voice pants out his own longing for sleep and rest. When Voice and Music weaken at one point, even go silent without being formally closed, the Opener reveals an emotional commitment to the story far beyond what he was prepared to admit to at the beginning. He goads them on, 'God God', and joins in himself until finally he and Voice are at one in the agitated rhythm: 'this time . . . it's the right one . . . finish . . . no more stories . . . sleep . . . we're there . . . nearly . . . just a few more . . . don't let go . . . Woburn . . . he clings on . . . come on . . . come on. . . .'

So it could seem that 'they' were right when they said, 'It's in his head', that Voice and Woburn have to be taken unequivocally as projections of the Opener, Woburn being the furthest he can get away from himself. But does that view take in the force of the sounds heard, as they are meant to be, with the physical ear? Would we not then be struck by the seeming autonomy of Voice and Music and the strange harmony between them which so puzzles the Opener: 'Is that mine too?' 'As though they had linked their arms.' The operatic element is easy to underestimate in reading, but in performance that flood of music and verbal sound could invest the Woburn story with a kind of freedom and independence, make it seem a thing on its own, as Woburn ends by seeming a character on his own, more there than the characters who present him, because so sharply visualised; the huge bulk, old coat and broad-brimmed hat, head sunk, the unseen face a vivid object of curiosity. Perhaps after all he might have to be thought of as 'out there', free-floating, the getting of him a deeper mystery than 'they' have understood.

Certainly in the other music play, as a recent hearing of the BBC production brought home to me, the impact of the musical sound can vitally affect interpretation. Again the idea of harmony between words and music is crucial, but in this play it is not an easy harmony: on the contrary it is the objective the characters painfully and ludicrously struggle to reach.

Words and Music opens with discord, Music aimlessly tuning, Words mindlessly elaborating on the theme of 'Sloth', both bitterly hostile to each other. 'My comforts! Be friends!' Croak pleads when he appears on the scene, but all he gets when he offers a new theme, 'Love', is the Sloth rigmarole repeated word for word, with Music doing a mocking equivalent. It's only when he stumbles on the theme of 'Age' that something real starts to happen: Words' fluency breaks down; he gropes his way reluctantly among images of physical decay – 'if you're a man . . . were a man . . . huddled . . . nodding . . . the ingle . . .' – then comes back to love but now very differently: under pressure from the harsh facts of life as it is, abstractions have given way to a vivid image, a beautiful face seen in moonlight; he has got through, it seems, to 'the face' Croak was muttering incoherently about when he first came in.

But still there seems to be a terrible block in the way of Words and Music fully realising that image and the vision of the well-head, the dark, silent consummation, that grows out of it. They both try to evade this reality, Music in histrionic sentiment and Words (apparently frightened off by the sentiment), in a return to pedantic, pseudo-scientific detachment. Between them they distort and impede the experience and yet it begins to glimmer through; the black-haired beauty in the silver night, the sense of youth and love welling up again in the imagination of age. John Beckett's music may have been rather austere for the earlier sentimental passages where a more flamboyant theatricality seemed indicated, but in the closing 'well-head' sequence it was powerfully, persuasively lyrical; in a severe style that took in the grotesque, drab images of age – the hag putting the pan in the bed – as well as the romantic memory of the piercingly beautiful face. When Words tried to follow that pure hymeneal sound in his cracked voice, getting gradually stronger and more confident as the music swelled out into the full vision of the well-head – 'All dark no begging/No giving no words/ No sense no need . . .' – the effect was moving. The play seemed to be escaping from its limitations into the full freedom of opera; against their own worst failings, Words and Music were somehow expressing Croak's vision for him.

Whether Croak himself thinks so, it is rather hard to know. On this point criticism is understandably divided. He certainly interrupts them very noisily, dropping his club and shuffling off with one of his immense groans, drawing a shocked 'My Lord!' from Words. Some critics, like Alec Reid, have taken that exit and the groan as a sign that Words and Music stay specious to the end and Croak is giving them up as incorrigible,[5] for others, a harmony of sorts is achieved, though it seems usually to be thought of as a rather chilly one, a 'grey epithalamium', in Hugh Kenner's phrase.

Certainly in Felix Felton's performance, Croak's final groan was no different from all those earlier exasperated explosions: to judge from that alone, the harmony was not real. And yet for the listener it was real; the coming together of music and cracked hesitant voice, the gradual swelling out to a grave crescendo was both convincing and affecting. So perhaps it was the groan that was wrong: perhaps Croak should have an operatic repertoire of groans to match the shifts of mood and feeling in the words and the music; then his later responses might have expressed sad realisation rather than the same irritation he started with. An impossible task for an actor, one might say: it would certainly be a tough one; and yet a suggestion that it might have been managed was made by the marvellously expressive, long-drawn-out sigh that Patrick Magee as Words produced for the play's last sound.[6]

We can't expect to pursue these tantalising questions far without hearing real sounds. In his power to make us feel that this is so, to make us crave productions, turn us (in imagination or fact) into producers or performers, Beckett continually brings home to us the concreteness of his art, its perfect theatricality. In the stage and radio plays alike, imaginative involvement in the fine detail of the performing process is the best illumination we can get.

NOTES

1   John and B. S. Fletcher (eds), *Fin de partie*, Methuen Educational, London, 1970, p. 12.
2   John Gruen, 'Beckett talks about Beckett', *Vogue* (London), February 1970.
3   James Knowlson, *Light and Darkness in Beckett's Theatre*, Turret Books, London, 1972.
4   R. L. Admussen, 'The manuscripts of Beckett's *Play*', *Modern Drama*, vol. 16, 1973.
5   A. Reid, *All I Can Manage, More Than I Could*, Dolmen Press, Dublin, 1968, p. 87.

Since this was written, a new version has been made by the University of London Audio-visual Centre. Humphrey Searle's Music is a volatile character in tune with Patrick Magee's Words: they have a different relationship with the more variable Croak of Denis Hawthorne.

Quotations are from the following (Faber & Faber) editions: *Waiting for Godot*, 1965; *Endgame*, 1964; *All That Fall*, 1957; *Krapp's Last Tape* and *Embers*, 1965; *Happy Days*, 1966; *Play, Words and Music* and *Cascando*, 1968; *Not I*, 1973. As the plays are so brief, I have not thought it necessary to give page references.

Select list of Beckett's principal works

Date and place of first publication in book form are given for the works listed in the main sequence and of first publication in English when this is different: some later English editions have been included, when they had revisions or additions of interest or are likely to be more generally available than earlier ones. As this is a list primarily for English-speaking readers, all English translations of French works have been given, but not vice versa. English translations follow immediately after their French originals; plays occur in sequence according to their date of first production. For quick reference to the French translations of English works, see the *New Cambridge Bibliography of English Literature*, vol. 4. For a comprehensive bibliography, see R. Federman and J. Fletcher, *Beckett: His Works and His Critics*, University of California Press, Berkeley and Los Angeles, 1970.

A continuing bibliography is published by the Minard Press, Paris; editor, R. Davis. *Essai de bibliographie des œuvres de Samuel Beckett*, Minard (Lettres Modernes), Paris. Cumulative, continuing bibliography: 1st edn, 1971 (Collection Calepins de Bibliographie; 2nd edn, 1974 (Collection Bibliotheque)).

See also the select bibliography of the shorter fiction at the end of chapter 4, on pages 81–3.

'Dante . . . Bruno, Vico . . . Joyce' (in *Our Exagmination round his Factification for Incamination of Work in Progress*), Shakespeare & Co., Paris, 1929.

Proust, Chatto & Windus, London, 1931; John Calder, London, 1965 (with *Three Dialogues – Beckett and Georges Duthuit* – this English version first published in book form in *Bram Van Velde*, New York, 1960).

More Pricks Than Kicks, Chatto & Windus, London, 1934; Calder & Boyars, London, 1970.

Murphy, Routledge & Kegan Paul, London, 1938; Pan Books, London, 1970.

Malone meurt, Editions de Minuit, Paris, 1951.

Malone Dies, Grove Press, New York, 1956; Calder & Boyars, London 1959 (with *Molloy* and *The Unnamable*).

Molloy, Editions de Minuit, Paris, 1951.

Molloy (English version), Olympia Press, Paris, 1955; Calder & Boyars, London, 1959 (with *Malone Dies* and *The Unnamable*).

En attendant Godot (Théâtre de Babylone, Paris, 5 January 1953), Editions de Minuit, Paris, 1952; Harrap, London, 1966, ed. C. Duckworth.

Waiting for Godot (Arts Theatre, 3 August 1955; Criterion Theatre, September 1955), Grove Press, New York, 1954; Faber & Faber, London 1956, 1965 rev. and unexpurgated.

L'Innommable, Editions de Minuit, Paris, 1953.

The Unnamable, Grove Press, New York, 1958; Calder & Boyars, London, 1959 (with *Molloy* and *Malone Dies*).

Watt, Olympia Press, Paris, 1953; Calder & Boyars, London, 1963 (written 1941–2).

Nouvelles et textes pour rien, Editions de Minuit, Paris, 1955.

Stories and Texts for Nothing, Grove Press, New York, 1967 (also in *No's Knife: Collected Shorter Prose 1945–1966*, Calder & Boyars, 1967).

All That Fall (BBC Third Programme, 14 January 1957), Faber & Faber, London, 1957.

Acte sans paroles (Royal Court Theatre, 3 April 1957), Editions de Minuit, Paris, 1957.

Act Without Words, Faber & Faber, London, 1958 (with *Endgame*).

Fin de partie (Royal Court Theatre, 3 April 1957), Editions de Minuit, Paris, 1957.

Endgame (Cherry Lane Theatre, New York, 28 January 1958; Royal Court Theatre, 28 October 1958), Faber & Faber, London 1958 (with *Act Without Words*).

From an Abandoned Work (BBC Third Programme, 14 December 1957), Faber & Faber, London, 1958.

Krapp's Last Tape (Royal Court Theatre, 28 October 1958), Faber & Faber, London, 1959 (with *Embers*).

Bram Van Velde, Georges Fall, Paris, 1958.

Bram Van Velde (English version), Grove Press, New York, 1960 rev. ed. (with *Three Dialogues – Beckett and Georges Duthuit*).

Embers (BBC Third Programme, 24 June 1959), Faber & Faber, London, 1959 (with *Krapp's Last Tape*).

Act Without Words 2 (Institute of Contemporary Arts, 25 January 1960), Grove Press, New York, 1960 (in *Krapp's Last Tape and Other Dramatic Pieces*; Faber & Faber, London, 1967 (in *Eh Joe and Other Writings*)).

Happy Days (Cherry Lane Theatre, New York, 17 September 1961; Royal Court Theatre, 1 November 1962), Grove Press, New York, 1961; Faber & Faber, London, 1962.

Comment c'est, Editions de Minuit, Paris, 1961.

How It Is, Calder & Boyars, London, 1964.

Poems in English, Calder & Boyars, London, 1961.

Words and Music (BBC Third Programme, 13 November 1962; a second version with new music, by University of London, December 1973), Faber & Faber, London, 1964 (in *Play and Two Short Pieces For Radio*).

Play (Ulmer Theater, Ulm-Donau, 14 June 1963, in German trn; Old Vic, 7 April 1964), Faber & Faber, London, 1964 (in *Play and Two Short Pieces For Radio*).

Cascando (ORTF, Paris, 13 October 1963), Suhrkamp Verlag, Frankfurt, 1963 (in *Dramatische Dichtungen*).

Cascando (English version) (BBC Third Programme, 28 October 1964), Faber, London, 1964 (in *Play and Two Short Pieces For Radio*).

220

Play and Two Short Pieces for Radio, Faber & Faber, London, 1964.

Come and Go (Schiller Theatre, Berlin, September 1965, in German trn.; Abbey Theatre, Dublin, 28 February 1968), Suhrkamp Verlag, Frankfurt, 1966; Calder & Boyars, London, 1967.

Film (Venice Biennale, 4 September 1965), Faber & Faber, London, 1967 (in *Eh Joe and Other Writings*), 1972 (with complete scenario, illustrations and production shots).

Imagination morte imaginez, Editions de Minuit, Paris, 1965.

Imagination Dead Imagine, Calder & Boyars, London 1965.

Eh Joe (BBC Television, 4 July 1966), Faber & Faber, London, 1967 (in *Eh Joe and Other Writings*).

Assez, Editions de Minuit, Paris, 1966.

Bing, Editions de Minuit, Paris, 1966.

Ping and *Enough* (English versions of above), Calder & Boyars, London, 1967 (in *No's Knife*).

Eh Joe and Other Writings, Faber & Faber, London, 1967.

No's Knife: Collected Shorter Prose 1945–1966, Calder & Boyars, London, 1967 (contains *Stories and Texts for Nothing, From an Abandoned Work, Enough, Imagination Dead Imagine, Ping. Enough* and *Ping* first printed in this volume).

Poems, Paris, 1968. Contains all the French poems.

Breath (Eden Theater, New York, 16 June 1969; Close Theatre Club, Glasgow, October 1969), Faber & Faber, London, 1972 (in *Breath and Other Short Plays*).

Sans, Editions de Minuit, Paris, 1969.

Lessness (English version of above), Calder & Boyars, London, 1970.

Le Dépeupleur, Editions de Minuit, Paris, 1970.

The Lost Ones (English version of above), Calder & Boyars, London, 1972.

Mercier et Camier, Editions de Minuit, Paris, 1970 (novel, written 1946–7).

Premier Amour, Editions de Minuit, Paris, 1970 (short story, written 1946).

First Love, Calder & Boyars, London, 1973.

Not I (Lincoln Centre, New York, 22 November 1972; Royal Court Theatre, 16 January 1973), Faber & Faber, London, 1973.

Select list of critical writings

CHEVIGNY, B. G. (ed.), *Twentieth Century Interpretations of Endgame: A Collection of Critical Essays*, Prentice-Hall, Englewood Cliffs, New Jersey, 1969. Chiefly reprinted articles, including translation of T. W. Adorno's *Versuch das Endspiel zu verstehen*.

COE, R. N., *Beckett*, Oliver & Boyd, Edinburgh (Writers and Critics Series), 1964. Especially helpful on philosophical aspects of Beckett's art.

COHN, R., *Beckett: The Comic Gamut*, Rutgers University Press, New Jersey, 1962.

—— (ed.), *Casebook on Waiting for Godot*, Grove Press, New York, 1967. Collects early reviews, theatrical reminiscences and some criticism.

DUCKWORTH, C. (ed.), *En attendant Godot*, Harrap, London, 1966. The Introduction gives a full account of the growth of the text.

ESSLIN, M., *The Theatre of the Absurd*, London, 1968 rev. ed.

—— (ed.), *Samuel Beckett: A Collection of Critical Essays*, Prentice-Hall, Englewood Cliffs, New Jersey, 1965. Reprinted articles and extracts from books, including some *loci classici* of Beckett criticism. See especially G. Anders, 'Being Without Time: on Beckett's play, *Waiting for Godot*'; H. Kenner, 'The Cartesian Centaur'; A. Robbe-Grillet, 'Beckett, or "Presence" in the Theatre'; D. Wellershof, 'Failure of an Attempt at De-mythologisation: Beckett's Novels'.

FEDERMAN, R., *Journey to Chaos: Samuel Beckett's Early Fiction*, University of California Press, Berkeley and Los Angeles, 1965.

FLETCHER, J., *The Novels of Samuel Beckett*, Chatto & Windus, London, 1964, rev. ed. 1970.

—— with FLETCHER, B. S., *Fin de partie*, Methuen, London, 1970. See the Introduction.

FRIEDMAN, M. J. (ed.), *Samuel Beckett Now*, University of Chicago Press, Chicago and London, 1970. New version of *Configuration critique de Samuel Beckett*, *Revue des lettres modernes*, no. 100, 1964. Includes check-list of criticism by J. R. Bryer and translations of French criticism. See especially: F. J. Hoffmann, 'The Elusive Ego: Beckett's M's'; B. Morrissette, 'Robbe-Grillet as a Critic of Beckett'.

HARVEY, L. E., *Samuel Beckett: Poet and Critic*, Princeton University Press, New Jersey, 1970.

HOFFMAN, F. J., *Samuel Beckett: The Language of Self*, Dutton, New York, 1964.

JACOBSON, J. and MUELLER, W. R., *The Testament of Samuel Beckett*, Faber & Faber, London, 1966 (first ed. Hill & Wang, New York, 1964).

JANVIER, L., *Beckett par lui-même*, Editions du Seuil, Paris, 1969.

KENNER, H., *Samuel Beckett: A Critical Study*, University of California Press, Berkeley and Los Angeles, 1968 (first ed., Grove Press, New York, 1961).

MÉLESE, P., *Samuel Beckett*, Paris, 1966.

REID, A., *All I Can Manage, More Than I Could: An Approach to the Plays of Samuel Beckett*, Dolmen Press, Dublin, 1969 rev. ed.

See also *Samuel Beckett: An Exhibition* (Catalogue of the exhibition held at Reading University Library, 1971), Turret Books, London, 1971. Includes illuminating material and comments on Beckett's life and on his writings in journals and unpublished writings.

Index